Peace, Prosperity, and Politics

The Political Economy of Global Interdependence

Thomas D. Willett, Series Editor

Peace, Prosperity, and Politics

EDITED BY

John Mueller

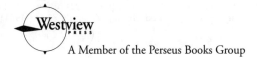

Westview
PRESS

A Member of the Perseus Books Group

337
P355

The Political Economy of Global Interdependence

Copyright © 2000 by Westview Press, A Member of the Perseus Book Group

Published in 2000 in the United States of America by Westview Press, 5500 Central Avenue, Boulder, Colorado 80301-2877, and in the United Kingdom by Westview Press, 12 Hid's Copse Road, Cumnor Hill, Oxford OX2 9JJ

Visit us on the World Wide Web at www.westviewpress.com

Peace, prosperity, and politics / edited by John Mueller.
    p.   cm.—(the political economy of global interdependence)
  Includes bibliographical references and index.
  ISBN 0-8133-6761-1 (hc.)
  1. International economic relations.   2. Free trade.   3. Peace.   4. World politics—20th century.   I. Series.   II. Mueller, John E.
  JC1359.P39 1999
  337 21—dc21
                                                                        99-046218

10   9   8   7   6   5   4   3   2   1

Contents

Figures and Tables

1

Introduction:
Prospects and Problems
in the New Century

JOHN MUELLER AND ARTHUR A. STEIN

As we abandon the old century and enter a new one, it seems clear that there are at least four international developments that could have crucial consequences.

First, the leading countries confront no compelling or immediate major threats of a military sort; that is, there is little or no danger that anything resembling World War III will break out. The end of the Cold War transformed the distribution of global power with the collapse of the Soviet Union. Russia is smaller and less powerful than the Soviet Union was, and it doesn't have the imperial control over Eastern Europe the Soviet Union had (though it does still possess much of the nuclear weapons capacity that some international relations theorists have seen to be determining of international structure). And arguments heard as recently as the early 1990s about the decline of U.S. power have been replaced by ones that characterize the United States as the sole remaining superpower and the international system as unipolar.

Second, the Cold War concluded with the demise of a dramatic ideological struggle in world affairs. As Fascism died in World War II, the end of the Cold War witnessed the collapse of state Communism. The result seems to constitute the triumph of liberalism—democracy and market capitalism—and the recognition of the failure of alternative economic and political systems. Currently at least, all the leading countries see the world in essentially the same way.

Third, and substantially in consequence of the first two developments, there has been an enormous expansion of international trade and of multinational economic interconnections. Of considerable potential importance, these interconnections in many cases supersede—and perhaps render obsolete—older relationships of a political sort. The Cold War, like hot war, disrupted the flows of capital, commerce, and people, and its collapse makes possible the creation of a truly global marketplace, one in which exchange leads to the most efficient allocation of resources.

And fourth, the prospects for growth and economic development are further enhanced by rapidly expanding technological improvements in communications and in information flows that facilitate economic and non-economic international interconnections, ones that substantially skirt standard political arrangements.

The combined effect of these developments is to transform world affairs. The security environment in which states operate seems radically to have changed, and this makes possible a reallocation of national effort from security to material concerns. Thus there is a reasonable prospect for an unparalleled era of prosperity and peace.

But less benign forces also persist. The collapse of the Soviet multinational empire has witnessed the rise in some places of ethnic conflict and has perhaps created new political space for such conflicts to flourish. In addition, it is possible that we are merely enduring a brief hiatus before a new challenge to the international order is launched, perhaps by China or Russia or by another emergent or resurgent state.

Some states thus face the prospect of a virtuous circle in which reduced threat stimulates greater prosperity which in turn heightens the degree of security and peace. Yet other states may confront a vicious cycle in which conflict and turmoil destroy wealth and reduce investment that in turn fosters still greater violence, and in which ethnic conflicts, religious feuds, and border wars may fill the vacuums left by the diminished role of the distant and distracted superpowers. Similarly, the positive prospects of the global economy are not yet, and may not soon be, available for all nations and all regions of the world. The result is that politics—political choice—remains important.

The new international condition poses problems for policymakers and scholars alike. Both now find a world quite different from that which they experienced during the Cold War. What often seemed to be the certainty of bipolarity, and of military and ideological superpower competition, has been replaced with a less anchored and perhaps more fluid environment. Moreover, the ability of states to control outcomes may grow weaker under the onslaught of global economic forces. Scholars face new challenges to the adequacy of their formulations for explaining the end of the old world and the beginning of the new one being born.

In this book, a group of political scientists, economists, and historians assess these important developments. Despite disciplinary and other differences, the authors are in broad agreement that important historical changes are occurring in the nature of international politics, and they agree about some of the ways to think about them. They differ in their perspectives and proffer different speculations about the new era and about the consequences and difficulties of the emergent relationship between politics and economics. They also vary in the degree to which they are optimistic or pessimistic about the way things appear to be going.

The Rosecrance Connection

This collection began with a call to colleagues, students, and friends of Richard Rosecrance to delineate the factors that will be central to world politics in the next century.[1] The resulting essays were written in his honor, and, not surprisingly, they form a testament to themes that run through his work and to his intellectual contributions as an author, colleague, and teacher.

The essays deal with a variety of issues of history, of national security, and of political economy—areas with which Rosecrance has been concerned throughout his career. In particular, the essays focus on the need for a dynamic perspective, a recurrent theme in his work and a regular admonition to his colleagues and students. His first book, *Action and Reaction in World Politics*, looked at the changing role of domestic politics on international politics during the last two centuries. His *The Rise of the Trading State* focused on the changing relationship between commerce and conquest. And his new *The Rise of the Virtual State* extends the analysis into a new technological era.[2] In various ways, the essays explore that analysis and its implications for the next century. In his contribution, Rosecrance himself pursues the analogy of states with firms and explores the implications for international politics.

Elements of Agreement and Disagreement

The contributors are drawn from different disciplines. Although the majority are political scientists, the authors include economists (Lal, Kaysen, and Yardeni) and a historian (Schroeder). Most are academics, but they include one whose analysis is done predominantly in the private sector (Yardeni), and some of the academics have had extensive experience in international institutions (Lal at the World Bank) and in national government.[3]

Notwithstanding the disparate subjects and approaches developed, the essays in this volume all discuss and describe a variety of ways in which international politics is changing and assess forces whose consequence will be a much different international politics in the next century. This stands in marked contrast to the static nature of much theorizing in international relations where scholars often argue that, since it is unlikely that international anarchy will be replaced by world government, the only thing that can change is the distribution of power: The balance of power works in this century, it is claimed, and will work in the next century the way it has worked in prior centuries. This type of theorizing, static and synchronic, can be found in all the social sciences. Even when such scholars recognize that their propositions are temporally bounded or specific to some particular structure, they do not focus on what factors lead to change over time.

Many of the essays in the volume also forecast continued differentiation between, and specialization of, states. Rosecrance has long argued against the conventional realist view that all states, except for their relative power, are fundamentally alike in their international perspective. Instead, he has sought to apply the insights of trade theory and to see the international system as one in which states could exchange and specialize. In this view, states can adopt particular strategies and change their foreign policy emphases in their allocation of resources and effort, and can allow a division of labor to emerge between them. Interdependence can and has existed between states in the international system.[4]

Many of the essays emphasize the importance of domestic politics for international cooperation and conflict.[5] For some, the centrality of the provision of wealth to the domestic politics of modern states has spilled over into their international politics. Others argue that the absence of a domestic political alternative to market capitalism is a driving factor in international politics and that domestic politics remains central to foreign policy.

The contributors sometimes focus on different prospective motivating forces of historical change. Some emphasize the political, some the economic, and some the technological. Moreover, some point to the globalization of international politics while others stress its tendency to bifurcate the international arena.

Many of the essays envision greater opportunities for enhancing state power, wealth, and status in the altered international environment.[6] And some suggest that prosperity and the continued pursuit of material wealth will likely by itself make for a more peaceful world. Indeed they emphasize that economic globalization is limiting the scope of the political, a development they find to be all to the good because the reduced ability of states to interfere in market transactions makes for the more efficient creation of wealth, something that limits and constrains political conflict and may reduce the prospects for war.

Others are more inclined to stress that peace and prosperity depend on politics. Historically, patterns of stability often seem to be determined by the political arrangements among the leading countries and by the conception of peace they happen to agree on.[7] In addition, some argue that an international society has emerged in which states must necessarily justify and explain their actions.[8] Central to a more pacific global order may be the existence of quasi-judicial international institutions that provide the social lubricant necessary in any society in which actors face exigent circumstances.

Some of the essays emphasize the development of ideas as the motor forces behind the economic policies that underlie globalization: The maturation of economics as a science has been a hallmark of the twentieth century and, by virtue of this science, policymakers now know what to do. For others, the twentieth century has been an era of economic experimentation that has left in its wake many failures and economic basket cases, and those states that have made the greatest strides are the ones that have learned and adopted the appropriate policies, a path that is open to others. Thus, the growth of economic science and the emergence of what may be a scholarly consensus about appropriate economic policies could be a progressive vision of intellectual growth and development. Or it could be a return to a more classical set of economic arguments after a century of failed experiments with alternatives to liberalism, a product not so much of intellectual advance as of painful learning.

Most of the essays seem to suggest that states will remain the central actors of world politics. Nevertheless, a number of the essays stress that the states of the next century will be different, and they see market forces as changing the nature of states as they increasingly become constrained by global economic and technological forces beyond their control. In some cases, states will opt, or be forced to opt, for international institutions and arrangements that will diminish their sovereignty.

There is also some disagreement about the implications of, and the continued prospects for, the depoliticization of markets. Some see the continued triumph of market capitalism and a reduced role for the state. Others voice misgivings about the consequences of a return to laissez-faire through globalization and about the instabilities of global capitalism. They are concerned about the social costs of rising inequality, domestically and internationally, and see the prospect of a world increasingly divided between the haves and the have-nots with attendant increases in domestic and international conflict.

Even more generally, some of the essays raise the possibility of a dangerous rift between the political and the economic. They ask, for example, how we can square an economically successful China with a politically dissatisfied one.

The authors thus disagree about whether international politics is witnessing increased globalization and integration or fragmentation and regionalization. Some of the essays suggest that the transformations that are occurring are systemic and global, and they argue that the growth of market exchange and the new communications revolution has impelled much of this process. Others emphasize that globalization, prosperity, and institutionalized international cooperation apply only to a subset of nations. The rich, advanced industrial nations are indeed interested in getting wealthy and now confront a quite benign security environment. Yet large parts of the world are economically backward, falling behind, and embroiled in a variety of intra- and interstate conflicts.

Indeed, it could be argued that Rosecrance's delineation of a choice between commerce and conquest characterizes a bifurcation of the world and its politics. In one world, trading states exchange with one another in a secure environment while in the other states pursue territorial strategies and are embroiled in conflicts that preclude a choice of a trading strategy for them. A zone of peace and prosperity may come to prevail among the advanced societies, but this may fail, for reasons of structure or choice, to encompass the entire world in the medium-term future.

Finally, the papers vary in tone. Most are optimistic though some provide caveats and qualifications and express some pessimism. Most of the pessimists remain hopeful and most of the optimists remain cautious. Only a few are unabashedly triumphal.

Some see the future as technologically or economically determined, but most emphasize the role of political choice, and thus they stress possibilities rather than certainties. We now confront the prospect of a bright future, more prosperous and peaceful than the past century. But it will be accompanied by turmoil and conflict in many areas. And if those who emphasize politics are correct, a more prosperous and peaceful future remains a matter of choice. We retain the ability to foul it up, and we must attempt intelligently to manage the turbulence that remains.[9]

The Essays

The essays in this volume focus on the future, but are respectful of history and of the need for dynamic explanation.

Richard Rosecrance begins the discussion. Following the logic of the theory of international trade, he suggests that a new division of labor engendered by the process of market exchange is reshaping nations and their role in the world economy. It seems likely that countries, like firms, will increasingly come to specialize. Combined with new technological developments, this will lead to a situation in which the instruments available for combating or dissuading major military conflicts will become far more numerous and powerful than in the past. Most importantly, Rosecrance argues that modern states are experiencing the same downsizing and flattening that firms are undergoing, with profound consequences for foreign policy and international stability.

Economist Deepak Lal argues that economic grief in the past has chiefly stemmed from the overruling of market forces by politicians. However, as the world market has expanded and become integrated, politicians are less able to interfere. Capital, including human capital, which is increasingly important, can simply pack up and leave and take the politicians' tax base with it. That is, bad economic policies can lead to an almost instantaneous reduction of a nation's wealth and are accordingly readily punished. Partly as a result, the world may be returning to the classical liberal international order of the nineteenth century.

Political scientist John Mueller concludes that economists have now finally gotten on top of their subject so that the advice they render is more likely than not to be sound and that policymakers have, often reluctantly, become willing to accept that advice. The prospects for an unprecedented expansion of economic growth and well being accordingly seem high, although he argues that this development will not particularly enhance happiness, or at any rate professions of happiness.

Economist Edward Yardeni celebrates the ending of the fifty-year era embraced by World War II and the ensuing Cold War—a period he characterizes as an unprecedented trade barrier. With its eradication, the world market has been freed up and has massively expanded. Aided by quickly developing and massively improving new technologies, the world economy is in a good position to capitalize on these developments to the general benefit.

Lawyer and political scientist Alan Alexandroff assesses the blurring of national political sovereignty that must emerge as the world enters an era dominated by economics. As a prototype of things to come, he analyzes the relationship between the United States, Canada, and Mexico, in which a consensual, but politically controversial, economic rebalancing has led to a slow melting of sovereignty for all three states.

Economist Carl Kaysen reflects on the twentieth century and projects that we may be in for a half-century of peace and prosperity because of four ongoing transformations in the underlying forces shaping the world. These are changes in international political organization, changes in ideology (particularly the triumph of capitalism and democracy), changes in social organization toward a world society facilitated in part by improved communication technologies, and increasing sophistication of military technology and organization. At the same time he assesses some possibilities for breakdowns in this bright picture. Most plausible is the emergence of an aggressive and expansive China or Russia, but he deems this unlikely on balance, in part because both countries are deeply dependent on international trade and investment. In all this, Kaysen holds, political choice will remain important.

Political scientist Joseph Grieco deals extensively with the atavistic—even economically irrational—way China sometimes has behaved in international affairs, and he compares this with the approaches taken by two major beneficiaries of the modern world order, Germany and Japan. He suggests China may show signs of territorial discontent because there has been so much turbulence in the relative capabilities of the countries of East Asia and because there is less regional social capital, or mutual trust, in the area.

Political scientist Ronald Rogowski voices misgivings about some aspects of international economic developments. As the world economy comes more and more to depend on the effective development and efficient use of human capital, there will be great benefit for many, but he anticipates that this process will also lead to an economic divergence of nations and regions. He sees immigration, particularly of the most able, from backward regions and a heightened welfare cost to political failure (caused by an underinvestment in human capital) even as great social benefits accrue to those areas well governed. This could lead to an increasing division between wealthy democracies and impoverished non-democracies and to military turmoil in what used to be known as the Third World.

Political scientist Michael Brown focuses on the last of these problems: internal and communal conflict. However economically irrational they may often be, such conflicts remain the most pervasive—indeed, almost the only—form of armed violence in the world. At times, he argues, these can have important and problematic implications—economic and otherwise—for the wealthy leading countries. He assesses policies those countries might apply to deal with the turmoil, and he also considers the effects of economic development—or the lack thereof—in causing or exacerbating such conflicts.

Political scientist Cherie Steele considers the effects on the international system of technological change which, she argues, is often determining. A new system, she suggests, is indeed emerging, and most of the incentives increasingly favor economic strategies—trading perspectives rather than territorial ones. As a result, states may well become smaller and more specialized and, perhaps, culturally based. However, unequal resources, uneven economic growth, and a continuing shift from traditional manufacturing toward information-based technologies may exacerbate core-periphery problems, sometimes leading to the violent flaunting of emerging international norms by those left behind. Moreover, technological imperatives could change and begin to promise greater returns for military strategies than for cooperative, economic ones.

Political scientist Arthur Stein asks why states justify their behavior. As he puts it, "anarchy should mean not having to say you are sorry." He lays out reasons why states might want to explain their choices. He argues that justification in international politics demonstrates the importance of domestic politics to foreign policy and the existence of an international society with shared values. He also argues that justification is an important component of international institutions and regimes and the basis of an international society that approximates how domestic society functions.

Historian Paul Schroeder compares the end of the Cold War to similar international periods following 1643 and 1811. During the Cold War, he argues, the major contestants were working out their differences within an essentially peaceful context—peaceful coexistence was a central purpose from its very beginning. He finds the permanent pacification and integration of Western Europe during the Cold War to be particularly important because the very concept of peace was redefined, expanded, and transformed in the process. From this perspective the end of the Cold War can be characterized as the adoption by the Communist world to this expanded and transformed definition of peace. Because this process is supported by such institutions as democracy, free trade and communication, market-based economics, and the rule of law, this could be a real breakthrough to general world peace, unlike the temporary and partial ones that took place in earlier centuries. Historical experience suggests, however, that this breakthrough could still break down—ideas remain important and bad ones can still be developed and gain acceptance. The chief dangers, as in the past, are from internal decay and disintegration, and Schroeder suggests that the unfettered market place is a bad and dangerous master in world affairs and that eternal politics will be the price of peace.

International relationships can remain largely static for long stretches of time, and then change dramatically at critical points. The world is now at one of those historic turning points, and a new structure is being born—or invented. The essays in this volume suggest that the coming century poses both challenges and opportunities in international politics, and that there is political and economic space for important new possibilities. We may be moving into an era of peace and prosperity, but attaining that result requires getting the politics right.

Notes

1. Important in this process were the work and contributions of Martin Sherwin. Additionally, the contributors owe thanks to Michael Blakley for exemplary work on arrangements for a memorable and productive conference in January 1997.

2. *Action and Reaction in World Politics: International Systems in Perspective* (Boston: Little, Brown, 1963; reprinted, Westport, CT: Greenwood Press, 1977); *The Rise of the Trading State: Commerce and Conquest in the Modern World* (New York: Basic Books, 1986); *The Rise of the Virtual State: Wealth and Power in the Coming Century* (New York: Basic Books, 1999). Other works discuss these issues as well. His international relations textbook, *International Relations: Peace or War?* (New York: McGraw-Hill, 1973), stands out for its historical discussion and analysis. When Rosecrance created an events database, it was the only one not focused on current events and the era of the Cold War, as he found the Bismarckian period appropriate both for testing many international relations theories and for generating lessons for more modern times. See, among other articles, Richard Rosecrance, Alan Alexandroff, Brian Healy, and Arthur A. Stein, "Power, Balance of Power and Status in Nineteenth Century International Relations," *Sage Professional Papers in International Studies* no. 29 (1974); Ronald Goodman, Jeffery Hart, and Richard Rosecrance, "Testing International Theory," in Edward E. Azar and Joseph D. Ben-Dak, eds., *Theory and Practice of Events Research* (New York: Gordon & Breach, 1975).

3. Rosecrance's interdisciplinary orientation has also included psychology. He is the only political scientist, for example, to have noted the importance of structural balance theory for international relations. See Richard Rosecrance, *International Relations: Peace or War?*; and H. Brooke McDonald and Richard Rosecrance, "Alliance and Structural Balance in the International System: A Reinterpretation," *Journal of Conflict Resolution* 29 (March 1985): 57–82.

4. Richard Rosecrance, *The Rise of the Trading State*; Richard Rosecrance and Arthur A. Stein, "Interdependence: Myth or Reality?" *World Politics* 26 (October 1973): 1–27; Richard Rosecrance, "International Interdependence," in Geoffrey L. Goodwin and Andrew Linklater, eds., *New Dimensions of World Politics* (New York: Halsted Press, 1975); Richard Rosecrance, Alan Alexandroff, W. Koehler, J. Kroll, S. Laquer, and J. Stocker, "Whither Interdependence?" *International Organization* 31 (Summer 1977): 425–471. There is a long-standing tendency in international relations to treat states as analogues of firms and to borrow ideas from economics. Rosecrance argues that the realist mainstream has only borrowed arguments about competition and that other ideas can be more fruitfully applied. See Richard Rosecrance, "International theory revisited," *International Organization* 35 (Autumn 1981): 691–713, as well as his delineation of a political analogue for the virtual corporation in his "The Rise of the Virtual State," *Foreign Affairs* 75 (July/August 1996): 45–61.

5. On this issue, see, in particular, Richard Rosecrance and Arthur A. Stein, eds., *The Domestic Bases of Grand Strategy* (Ithaca, NY: Cornell University Press, 1993).

6. Rosecrance has long emphasized the importance of reward and positive inducements in contrast to threat and sanctions as the basis for altering state behavior. During the Cold War, he noted that deterrence could be more easily achieved by increasing the payoffs states obtained in the status quo and thereby reducing their incentive to challenge the status quo. This conclusion emerged readily from the standard deterrence equations that others used merely to determine which weapons systems were more or less stabilizing. Richard Rosecrance,

Strategic Deterrence Reconsidered (London: International Institute for Strategic Studies, 1975); Richard Rosecrance, *International Relations: Peace or War?*; Richard Rosecrance, "Reward, Punishment, and Interdependence," *Journal of Conflict Resolution* 25 (March 1981): 31–46.

7. This emphasis also picks up on a Rosecrance theme, namely the importance of the relations forged between great powers at the end of major global wars. For his arguments about the prospect for a new concert of powers in the wake of the Cold War, see Richard Rosecrance, "A New Concert of Powers," *Foreign Affairs* 71 (Spring 1992): 64–82. For earlier reflections, see Richard Rosecrance, ed., *America As an Ordinary Country: U.S. Foreign Policy and the Future* (Ithaca, NY: Cornell University Press, 1976).

8. Rosecrance has emphasized that states copy one another and that an international form of socialization takes place: Richard Rosecrance, "The Political Socialization of Nations," *International Studies Quarterly* 20 (September 1976): 441–460.

9. Unlike many scholars of international relations, Rosecrance has emphasized the utility and the centrality of scholarly analysis as a way of informing public policy. Among others, see his recommendations for U.S. policy in Richard Rosecrance, *America's Economic Resurgence: A Bold New Strategy* (New York: Harper & Row, 1990); and his suggestions to Japan in Richard Rosecrance and Jennifer Taw, "Japan and the Theory of International Leadership," *World Politics* 42 (January 1990): 184–209.

2

Corporations and States: Factor Flows in the Twenty-First Century

RICHARD ROSECRANCE

The Units

States and Firms: The Conventional Theory

The conventional theory of international politics compares the rivalry among states to the competition of firms in an industry.[1] The two disciplines of microeconomics and international politics are seen as operating according to similar principles. The relevant unit, whether state or corporation, seeks to succeed in a wider market.[2] The firm was a hierarchical organization that made products for the consumer. It designed and manufactured components and then assembled them to create a final product. Firms financed, marketed, and transported goods to prospective buyers.

Similarly in the conventional view, states were hierarchical organizations that performed services for their members.[3] They protected their populations from outside threats and sought to guarantee domestic peace. Governments were created and instituted to provide social services for individuals. Through taxation, they offered municipal and national services to citizens in the fields of police, welfare, health, and education. They established the legal environment in which individuals and corporations could exchange goods and services.

Firms contracted with suppliers and buyers, but they also competed with other firms in the same industry, each seeking to provide a complete product to consumers. In the conventional theory, states might equally reach agreements with one another in arms control or trade, but they remained competitors for influence and power in the system as a whole. They did not willingly agree to the establishment of a hierarchy that placed one of their number above the rest; nor did they develop a stable division of labor among themselves internationally.[4] In the conventional view, states were similar units. They did not perform differentiated functions. Like firms, however, they might occasionally enter into market-sharing or spheres of influence arrangements.

States and Firms: A Revised View

Yet, the conventional analysis provides only one possible view of the link between economic competition and international politics. The theory of international trade (which, unlike the theory of the firm, actually deals with countries) offers reasons for nation-states to specialize in the production of goods and services internationally according to their respective comparative advantages. Countries derive benefit from free trade in which they purchase goods from others that they produce relatively less efficiently at home. According to the theory of international trade, states can achieve a division of labor internationally, which is not altogether different from the economic division of labor among producers within domestic society.[5]

The Theory of the Firm.   A new division of labor engendered by the process of market exchange could thus reshape nations and their role in the world economy in accordance with the theory of international trade. Ronald Coase held that the firm was an equally flexible and adaptable entity.[6] It exists only because individuals face intractable information and transaction problems in directly contracting with one another for the production of goods and services. A firm bundles a series of components or services into a complete and integrated product. By bringing together the individuals or suppliers who produce the components that make up a product, the firm provides a vital service, for which, of course, it exacts a return, earning a profit.[7] If individuals possessed enough information and contracting ability, however, they might do the work on their own.[8]

Consider a homeowner who wishes to add a bedroom or patio to her house. She may decide to perform the functions of contractor herself, or she may hire a prime contractor to oversee and coordinate the activities of separate subcontractors—bricklayers, carpenters, plumbers, and electricians—paying the former a fee in return. If she hires a prime contractor, that contractor acts like a corporation would, integrating a series of services and products together.

The size and function of the firm are always subject to change with alterations in technology, information, and transaction costs, and the willingness of individuals directly to contract with each other.[9] The firm is no more static in its contractual relationships than is the nation-state.[10] If an individual purchaser could seek out individual suppliers of subcomponents, she would not have to rely on a corporation to provide them.[11]

One effect of information technology (IT) is to short-circuit the complex communication channels of traditional firms, allowing individuals to find what they need and to purchase it directly without engaging the services of corporate middlemen.[12] The World Wide Web and the Internet provide such linkages and the requisite information. An adept individual with access to a good communications network can thus duplicate many of the functions of travel agent, banker, insurance adviser, stock broker, and real estate agent. Another effect of superior ITs is to give senior managers data that they never before possessed, allowing them to dispense with the expertise and services of middle management. Finally, if physical capital can be substituted for routine work through robotics or other technologies, only the most skilled and educated workers need be retained. Partly as a result of the widespread availability of information, therefore, transaction costs have been greatly reduced, and firms have become leaner as a result, dispensing with unneeded management and labor.

To save on costs, companies have also reduced the number of vertical levels in their organization.[13] Finding new and reliable suppliers, firms no longer have to produce all their subcomponents in-house. They can contract out their production, saving expenses on large endowments of plant, equipment, and land. "Just-in-time" methods bring materials to the plant when a specific process occurs, saving on storage and warehousing costs. The net result is an efficient "downsizing" of corporations, which then have extra funds for investment in new products.

At one extreme end of this continuum of downsizing lies the "virtual corporation," an entity that performs headquarters functions—research and development, product design, financing, marketing, insurance, and transport—but which does not actually manufacture products.[14] Proceeding along a route outlined by Ronald Coase, the firm subcontracts production to another company, saving on in-house costs. As this process proceeds, companies form industrial alliances to produce products. This partly mitigates the competitive relationship between them. "Headquarters" companies design products to be made somewhere else. In the new locution of Silicon Valley, these are designated as "fabless" firms (without fabrication capabilities). In response, "foundry" (or "fab") companies emerge—firms that produce goods for other companies but have no distinctive products of their own.[15] Their production facilities have to be joined with other firms' product design for a new line of merchandise to be created. Relations between "fabless" and "foundry" companies are even more cooperative than those between traditional companies that do contract work for each other. "Foundries" will never compete in product design with "fabless" firms, and thus strategic alliances with them will be more dependable.

IT affects transaction costs in two ways. It reduces the necessary activity of the firm itself, returning sovereignty to individual buyers and sellers of goods who can now contract directly with one another, without the intermediary of the corporation. Second, new information makes a firm more efficient, allowing it to contract with others for subcomponent production or even for production as a whole. In both instances, the market gains while in-house costs decline.

The Theory of International Politics.   Just as firms have downsized along Coasian lines, so some states have recognized that they do not have to produce everything at home. The rapid development of foreign, direct investment since World War II is in part a reflection of the new trend. At particular stages of production, states like firms find it convenient and economical to produce their goods within other countries, benefiting from cheaper labor and closer proximity to the international marketplace. All major industrial countries have moved in this direction, including the United States, European countries, and most recently Japan. The United States began heavily to invest abroad (particularly in Europe) in the 1960s and 1970s. In the late 1970s and 1980s, European investment reciprocated, going largely to America. Since then, the United States and Europe have directed investment to East Asian countries and China. Now Japan has begun to diversify its production and to invest overseas—in the United States, the emerging markets of East Asia, and also particularly in mainland China. As a result, manufacturing has fallen as a proportion of Gross Domestic Product (GDP) in all developed countries. Services have now risen to 70 percent or more of GDP in many first world economies. And the trend is increasing.

As we have already seen, the most dynamic new players have been countries and regions that have moved fully to embrace high technological services as their future industrial advantage.[16] These countries—and there are more on the way—have emerged as "virtual states"—states that concentrated on headquarters or "head" functions and that produce their goods through reliable contracts with production or "body" nations somewhere else. The return on the high-level services performed by "head" nations has on the whole been greater than the return on manufacturing of a traditional sort.

In part, of course, this shift is simply a change in market incentives that brings corresponding changes in corporate strategy among modern firms. The state is in part a bystander in the process. At the same time, states can either accept or resist the change. Like Great Britain, Holland,

Switzerland, Hong Kong, and Singapore, they can seek to benefit from the shift, moving to gain new comparative advantage through services and a more highly educated and technical management and workforce. Or they can try to protect domestic industry (as France, Italy, and Japan did in the past), keeping production largely at home. As states move to accommodate and foster the industrial trend, they change their role as players in international relations.

In this way there has been a growing alteration in the function of the state, analogous to the shift in the nature of the corporation or firm. In both cases, the organization has become more horizontal and more (not less) dependent on relationships with suppliers. As firms and states contract out production, they develop crucial economic links with foreign entities. Their stake in the continuance of such relationships rises.

Further, state control of consumer decisions declines. The market rises as a direct provider of services and the state contracts its role in the market. This means that individual citizens are less beholden to the state for their long-term welfare. Individual sellers of their labor must rely more on themselves and the market and less on the safety net provided by the state.

States and Firms: The Consequences of the Modern Theory of International Politics

The conventional view holds that the theory of the firm is the theoretical starting point for the theory of the state acting in international politics. When the firm undergoes a transformation in its relations with suppliers and subcontractors, the nature of interfirm competition changes. Industrial alliances emerge. There is a greater division of labor even among erstwhile competing firms. Firms are no longer entirely "like units" but have undergone some differentiation. The firm—traditionally a vertical entity bundling all subcomponent production in-house—then emerges as a contracting, horizontal entity in which many subcomponents have to be bought from suppliers or even from competitors. Flatter firms are more efficient and more profitable, but they also depend more on each other.

In similar ways, there is a process of downsizing affecting contemporary states that now purchase vital components abroad. They increasingly produce goods abroad. Foreign, direct investment creates interdependence based on production that is far stronger than past interdependence based solely on trade. There is a differentiation of production and the beginnings of a division of labor among states. The theory of international trade augurs in favor of such outcomes.

Ronald Coase foresaw the possibility that firms would become less necessary as transaction costs declined and information became cheaper and more available.[17] We are now witnessing the unbundling of the state for similar reasons. The consequences for international politics are fundamental ones. The theory of the firm initially presumed no differentiation of function among firms competing in a single industry. This assumption is no longer fully true. Industrial alliances, international production arrangements, and subcontracting of component production all make the classical theory of the firm obsolescent, if not obsolete. The conventional theory of international politics also inveighed against their being any division of labor among states. The emergence of foreign direct investment, virtual states, connections between "head" and "body" nations show that, contrary to conventional theory, states are becoming increasingly "unlike" units. Cooperation amongst them thus can now be founded on the beginnings of a division of labor internationally.

In addition, the citizen emerges with a greater independence of the state and greater contracting ability. In these circumstances, citizens may be less willing to pay for state-oriented foreign-policy activities if they appear to conflict with their own economic and contracting interests.

The Interaction of Units

In the conventional theory of international politics, states typically created a balance of power against potential aggressors. They formed alliances against states bent on political or military expansion.[18] Or they rearmed, using "internal balancing" to deter conflict.[19] The conventional theory assumed that nation-states controlled territory and that they needed to prevent an aggressor from seizing new land, thereby upsetting the balance of power. Alliances hemmed the aggressor in, and the rearmament of target countries made it difficult to take a new province away. In the conventional approach, territory was one of the important elements in political and military power.[20]

Stocks and Flows

Few denied that nations could gain power through stocks of raw materials, population, and territory. Many wars (to say nothing of the colonial acquisitions of nineteenth-century imperialism) were based on the territorial assumption. Territory and population lent power to their holders. But stocks were not the only elements in economic or military power. If a nation controlled or could benefit from "flows" of goods, capital, and technology, it could also become powerful.

In the economic assumptions of the post-medieval period, any successful country could control "flows" by fiat. It could keep goods at home, and it could prevent imports from coming in. When this was seen to be self-defeating, however, mercantilist principles still dictated that a nation should run a uniform trade or payments surplus with exports exceeding imports. The country could then gain gold or foreign exchange to carry on its wars. In the nineteenth century, countries recognized that export-led growth could be an important addition to domestic demand, facilitating rapid economic expansion. Even before Great Britain came to control about one quarter of the world's land area in 1897, it had rapidly developed to become the world's premier industrial power through exports of manufactured goods. It did so on a relatively narrow insular base. Flows were then becoming important equally with stocks.

Before World War I, Great Britain enjoyed enormous prosperity, not because of its export surplus (which by then had turned into a deficit) but because of financial flows and income from foreign investment that provided an overall surplus on current account. At that point, British power derived more from favorable flows of purchasing power than it did from stocks of raw materials, food, or population.

The "flow" of goods, capital, and technology, therefore could at least theoretically compensate for any deficiency of "stocks." If a country lost a province, perhaps it could make up the deficit by rapid economic growth.[21] It might gain access to new resources and wealth through foreign trade. The losers of World War II were deprived of territory. Japan lost her empire in East Asia and her position in Manchuria and China. Germany was divided and stripped of gains in the East. Italy was forced to disgorge Ethiopia and Albania. All the losers' colonies were taken away and distributed to others. Two or three decades after World War II, however, the losers had more than compensated for their losses of "stocks." "Flows" of goods and purchasing power lent them higher growth rates than achieved by the victors.

What difference does the pervasive shift from stocks to flows make for the interaction and "balancing" process in world politics? It means fundamentally that losses of stocks can be compensated for in many ways, only one of which is gaining other stocks. Flows of factors of production: capital, labor, and information can provide an equilibration that does not occur in "stocks." No territory changes hands yet one party may gain.

The Greater Flexibility of Interaction

The increasing emphasis on flows means that territorial gain for one power is less important in the international scheme of things.[22] Smaller countries may sometimes do better than larger ones. Peter Katzenstein has convincingly portrayed the small countries of Europe as efficient, outwardly looking entities, ready to meet the challenge of global competition. The smaller nations of East Asia have been even more successful and productive. In contrast, larger states seeking to monopolize their own domestic markets may not feel as strong a need to develop cutting-edge industries. They may therefore fail to create industries or services of the highest quality.

This suggests that responses to presumed international "threats" could be more varied and less exigent than presumed in the past. Despite the apparatus of military power that Western countries mobilized against the Soviet Union after World War II, they did not seek to take away Soviet territory. The great advantage of Western and democratic nations was in their mastery of flows, not stocks. It was the failure of the Soviet Union to match the standard of world technology and economic growth that ultimately doomed the Soviet experiment. In a world in which the importance of flows may be greater than stocks, arms races, new alliances, and military threats are not the only means of regaining a balance internationally.

The Uncertainty of Interaction:
The Inability of Governments to Command Flows

There is a further reason for nations not to despair if a rival appears to do well. In liberalizing societies, governments cannot simply command key flows of production and purchasing power. They cannot force multinational corporations or labor power to migrate to their shores. They cannot command finance to do their bidding. Mobile factors of production can leave an economy as well as enter it if the environment is not a hospitable one. If flows are as or more important than stocks, therefore, it is often unclear which nations are winning and which losing. In the 1970s many thought the Soviet Union was gaining. But it was not. It failed to command or attract the mobile factors of production and information capital that ultimately proved to be all important in deciding its competition with the West. Those who believe that there must be a conflict between the United States and Japan also bank too much on particular trends in growth rates or political attitude. These can and have been frequently reversed. Increasingly uncontrolled by governments, changes in flows can be of enormous significance. One does not need to "balance" against a nation that is losing factors of production to China or other countries.

Flows and Modern Nation States

There is a relationship between the "flatness" of the corporation or the state and its reliance on stocks and flows. Vertically organized corporations depend least on contractual arrangements with other firms to purchase components. Territorial states producing all needed commodities at home have little use for international trade or finance. But as firms and states covet greater efficiency, they become streamlined and downsized; they find it in their economic and political interests to contract for some of the things they need from outsiders. The importance of flows rises in comparison to territorial stocks.

International Conflict and the Modern State

It does not follow that countries benefiting from a division of labor sustained by flows between them will never engage in conflict. Some countries are still at the territorial stage (with land as the major factor of production), and their quest for power involves seizure of other peoples' stocks of population and resources. The Gulf War represented such a quest on behalf of Iraq's Saddam Hussein. Few believe that large countries will never again become aggressive in world politics. Some think that China will sometime embark on a career of international expansion. The stability of Russia's fragile political institutions is in doubt, and a new Russian nationalism cannot be ruled out for the long-term future. There are some who contend that the collective representatives of Islamic Fundamentalism will eventually try to assault the liberties of the system and initiate a new cultural clash with Western and democratic states.[23]

New Means of Coping with Conflict

The major difference between the past potentiality for major conflict and the situation today and in the coming century is that the instruments to combat or dissuade such conflicts are far more numerous and powerful than in the past. At the same time the instruments that military aggressors possess (to conquer a province or an oil field) are much less efficacious ones.

To take the second first. Aggressors must be convinced that a military assault will yield commensurate political and economic dividends before they strike. They must also believe that control of new territory conveys a particular boon. This will not always be true. Larger states are sometimes weaker and less effective competitors than their smaller brethren. At the theoretical extreme, perhaps some states will one day seek to disgorge territory to become more efficient units.[24] Some continue to question whether the addition of East Germany has made Germany a more effective trading state. But even if new territory contributes more to strength than weakness, perhaps it cannot be governed. Israel has spent a great deal of time trying to extract benefit from its rulership of the West Bank and Gaza, almost entirely without success. Mobilized and subject populations resist. An imperial ruler of today's Afghanistan would inherit a hornets' nest. Who would want to try to conquer and assimilate Southeast Asia or Africa in the contemporary era? But if we assume that conquest somehow pays, how can expansion be deflected? There are many ways in which possible target states can strengthen themselves, and not only by the traditional means of raising arms or concluding new alliances. Economic development is their longer term means of strengthening the mobilization base, and that development can be secured through flows of capital and technology, as well as through internal demand. Indeed, the subtlest means of deflating an aggressor's presumption is by providing incentives that will lead critical factors of production to flow elsewhere. This is not some purely hypothetical example. It is precisely the means that will be used against China if it mistreats Hong Kong or bullies Taiwan. Foreign, direct investment could leave China in a mass exodus, undermining the competitiveness of her export industries and deflating her growth prospects. China would be materially weakened.

Policy Objectives Versus Policy Instruments

Jan Tinbergen stressed that policy instruments have to be sufficiently numerous and varied to attain requisite policy goals. Internationally in the past, the major means of balancing an aggressive power was by making war. This, however, was the least sophisticated method, and it was a generally unsatisfactory means of international adjustment. Alternatively, a state could rearm and seek to acquire allies. Now and in the future there are many other ways of strengthening oneself or weakening the potential adversary. To change the repertoire of stocks requires military methods. But flows can be redirected in many other ways. Economic competition is one such means. Interest rates, inflation rates, and stable currencies are in this respect weapons of war.

This does not mean that the future will not witness conflict among economic and political rivals. But it will be conflict sotto voce. Some have thought that one country would seek to disable another's data network, spreading viruses throughout its communications systems.[25] But this is a game that two can play. Industrial espionage gives intelligence organizations something to do in a future in which economic sophistication and strength will be very important. But even these possibilities merely transfer the state into a realm already populated by corporations, who certainly engage in peaceful competition with one another.[26] The chairman of General Motors still does not decide to kill the head of Toyota.

Even state rivalry transformed into something akin to industrial competition does not strike the same sparks it used to do.[27] Flattened corporations have to contract with one another. Less omnicompetent nations also need economic alliances with other countries as production and capital moves overseas. As Ronald Coase foresaw, corporations adjust as information proliferates, and transaction costs decline. Smaller corporations and streamlined states efficiently become more dependent on outside suppliers and sometimes even competitors. Individuals pursue international interests aside from government. Conflict among states continues but it also pales in comparison with the violence of yesteryear.

The Twenty-First Century

The return on services is now higher than the return on land or the return on manufacturing. Following this trend, most modern nations have diminished or relocated their manufacturing capabilities. While "head nations" have been created in consequence, new "body nations" have arisen to do the world's manufacturing. Few countries have today within their own territorial confines all the requisites of a sophisticated industrial, mining, and service capacity. They have learned instead to depend on others. When a Chinese textile or fashion house turns out dresses for the fall collection, they embody French, American, and Italian designs. When Daimler-Chrysler places its name on a car, it may include 80 percent foreign components. When IBM or Compaq stamps its company name on the computer, the product may have been put together by Ingram or other middleman assembler. As nations and corporations become thinner, flows between countries and firms become thicker. As specialization proceeds in both realms, interdependence rises. It is therefore possible that in the twenty-first century there will be no new omnicompetent national leader of the system, a new number one supplanting the United States, but rather a variety of nations and regions (like Europe) in which no one entity does everything well. If so, the very unitary notion of "power" will be disassembled into components, perhaps never to be put together again.

Notes

1. Kenneth Waltz contends: "International-political systems, like economic markets, are formed by the coaction of self-regarding units. International structures are defined in terms of the primary political units of an era. . . . Structures emerge from the coexistence of states. No state intends to participate in the formation of a structure by which it and others will be constrained. International-political systems, like economic markets, are individualist in origin, spontaneously generated, and unintended. In both systems, structures are formed by the coaction of their units" (*Theory of International Politics*, Reading, Mass: Addison-Wesley, 1979, p. 91).

2. Waltz notes, "In any self-help system, units worry about their survival, and the worry conditions their behavior. Oligopolistic markets limit the cooperation of firms in much the way that international-political structures limit the cooperation of states" (105).

3. Waltz observes, "Domestic politics is hierarchically ordered. The units—institutions and agencies—stand vis á vis each other in relations of super- and subordination" (81).

4. Waltz contends, "The states that are the units of international-political systems are not formally differentiated by the functions they perform. Anarchy entails relations of coordination among a system's units, and that implies sameness" (93).

5. See among others, R. Caves and R. Jones, *World Trade and Payments*. Boston: Little Brown, 1993.

6. In contrast, Waltz tended to assume that although they could be larger or smaller, foolish or prudent, states operating in a field of international relations would never change their basic character.

7. Coase points out that within a firm, "market transactions are eliminated and in place of the complicated market structure with exchange transactions is substituted the entrepreneur-co-ordinator, who directs production" ("The Nature of the Firm," *Economica*, November 1937, p. 388).

8. *The Economist* offers the following analysis of Coase's contributions: "In theory computers could wipe out the need for firms in the traditional sense altogether. In 1937 Ronald Coase . . . asked why workers were organised in firms instead of acting as independent buyers and sellers of goods and services at each stage of production. He concluded that firms were needed because of the lack of information and the need to minimise transactions costs. A world without firms in which production was organised entirely through markets would require full information and no transition costs; but in the real world it takes time and money to find out about the product being bought or sold. A firm resolves these problems. Mr. Coase argued that the size of firms is determined by the relative costs of bringing in services from outside and the overhead cost of providing them in house" (*The Economist*, September 28, 1996).

9. Oliver Williamson makes an essential distinction between the corporation's decision to "make or buy" a product or component. See particularly Oliver Williamson and Janet Bercovitz, "The Modern Corporation as an Efficiency Instrument: The Comparative Contracting Perspective," in Carl Kaysen (editor), *The American Corporation Today* (New York: Oxford University Press, 1996), p. 334.

10. Coase observes, "The amount of 'vertical' integration, involving as it does the suppression of the price mechanism, varies greatly from industry to industry and firm to firm" (389).

11. Coase formulates this point in the following way: "At the margin, the costs of organizing [an exchange transaction] within the firm will be equal either to the costs of organising in another firm or to the costs involved in leaving the transaction to be 'organised' by the price mechanism" (404).

12. In Coasian terms, "It is clear that the dynamic factors are also of considerable importance, and an investigation of the effect changes have on the cost of organising within the firm and on marketing costs generally will enable one to explain why firms get larger and smaller" (405).

13. See note 8.

14. See R. Rosecrance, "The Rise of the Virtual State," *Foreign Affairs,* July-August 1996.

15. Such firms are now emerging in Silicon Valley, Taiwan, and other places in East Asia. See for instance, "Pure Foundry, Pure Profit," in *Electronic Business Asia* December 1995.

16. See for example, "Services Becoming the Goods in Industry," *New York Times,* January 7, 1997, p. C1.

17. The effect of information technology is truly dazzling. According to one estimate, "Since the Second World War 60 percent of U.S. economic growth has derived from the introduction of increasingly efficient equipment, the most important of which have been information machines. Around 1950 computers entered the economy, essentially as calculating devices, and the cost of crunching numbers plummeted. Between 1950 and 1980 the cost of a MIP (million instructions per second) fell between 27 and 50 percent *annually.* In the 1960s computers became labor-saving devices for storing, sorting and retrieving data, the cost of which probably fell at an annual rate of 25 to 30 percent between 1960 and 1985" (*Newsweek,* October 28, 1996, p. 92).

18. Waltz argues, "We find states forming balances of power whether or not they wish to" (125) and, "The theory leads us to expect states to behave in ways that result in balances forming" (125). But see Rosecrance and Lo, "Balancing, Stability, and War: The Mysterious Case of the Napoleonic International System," *International Studies Quarterly,* December 1996.

19. In a bipolar world, internal balancing is likely. Waltz writes that the Soviet Union and the United States "balance each other by 'internal' rather than 'external' means, relying on their own capabilities rather than on the capabilities of allies. Internal balancing is more reliable and precise than external balancing"(168).

20. Waltz observes that state capability and rank depend on "size of population and territory, resource endowment, economic capability, military strength, political stability, and competence" (137).

21. Waltz himself speculates that the free world's "loss of China" in 1949 could be made up by several years of American economic growth ("The Stability of a Bipolar World" *Daedalus,* Summer 1964).

22. See particularly Richard Rosecrance, *The Rise of the Virtual State: Wealth and Power in the Coming Century* (New York: Basic Books, 1999).

23. See Samuel P. Huntington, "The Clash of Civilizations?" *Foreign Affairs,* 72, no. 3 (Summer 1993): 22-50.

24. Jane Jacobs expressed this thesis in *Cities and the Wealth of Nations: Principles of Economic Life.* New York: Random House, 1984. It has also been adverted to by Paul Krugman.

25. See Alvin and Heidi Toffler, *War & Anti-War: Survival at the Dawn of the 21st Century.* Boston: Little Brown, 1993.

26. Waltz also recognizes this. He writes: "Economically, the self-help principle applies within governmentally-contrived limits" (91).

27. This lack of sparks of course was not true in the seventeenth and eighteenth centuries, when the Dutch and British East India companies were in effect fighting organizations.

3

The World Economy at the End of the Millennium

DEEPAK LAL

Introduction

If a Rip van Winkle had gone to sleep at the end of about 1870 and woken up in the last few years, he would find that little has changed in the world economy. He would note the various technological advances in transportation and communications (airlines, telephones, and the computer) have further reduced the costs of international trade and commerce and led to the progressive integration of the world economy which was well under way after the first Great Age of Reform, when he went to sleep.

The terrible events of this century—two world wars, the Great Depression, and the battles against two illiberal creeds—Fascism and Communism—which led to the breakdown of the first liberal international economic order (LIEO)—created under British leadership after the repeal of the Corn Laws—would form no part of his memory. Nor would the various and varying fads in economic policy-both national and international—during this century make any sense (e.g. exchange controls), the use of quotas rather than tariffs as instruments of protection, centralized planning and associated controls on production and distribution, and restrictions on the free flow of capital.

Having read his De Tocqueville he would also not be surprised that the United States and Russia had become great powers in the latter part of this century. Nor, that it took the United States nearly a century to become the predominant power, just as it took Great Britain nearly a century from the mid-eighteenth-century conflict with France till the end of the Napoleonic Wars to achieve its predominance. His reading of De

Tocqueville would also allow him to see a natural progression from the
rise of Great Britain—which was in a sense the victory of an aristocratic
oligarchy over the divine right of kings—to that of the United States,
which is a victory of Demos over aristocracy. Whether this is an unmixed
blessing is open to question.[1]

He[2] would be surprised by two features of the current world economy.
For unlike the nineteenth century when there was free movement of
goods, money, and people, today there are relatively free flows of goods
and money but no free movement of labor. This is related to the second
surprising feature he would observe: the welfare states to be found in
most advanced countries, which as he would soon recognize, have created property rights in citizenship. This necessarily leads to restrictions
on immigration. For immigration creates new citizens with an automatic
right of access to the purses of existing citizens through the transfer state.
Having gone to sleep in 1870 before the great scramble for Empire by the
nations of Europe, and the universal spread of the Romantic movement's
ideal of nationalism, he would also not be surprised by the twin theses of
Richard Rosecrance who we are honoring in this work.[3] First, that the territorial imperative that had motivated competition between nation states
since the end of the wars of religion was replaced by the commercial
competition of trading states following the example of Great Britain in
the first great Age of Reform. Second, that as more and more developing
countries, particularly India and China with their vast pools of relatively
cheap labor, are brought into an integrated world economy, a new international division of labor is emerging, with developed countries mainly
providing services and developing ones manufactures. With this spatial
division between 'the head' and 'the body' of economic activity, trade is
becoming essential for the well being of all countries, thus reducing the
attractions of nationalism and war.

He would also not be surprised by the consensual economic policies
increasingly embraced around the world as they echo those of the standard textbook of nineteenth-century political economy—Mill's *Principles*.[4] Though he would be surprised by the technicalities in which the
discussions were conducted—particularly amongst the new breed of academic economists—he would have no difficulty in understanding and
endorsing their prescriptions: sound money, Gladstonian finance, and a
general acceptance of the nineteenth-century policy prescription of "lais-
sez faire." Having missed the heated discussions and theories concerning
planning, Keynesian macroeconomics, optimum taxation, and various
other fads and fashions, he could happily neglect the voluminous literature they spawned in the time he had been asleep.

But being of a curious bent he would probably have decided to read
some condensed account of what had happened to the world while he

was sleeping. He would have been astounded by the events of this century—of a world gone mad. He would have tried to find an explanation of what had gone wrong, and why and when the tide turned to enable the world economy to resume the progress that had stalled after he had gone to sleep. He would also wonder if the coming century would repeat the mistakes of the last, or if that age of universal worldwide peace and prosperity that seemed imminent toward the end of the great nineteenth-century Age of Reform was now in prospect. These are the themes I will explore on Rip van Winkle's behalf in the rest of this essay. But before that I need to provide some harder evidence than Rip's casual empiricism for his belief that the world economy has picked up where it left off in the late nineteenth century.

Remembrance of Things Past

There are two pieces of statistical evidence that show that the world economy is back to where it was in the late nineteenth century. The first concerns the integration of global, capital markets. The second is the integration of world commodity markets through trade and thus indirectly the world markets for labor.

Determining the extent of global, capital-market integration has spawned a vast literature surveyed masterfully by Obstfeld (1995). For our comparative historical purpose what we need is a statistical measure of this integration for which we can obtain historical data to see the trends in capital-market integration over the last century. There are essentially two routes—a price and a quantity route. On the price measure, if capital markets were globally integrated, the price of an asset must be the same wherever it is sold. In practice it is very difficult to test this implication because there is insufficient data on *identical* assets in different markets. One data set that Obstfeld (1995) has used is the onshore-offshore price differential on a given asset. But the Euro currency markets, which allow these comparisons, are a post-World War II invention, and we cannot make similar historical comparisons.

The second route (through quantity) is based on the argument that in a completely integrated, global, capital market, as the productivity of a country's investment is not necessarily linked to the determinants of its savings rate, a rise in the latter should lead to their most efficient deployment worldwide, which *ceteris paribus* should lead to a current account surplus and a capital outflow, and conversely if there is a rise in the productivity of a country's investment, to a capital account deficit and a capital inflow. Feldstein and Horioka (1980) use this to argue that, in such a world, the savings and investment rates in a particular country should not be systematically associated. They suggest a cross section regression of the form:

$$(I/Y)^j = a + b (S/Y)^j + u^j$$

where I/Y is the investment ratio; S/Y the savings ratio, and u is a random disturbance for each country j. If capital is completely immobile $b=1$, so that the lower the value of b from unity the greater the degree of capital mobility.

There are various problems with the implementation and interpretation of these types of regressions.[5] But, despite this, as the data on savings and investment rates is readily available, *faute de mieux*, at least an imperfect measure of capital market integration can be derived. There are moreover, two sets of data (with somewhat different countries covered) which allow us to obtain estimates of b from the late nineteenth century to the present. These were compiled by Taylor (1996) and Maddison (1991, 1992). Taylor has estimated the b coefficients for his historical data and we have done so for the Maddison data. The resulting values are charted in Figure 3.1.

A similar story emerges from all three trends in the b estimates, which is in consonance with the qualitative historical evidence we have on changing capital mobility over this long period.[6] What this shows is that till 1900 there was growing capital market integration, which was partially reversed in the early part of this century. There was a partial recovery in integration in the 1920s, but with the Great Depression and World War II there was further disintegration that continued into the post-war period till the 1960s. This was followed by some increased integration, but which did not become marked till the 1980s. So that now the index is roughly where it was in 1870 when Rip went to sleep!

To determine the degree of globalization of commodity markets, we will use the historical data on real-wage trends for a number of countries around the Atlantic basin, which has been put together by Jeffrey Williamson and his collaborators.[7] The Hecksher-Ohlin theory predicts that with growing integration of commodity markets through international trade there should be convergence in real-wage rates as the low wages of the labor abundant countries rise toward those of labor-scarce countries.

Figure 3.2 charts an index of the dispersion of real-wage rates (measured by the coefficient of variation) for the time series for the Atlantic economies derived by Williamson (1995) from 1830 to 1986 for 15 countries (4 in the New World, and 11 in the Old). There is *first* the period till 1845 when there was a sharp divergence of real wages because of continuing trade barriers, high transport costs, and modest international labor migration. Then, *second*, after the repeal of Corn Laws in Britain in 1846 and the subsequent creation of the first LIEO under British leadership there is a marked and continuing convergence in real-wage rates that continues till 1900. This was the period during which Rip went to sleep, when there were sharp

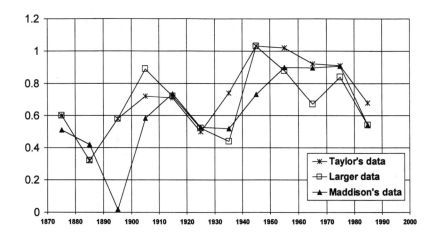

FIGURE 3.1   Comparison of Beta Coefficients, by Decade
NOTE: Taylor's data include Argentina, Australia, Canada, Demark, France, Germany, Italy, Sweden, UK, US. Larger data include Taylor's data plus India, Korea, Netherlands, Taiwan. Maddison's data include Australia, Canada, Denmark, France, Germany, India, Italy, Japan, Korea, Netherlands, Norway, Sweden, Taiwan, UK, US.

falls in transport costs[8] and trade barriers, and free international migration of labor and capital. With the creeping protectionism at the end of the century this trend comes to an end. There follows the *third* period from 1900 and the two World Wars, till about 1950, when there is a growing dispersion of real wages. This is the period in which the LIEO breaks down with the disintegration of world commodity and factor markets. The *fourth* period is the gradual reconstruction of a new LIEO under U.S. aegis from about 1960 to the present. A convergence in real wages begins and continues till the early 1970s, when there is a brief reversal, associated with the travails induced by the Organization of Petroleum Exporting Countries (OPEC) oil price shock. This is followed by continued convergence in the 1980s, so that the index is nearly back to where it was in 1900.

Since much of the convergence in the nineteenth century LIEO was fueled as much by international labor migration as by the integration of trade [see Williamson et. al (1996)], the more recent convergence in real wages is more likely to have been caused by trade integration, given the ubiquitousness of immigration controls limiting the international migration of labor.

It would seem therefore that Rip's casual empiricism is sound, and we can examine the three questions this rise, fall, and rise of the LIEO over the last 150 years raises.

32

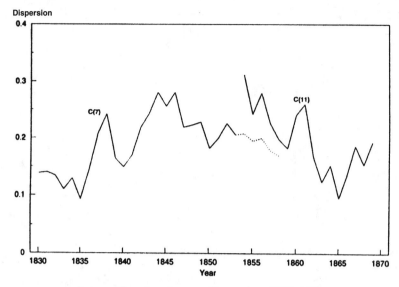

International real wage dispersion, 1830–1869.

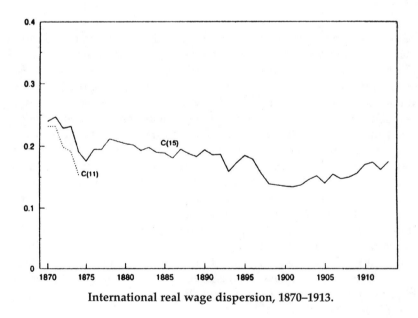

International real wage dispersion, 1870–1913.

FIGURE 3.2   Four Curves of International Real Wage Dispersion

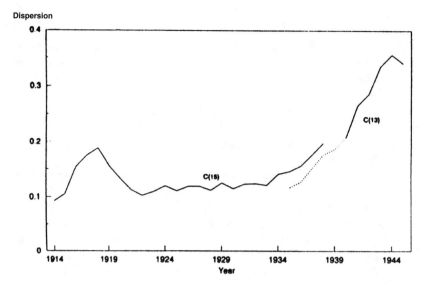

Dispersion

International real wage dispersion, 1914–1945.

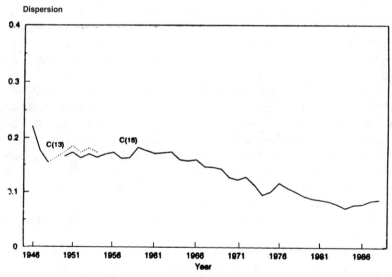

Dispersion

International real wage dispersion, 1946–1988.

FIGURE 3.2   (continued)

Why?

Broadly speaking the ghastly events of this century and the breakdown of the nineteenth century LIEO were caused by the rise of various ideas that questioned the economic and political liberalism[9] that underlay the nineteenth-century Age of Reform. To delineate them and to put them into historical and intellectual perspective, some distinctions made by the English political philosopher Michael Oakeshott are useful.

Oakeshott makes a crucial distinction between two major strands of Western thought on the State: the State viewed as a *civil* association, or alternatively as an *enterprise* association. Oakeshott notes that the view of the State as a civil association goes back to ancient Greece. The State is seen as the custodian of laws that do not seek to impose any preferred pattern of ends (including abstractions such as the general [social] welfare, or fundamental rights), but merely facilitates individuals to pursue their own ends. This view has been challenged by the rival conception of the State as an enterprise association—a view that has its roots in the Judaeo-Christian tradition. The State is now seen as the manager of an enterprise seeking to use the law for its own substantive purposes, and in particular for the legislation of morality. The classical liberalism of Smith and Hume entails the former, whilst the major secular embodiment of society viewed as an enterprise association is socialism, with its moral aim of using the State to equalize people. Equally, the other major ideological challenge to classical liberalism in this century, Fascism (national socialism), also viewed the State as an enterprise association. Both bred collectivist moralities as a reaction to the morality of individualism.

Oakeshott (1993) notes that as in many other preindustrial societies, modern Europe inherited a "morality of communal ties" from the Middle Ages. This was gradually superseded from the sixteenth century by a morality of individuality, whereby individuals came to value making their own choices "concerning activities, occupations, beliefs, opinions, duties and responsibilities" and also came to approve of this "self-determined conduct" in others. This individualist morality was fostered by the gradual breakdown of the medieval order, which allowed a growing number of people to escape from the "corporate and communal organization" of medieval life.

But this dissolution of communal ties also bred what Oakeshott terms the "anti-individual," who was unwilling or unable to make his own choices. Some were resigned to their fate, but in others it provoked "envy, jealousy and resentment. And in these emotions a new disposition was generated: the impulse to escape from the predicament by imposing it upon all mankind." (p. 24) This, the anti-individual sought to do through two means. The first was to look to the government to "protect him from the necessity of being an individual." (p. 25) A large number of government activities epitomized by the Elizabethan Poor Law were devoted from the sixteenth century onwards "to the protection of those who, by circumstance or temperament, were unable to look after themselves in this world of crumbling communal ties." (p. 25)

The anti-individual, secondly, sought to escape his "feeling of guilt and inadequacy which his inability to embrace the morality of individuality provoked" (p. 25) by calling forth a "morality of collectivism", where "'security' is preferred to 'liberty', 'solidarity' to 'enterprise', and 'equality' to 'self-determination'." (p. 27) The individualist and collectivist moralities were different modifications of the earlier communal morality, but with the collectivist morality in addition being a reaction against the morality of individualism.

This collectivist morality inevitably supported the view of the State as an enterprise association. While this view dates back to antiquity, few if any premodern states were able to be "enterprising", as their resources were barely sufficient to undertake the basic tasks of government—law and order and external defense. This changed with the creation of centralized "nation-states" by the Renaissance princes and the subsequent Administrative Revolution, as Hicks (1969, p. 99) has labeled the gradual expansion of the tax base and thus the span of control of the government over its subjects lives. Governments now had the power to look on their activities as an enterprise.

There have been three versions of collectivist moralities Oakeshott identifies with the State viewed as an enterprise association. Since the truce declared in the eighteenth century in the European wars of religion, the major substantive purposes sought by States seen as enterprise associations are "nation-building" and "the promotion of some form of egalitarianism". These correspond to what Oakeshott (1993) calls the *productivist* and *distributivist* versions of the modern embodiments of the enterprise association, whose *religious* version was epitomized by Calvinist Geneva, and in our time is provided by Khomeni's Iran. Each of these collective forms conjures up some notion of perfection, believed to be "the common good".[10]

Combining these insights with those of the great Swedish economic historian Eli Hecksher's *Mercantilism* allows us to provide a thumbnail sketch of the rise fall and rise of economic liberalism during the last two hundred years.

The precursor of the nineteenth century LIEO was the system of mercantilism. It arose, as Hecksher has shown, from the desire of the Renaissance princes of Europe to consolidate their power by incorporating various feuding and seemingly disorderly groups that constituted the relatively weak states they inherited from the ruins of the Roman empire, into a "nation". This was a "productivist" enterprise in Oakeshott's terms. The same nationalist motive also underlay the very similar system of mercantilist industrial and trade controls that were established in much of the postwar Third World.[11]

In the Third World, the jealousy, envy, and resentment that bred the European anti-individualist, was based not merely on the dissolution of the previous communal ties that industrialization and modern economic growth entail, but also because in these post-colonial societies, such emotions were strengthened by a feeling among the native elites, of a shared exclusion from positions of power during the period of foreign domination. It is not surprising therefore that the dominant ideology of the Third World came to be a form of nationalism associated with some combination of the productivist and distributivist versions of the state viewed as an enterprise association. Historically, these secular collectivist versions have led to dirigisme and the suppression or control of the market.

In both cases of "nation-building" (in post-Renaissance Europe, and the modern Third and Second Worlds) the unintended consequences of the similar system of mercantilist controls instituted to establish "order" was to breed "disorder". As economic controls became onerous, people attempted to escape them through various forms of evasion and avoidance. As in eighteenth-century Europe, in the post-war Third World, dirigisme bred corruption, rent-seeking, tax evasion, and illegal activities in underground economies. The most serious consequence for the State was erosion of its fiscal base and the accompanying prospect of the un-Marxian withering away of the State. In both cases economic liberalization was undertaken to restore the fiscal base, and thence government control over what had become ungovernable economies. In some cases the changeover could only occur through revolution—most notably in France.[12]

But the ensuing period of economic liberalism during the nineteenth-century's great Age of Reform, was short-lived in part because of the rise of another substantive purpose that most European states came to adopt—the egalitarian ideal promulgated by the Enlightenment. Governments in many developing countries also came to espouse this ideal of socialism. The apotheosis of this version of the State viewed as an enterprise association were the communist countries seeking to legislate the socialist ideal of equalizing people. The collapse of their economies under similar but even more severe strains than those that beset less collectivist neo-mercantilist, Third-World economies is now history, though I cannot help remarking on the irony that it took two hundred years for 1989 to undo what 1789 had wrought!

When?

If this account provides some reasons for the unraveling of the nineteenth-century LIEO, as well for its subsequent resurrection—gradually at first and more spectacularly in the last two decades—the dating of this change is of some importance. If asked to indicate what event or date marks an important turning point in this century, I would choose the OPEC coup of 1973. For its major unintended consequence was to set in motion various forces that undermined the intellectual consensus underpinning the dirigisme of most economies in the first two decades after World War II.

From the perspective of the Third World, the OPEC coup represented the ultimate politicization of economic decisions in the global economy. By forming commodity cartels it was hoped that the resource-rich countries of the developing world would hold the rest of the world to ransom. Demands arose for a new international economic order (NIEO) to replace the half-baked LIEO established in the wake of the collapse of the international system during the interwar and World War II period.

The partial restoration of the nineteenth-century LIEO after the World War II was based on three pillars created as the outcome of the Bretton Woods conference: the International Monetary Fund (IMF), the World Bank, and the General Agreement on Tariffs and Trade (GATT). They were institutionalized attempts to resurrect three of the important elements of the nineteenth-century LIEO that had collapsed in the early parts of this century: an international monetary system based on quasi-fixed exchange rates, flows of capital from developed to developing countries, and the freeing of trade and payments regimes.

Of these, the GATT was the most successful in resurrecting another LIEO. Under its auspices trade was progressively liberalized, which ushered in what has been termed the post-war "golden age." But even while world trade boomed, most developing countries, caught in the time warp of their import substitution strategies, did not reap its full benefits, claiming and getting their right to special privileges and exceptions in the emerging global free trade regime. The NIEO was their final attempt to replace this liberal trading order by one politically managed.

But within a decade the wind had gone from their sails. The supposed commodity power wielded by OPEC proved to be illusory. As market-oriented economists had predicted, any attempt by a cartel to artificially raise the price of its product would eventually come unstuck.[13] For such a price rise would first induce a search for substitutes, which would reduce the demand for the product, and second, lead to a search for alternative sources of supply. Both occurred. Various members of the cartel also succumbed to the temptation of increasing their share of the rationed output at the expense of the other members. Within a decade the oil price was no longer headline news. After the failure of another brief attempt at rigging it in the late 1970s, it has continued to decline in real terms ever since.[14] This effectively killed the illiberal dream of the NIEO. GATT has now successfully transformed itself into the World Trade Organization (WTO) after its latest Uruguay round, and developing countries are now its most loyal supporters.

In the monetary sphere, the IMF was created to supervise the new gold exchange rate system based on the adjustable peg. It replaced the nineteenth-century gold standard which, as the events of the interwar period had so painfully shown, could not be resurrected: essentially because of the inflexibilities in the workings of industrial labor markets, which did not permit the flexibility of domestic money wages and prices on which adjustments to economic shocks was predicated under the gold standard. The socialist "enterprise" association viewpoint was represented in the increasingly social democratic countries of the West by Keynesian prescriptions of aggregate demand management to maintain "full employment". Exchange-rate changes were then deemed to be necessary when a country could only cut its real wages to achieve this target through devaluation. The only country not permitted this 'luxury' was the United States—because it formed the base of the gold exchange standard through its fixed parity with gold.

The *first* consequence of the OPEC coup, which raised the costs of an essential input in all non-oil producing countries, and its partial monetary accommodation by most countries, was to raise their general price levels. At a time when the United States was already suffering from the inflationary excesses associated with the financing of the Vietnam war, this further push to the inflationary process (and the stagnation in output that accompanied it) made the U.S. balance of payments unviable. Devaluation was required to realign its domestic with the international price level. This was achieved by President Nixon's closing of the gold window, which in turn inflicted the *coup de grace* to the gold-exchange standard. The subsequent period has seen the institution of a worldwide free-floating, exchange-rate regime among the major economic powers, which has made it unnecessary to use dirigiste means to manage the balance of payments. This was the *first* benefit from the OPEC coup.

It also undermined the original mandate of the IMF, which has since, like Pirandello's six characters in search of an author, been looking around for a play. It has skillfully found a role in the ongoing adjustments from the plan to market underway in the Third and Second worlds. But this has a natural limit. The IMF's future cannot be bright, particularly (as argued below) in light of its most recent actions in South East Asia.

The *second* benefit from the OPEC coup was that, the ensuing stagflation exposed the fallacies of Keynesian macroeconomics. Gradually all Western governments realized that full employment could no longer be maintained by spending other peoples money. The classical prescriptions of sound money and deregulated labor markets (along with other supply side measures) were the only way to deal with stagflation.

The *third* consequence, and the most momentous for the Third World, arose from the disposition of their new-found oil wealth by the sparsely populated countries of the Middle East. The interwar collapse of world capital markets, which involved many defaults by Third World borrowers and led to their subsequent exclusion from western capital markets: through ubiquitous exchange controls in Europe—with the UK only abolishing them in 1979—and legal restrictions (e.g., the 'blue sky' laws in the United States). The World Bank, or the International Bank for Reconstruction and Development (IBRD) as its initial and still major component is called, was set up as a financial intermediary to fill this lacuna. Its intergovernmental ownership and guarantees allowed it to borrow at preferential rates in developed country markets and on-lend the money at near commercial interest rates to the Third World. For those countries deemed too poor to borrow at these rates a soft loan window was established with money subscribed by Western governments: the International Development Association (IDA). These governments had also established their own bilateral, foreign-aid programs, mainly to compete for political influence in the Third World during the Cold War, than to serve their professed aim of alleviating world poverty. As nearly all of these capital flows were mediated through multilateral or bilateral governmental channels, the access of developing countries to world capital markets was necessarily politicized. This was in stark contrast to the nineteenth-century pattern when private capital flowed from Europe to the rest of the world on market principles.

The OPEC coup set in train a chain of events that were to dramatically change this post-war politicization of the disposition of international capital. The OPEC countries could not conceivably absorb the large surpluses derived from the oil price rise domestically. They had to place them abroad. As Third World capital markets were underdeveloped, this in effect meant the West. But having obtained their newfound wealth through a political coup, the OPEC countries were fearful of placing it within the reach of government's whose citizens they had robbed. It could be confiscated: a not unreasonable fear as shown by the subsequent sequestration of Iranian assets by President Carter. So they placed their money in the offshore branches of the money center banks (the so-called Eurocurrency market). These offshore banks had developed outside the jurisdiction and reach of their parent monetary authorities and governments in the 1960s to allow intermediation of capital flows to communist Europe–which had been equally wary of dealing directly with institutions that would be subject to political pressure from its Cold War adversaries.

The consequent explosion in the liquidity of these Western offshore branches led them to a frantic scramble to on-lend this money. This recycling of the OPEC surpluses was also pressed by their governments, who were concerned by the worldwide deflationary consequences of an increase in the worldwide savings propensity caused by the transfer of income from relatively low to high savings propensity countries that the OPEC coup entailed. There were many eager borrowers in the Third World, in particular in the "inward looking" countries of Latin America. Thus the seeds of the debt crisis were sown.

This bank lending to the Third World was based on variable interest rates linked to the London Inter-Bank Offer Rate (LIBOR). When, in the late 1970s, the United States and subsequently much of Europe adopted sound money policies to deal with the stagflation that had plagued them since the OPEC coup, world interest rates and the cost of servicing debt rose dramatically. As most of the Third World borrowers—mainly in Latin America but not in East Asia—had borrowed to deal with their long-standing fiscal deficits, they now found themselves unable to service their debts. Starting with Mexico many in effect defaulted on their obligations. They were forced to recognize—as had the mercantilist states in the past—that the only way to restore their diminished control over the economy was through economic liberalization. Thus began the long drawn out process of reform whereby dirigiste "inward looking" regimes are gradually being replaced by more market friendly "outward looking" ones, all over the globe.

Economic liberalization has also provided many developing countries a new-found access to direct foreign and portfolio investments. For them this is a more desirable form of borrowing than bank borrowing at variable interest rates, because the associated currency and income risks are shared with the foreign investors. More sustainable forms of capital flows are thus now available to developing countries willing to change their nationalist attitudes to multinationals.[15] These market-based capital flows now dwarf the politicized flows from bilateral and multilateral agencies—whether they be IBRD loans or various forms of foreign aid (see Figure 3.3). The future of this politicized part of the world capital market is increasingly in jeopardy.[16]

Finally, the stagflation resulting from the OPEC coup also led to the replacement of demand management by supply-side policies in most developed countries. Beginning with the Thatcherite revolution in the UK, the worldwide movement toward privatization, and deregulation—in

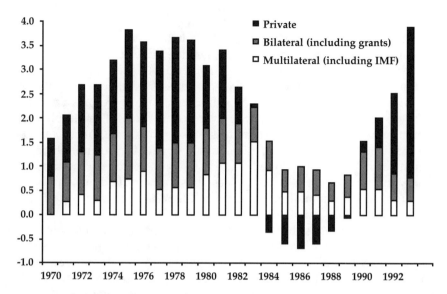

FIGURE 3.3 Net Flows to Developing Countries, 1970–1993 (Percentage of recipient GNP)

particular of labor markets—is reversing nearly century old trends and the habits and intellectual beliefs they had engendered. With the collapse of the Communist economic system,[17] dirigisme for the first time in a century is in worldwide retreat. It is a supreme irony that the unintended consequences of the final push to set up a politicized planned global economy initiated by the 1973 OPEC coup should have instead led to this new era of economic liberalization.

What Next?

What of the future? Is this new worldwide Age of Reform likely to be more permanent than its nineteenth-century predecessor? There are auguries—favorable and unfavorable.

Fears. To take the latter first. The desire to view the State as an enterprise association still lingers on, as part of social democratic political agendas in many countries. It has ancient roots and is unlikely to die. It has now adopted a new voice, which Ken Minogue (1993) has labeled "constitutional mania". This emphasizes substantive social and economic rights in addition to the well known rights to liberty—freedom of speech, contract, and association—emphasized by classical liberals. It seeks to use the law to enforce these "rights" based partly on "needs", and partly on the "equality of respect" desired by a heterogeneity of self-selected minorities differentiated by ethnicity, gender, or sexual orientation. But no less than in the collectivist societies that have failed, this attempt to define and legislate a newly discovered and dense structure of rights (including for some activists those of plants and animals) requires a vast expansion of the government's power over people's lives. Their implementation moreover requires—at the least—some doctoring of the market mechanism. Then there is the global environmental scare and the population scare. Finally the United Nations (UN) has taken up the cause of the world's poor and is seeking to establish a worldwide welfare state through a UN economic security council. Classical liberals can clearly not yet lay down their arms!

Equally worrying is the "Delors" vision of Europe, which seems to be a form of mercantilist nation-building, in the manner of the Renaissance princes documented by Hecksher.[18] Many voices are also resurrecting the threat from pauper labor imports to U.S. and European living standards (particularly of the low skilled), and thence their social harmony. This is particularly worrying as it echoes various fears in the late nineteenth century of the social disruptions and discontent caused by the Industrial Revolution. Though recent historical work has questioned the bleak picture painted by novelists such as Dickens,[19] their fears were nevertheless influential in propagating the dirigiste cause, which led to the gradual unraveling of the nineteenth-century LIEO as the distributive consequences of trade integration led to the rise of protectionist political coalitions in the United States, Germany, and France after 1870.[20]

Another great structural change is taking place in Western economies, whose short-term consequences could be equally painful and trigger another dirigiste reversal of the emerging LIEO. It may be worth spelling this out. Hicks saw the substitution of fixed for circulating capital as the distinguishing feature of the Industrial Revolution.[21] But, as Ricardo in his chapter on "Machinery" noted, during the period of adjustment there could be a reduction in employment and output; though at the end of the process the productive power and hence the level and growth rate of output and employment would be higher. This explains why it took a long time in Great Britain for the Industrial Revolution to raise overall living standards, and why during the period of adjustment, the older handicraft workers (using circulating capital in various forms of the 'putting out' system) initially suffered, until they were eventually transformed into much richer industrial workers.

Today a similar process is underway in the West, with the increasing substitution of human for fixed capital in its newly emerging "information age" service economies. This process has been accelerated by the emerging

LIEO as the unskilled labor-rich countries of Asia—particularly China and India—go through their Industrial revolutions, and increasingly specialize in the production for export of those manufactures on which workers— particularly the low skilled—had depended in the past in the West. The on- going substitution of human for fixed capital is an unavoidable means for maintaining and raising living standards in the West. But during the process of adjustment it may cause severe social strains.

In this adjustment process it is inevitable that initially the premium on human capital should rise, as this provides the signal for workers to up- grade their skills. This rising skill premium accompanied by stagnation in the wages of the unskilled is evident in all Western countries. Those countries, mainly in Europe, which have prevented this signal from working, have found that, instead of low and stagnant wages for the un- skilled they have the much worse problem of high and rising unemploy- ment. Despite the siren voices calling for protection from Third World imports to ease these problems, for the West to follow their advice would be a snare and a delusion. But, as the rise of protectionism based on the equally deluded infant industry arguments of Hamilton and List in the late nineteenth century demonstrates, such snares are not always avoided. At a time when the Third and Second Worlds have enthusiasti- cally embraced the LIEO it is the temptation for harried Western govern- ments to turn their backs on the world they have created that constitutes the greatest threat to the future of the new global LIEO.[22]

Then, there is the creeping and continuing dirigisme to promote vari- ous "social policies" in many Western states (including the United States). These include demands for the inclusion of environmental and labor standards in the WTO (which has replaced GATT), as well as recent attempts to thrust Western moral values (democracy and human rights) down foreign throats—using the threats of unilateral trade restrictions. All these inevitably poison international relations. The nagging bad tem- per generated could lead to a gradual erosion of the liberal international economic order, as in the late nineteenth century.

Meanwhile there are more immediate worries that the recent financial crises in Asia might lead to a backlash against the globalization of capital flows in developing countries.[23] There is a pervasive fear in the Third World that continuing capital market liberalization will lead to a greater volatility in their national incomes damaging growth performance. The recent Asian crisis, which has taken the stripes off so many of the region's tigers, has merely accentuated these fears. Mahathir's recent reimposi- tion of stringent capital controls in Malaysia maybe the harbinger of a trend toward the resucitation of economic nationalism.

This fear of volatility is an ancient worry of the Third World, earlier ex- pressed as the purported adverse effects on growth of the export instability engendered by primary product exporting countries integration in the world economy.[24] In the 25-country study covering the period since World War II, Myint and I could find no statistical evidence that the volatility of annual growth rates effected overall growth performance—a conclusion in consonance with the numerous studies of the effects of export instability on growth. Thus Hong Kong has had one of the most volatile growth rates amongst developing countries, while India one of the most stable—but the long-run growth performance of Hong Kong puts the Indian one to shame. Thus, though there may undeniably be greater volatility in national incomes of countries integrating with the world economy, this need not damage their long-run growth rates.

But what of the lessons against globalization many in the Third World seem to be drawing from the recent Asian crisis? This appears to be a misreading of the causes of the crisis, and how future ones can be avoided. There were three main causes of the crisis: (i) the exchange rate regime; (ii) the moral hazard in the domestic banking systems caused by the 'Asian model'; (iii) the international moral hazard created by the actions of the IMF.

To elaborate and explain. The first cause was the quasi-fixed exchange rate regimes in many of the countries. It is increasingly becoming clear that with a globalized capital market only two exchange regimes are viable: a fully floating exchange rate or a rigidly fixed rate one as in the currency board of Hong Kong.[25] The reason is that these are the only ones that allow automatic adjustment to external and internal shocks without any need for discretionary action by the authorities.[26] In a world that requires instantaneous responses to the actions of a highly decentralized but integrated world capital market mediating these shocks, the authorities do not have the time or the means to obtain the requisite information to deal with these shocks in a centrally planned manner. They often end up by being the problem rather than the solution if they try to manage their exchange rates in this volatile and unpredictable world economy, leading to serious misalignments of the *real* exchange rate.[27] An automatic adjustment mechanism is therefore preferable to a discretionary one.

The second cause was a systemic flaw in the 'Asian' model of development. A central feature of this model—as seen most clearly in Korea but presaged by the development of Japan—is a close linkage between the domestic banking system, industrial enterprises (particularly the biggest) and the government. The fatal flaw in this 'Asian model'—as shown by the recent travails of both Korea and Japan—is that, by making the banking system the creature of the government's will, it creates tremendous moral hazard in the domestic banking system. The banks have no incentive to asses the credit worthiness of their borrowers or the quality of the investments their loans are financing, as they know—no matter how risky and over extended their lending—they will always be bailed out by the government. This can lead in time to a mountain of bad paper and the de facto insolvency of a major part of the banking system, as has happened in Korea and Japan—not to mention the corruption that is inevitably involved in this type of development. But "as the example of the U.S. savings and loans crisis shows" this collapse of the banking system can ultimately be cleared up if there is the political will. Korea does have the will, and should bounce back fairly shortly. By contrast, Japan, which inherited a political system based on institutionalizing political paralysis from the Meiji oligarchs, shows no sign as yet of grasping this nettle and its prospects must therefore remain a cause for continuing concern.

Third, the problem of moral hazard for the domestic banking system created by this 'Asian' model have been aggravated by the actions of the IMF and the entrance of foreign bankers as lenders in the newly liberalized capital markets. Of the three types of capital flows that can be distinguished—direct foreign investment, portfolio investment, and bank lending—the income and foreign currency risks of the first two types of flows is shared by the lender and the borrower, as the 'investments' are denominated in domestic currency. By contrast foreign bank loans are usually denominated in dollars and the interest rate is linked to LIBOR. This means that, if faced by a shock requiring a devaluation (in a adjustable peg exchange rate regime), the domestic currency burden of the foreign bank debt rises pari passu with the changing exchange rate. If this debt is incurred by the private sector, this rising short-term debt burden need pose no problem for the country. For, if the relevant foreign banks run, the borrowers can always default on their debt.

But now enter the IMF. The foreign banks faced by a default on their Third World debt have ever since the 1980's debt crisis argued that this poses a systemic risk to the world's financial system, and asked in effect for an international bailout to prevent this catastrophe. Since the 1980's debt crisis and most clearly in the Mexican crisis in the early 1990s and the recent Asian crisis, the IMF has been more than willing to oblige, as since the demise of the Bretton Woods system it has been searching for a new role. With the debt crisis of the 1980s and the more recent Mexican and Asian crises it has increasingly become the international debt collector for foreign money center banks, as well as an important tool of U.S. foreign policy.

The crisis in Indonesia provides the clearest example of this metamorphosis of the Fund. Before the Thai crisis hit the region the Indonesian economy had been fairly well managed despite the 'cronyism' of its capitalism. It had provided exceptional growth rates, with a sensible deployment of its oil revenues—unlike many other comprators (e.g., Nigeria)—and which had made an impressive dent in its mass poverty. At the time of the Thai crisis, its economic fundamentals were sound: it did not have a massive trade or budget deficit, it had a flexible exchange rate, its debt burden was not onerous, and its foreign bank debt was all private.

When the contagion from Thailand spread, the foreign banks (mainly U.S. and Japanese banks), which had made loans to the Indonesian private sector, ran, leading to a depreciation of the rupiah and a massive increase in the domestic currency costs of servicing this short-term debt. Many of the borrowers would then have defaulted, and that would have been that. But enter the IMF. Under pressure from the governments of the foreign banks it deemed that such private sector defaults would pose a risk to the world's financial system, and under the cover of an IMF program, the Indonesian government was in effect forced to take on these private debts. The money from the IMF paid off the foreign lenders, and the general taxation of the Indonesian populace will have to repay the IMF. The Indonesian people have thus through the aegis of the IMF bailed out the foreign banks.

These actions of the IMF—ever since the 1980's debt crisis—have generated serious moral hazard in foreign bank lending. With the increasingly confident expectation that they will be bailed out through the IMF no matter what the quality of their lending to Third World countries, foreign banks have no incentive to act prudently in their foreign lending.[28] When this international moral hazard is coupled with the domestic moral hazard associated with the politicized domestic banking systems of the 'Asian' model—as in Korea—there is double jeopardy. Foreign banks lending to domestic banks that know they will be bailed out will over-lend, leading to ropy investments and an eventual debt crisis for the country.

With measures to remove the domestic moral hazard being widely adopted in the region, the international moral hazard from the IMF's operations would still remain. What is to be done? The best solution would be to shut down the IMF. Its original mandate ended with the Bretton Woods exchange rate system. Since then, its continuance, though in the interests of its rent-seeking international bureaucrats, is no longer in the interests of the world economy.

Being realistic it is unlikely that the IMF will be shut down—after all the redundant United Nations Educational Scientific and Cultural Organization (UNESCO), International Labor Office (ILO), and United Nations Industrial Organization (UNIDO) have not been, even though their major financiers at some stage sought to do so. In the circumstances, to avoid the socialization of the private risks associated with volatile foreign bank lending in the presence of this international moral hazard is for local central banks to ensure that all such borrowing is suitably hedged. If they lack the requisite capital markets for such hedging some of them might consider a second best 'control' on such capital flows till these markets are developed. This would lay down that all short-run foreign bank loans taken out by residents must be denominated in local currency. By raising the costs of such borrowing this will be equivalent to a market determined tax on such flows. Second, it would mean the foreign banks would now have to share in the foreign exchange risk, and at times of contagion instead of running might pause and refinance their long-term viable borrowers.

Hopes. Against these dangers there are many hopeful signs. As in pre-modern times, today's states are finding it more and more difficult to find the resources to continue (or increase) their enterprise. This is partly because of the worldwide growth in tax-resistance,[29] and most important the virtually complete integration of international financial markets. The latter has strengthened the former. Nor is a reimposition of exchange controls to stop this process likely, if for no other reason than that it would now have to be adopted and enforced worldwide.

The instincts of the State through most of human history have been predatory. The integration of world financial markets provides a bulwark against these base instincts—like tying Ulysses to the mast. Every government is now concerned about the rating of its country and its enterprises by world capital markets. Bad policies—or at least those disapproved of by world capital markets—can lead to an instantaneous reduction in a country's wealth, and the terms on which it can acquire the means to increase it—a painful lesson many South East Asian countries have recently learned. The worldwide movement toward fiscal rectitude and the creation of an economic environment that is transparent and rewards efficiency is no longer a matter of choice but necessity. With massive global flows of capital triggered at the press of a button, governments are now faced with an instantaneous international referendum on their economic policies. The Central Bank or Treasury proposes, but the money market disposes!

The same actual or incipient fiscal crisis that has ultimately prevented the State from giving in to the "enterprise" voice, or led to forced reversals in its past dirigisme, also threatens the major form of its continuing enterprise in the West—the welfare state. The partial dismantling of the New Zealand welfare state and its continuing erosion in that social democratic beacon of hope, Sweden, are surely more than straws in the wind.[30]

Finally, there is the recent spectacular movement from the plan to the market in China and India. The future progress of these ancient civilizations raises unresolved questions about the relationship between culture, democracy, and development.[31] Can the market survive in polities that are undemocratic? Will globalization necessarily lead to the worldwide spread of a homogenized Western culture? On the latter I have my doubts, partly because the very mainspring of Western culture—its individualism—is paradoxically leading to social decay and decadence in the West.[32] There is a triumphalist tendency in the West, most noticeable in the United States, to identify its cultural and political forms as necessary conditions for its economic success. This raises complex issues that I cannot go into on this occasion.[33] There is, however, one point that needs to be stressed, and that concerns the first of the questions posed in this paragraph. Many, including the major contemporary advocate of the classical liberal order—Hayek[34]—have posited a necessary connection between economic and political liberty (nowadays translated into the market cum democracy). I disagree.[35] Oakeshott's distinction between a civil and enterprise association is more useful in judging the sustainability of a market order. For after all, till 1997, the only "country" that was clearly a civil rather than enterprise association—in Oakeshott's terms—was Hong Kong, and it was a colony, now extinguished!

Given these contradictory trends in the global economy, I think we can be certain that the Polyannaish hopes of an "end of history" are premature. Mankind is unlikely in the next millennium, no less than in the past, to escape the ancient Chinese curse: "May you live in exciting times".

Notes

1. See Lal (1996b), (1998c).

2. I assume that Rip van Winkle was a male, but in this politically correct, androgynous age, if the reader likes whenever I write 'he' that should also imply 'she'.

3. Rosecrance (1986), (1999).

4. See Lal (1994a).

5. See Obstfeld (1995) for details.

6. See Taylor (1996) p.13 for details and references. For the current period see Obstfeld (1995) and Goldstein et al. (1993).

7. See Williamson (1995), O'Rourke, Taylor, and Williamson (1996), and Williamson (1996) for an overview.

8. O'Rourke et al. (1996) (p.509) find that between 1870 and 1910, freight indices for railroads and ocean shipping dropped from 41 to 53 percent. This led to considerable price convergence for tradable goods. O'Rourke and Williamson (1994) find the spread between grain prices in Liverpool and Chicago fell from 60 percent in 1870 to 14 percent in 1912; for meat and animal fats from 93 to 18 percent, for iron products from 80 to 20 percent, and for cotton textiles from 14 to 1 percent over the same period.

9. I use the term liberalism in the sense of classical liberalism and not in its current American sense, which makes it synonymous with some forms of socialism.

10. Sugden (1993), in his review of Sen (1992), makes much the same distinction between the two divergent views of public policy embodied in the techno-

cratic "market failure" school and in the neo-Austrians and the Virginia public choice school.

11. See Lal and Myint (1996), Chap. 7, on which much of this section is based.

12. See Aftalion (1990).

13. The one contemporary cartel that has bucked this trend is the diamond cartel run by De Beers, which was originally created by Cecil Rhodes. See "The Diamond Business," *The Economist*, December 20, 1997, pp. 113–115, for an account of how the cartel resisted the trend, and why it might not be able to in the future.

14. Having risen from $4 in 1972 to $30 in 1983, it collapsed in 1986 and is now about $20.

15. The costs and benefits of direct foreign investment are outlined and case studies for India and East Africa presented in Lal (1975).

16. See Lal (1996a). Source for Figure 3.3: Rodik (1995), p. 170.

17. It is still unclear to what extent the collapse is due to internal factors resulting from the economic consequences of past dirigisme, which impels reform (see Lal [1993]), or external factors such as the threat of Star Wars, which upped the ante in terms of unsustainable defense expenditures for the Soviet Union. Certainly Deng's reforms in China were motivated by a threatened internal economic collapse rather than any external factors.

18. See Wolf (1994).

19. See Hayek (1954).

20. See Rogowski (1989).

21. See Hicks (1969), esp. the Appendix, and Lal (1978), Appendix A.

22. This fear is also echoed by Williamson (1996).

23. The remainder of this section is based on Lal (1998a, 1998b).

24. See Lal (1983).

25. The reason the Hong Kong currency board seems to be under some threat at the time of writing (Sept. 1998) is that the authorities took inappropriate actions, which broke the rules of the currency board. These actions were unsuccessfully aimed at propping up the Hong Kong property market, but in the process have raised doubts about the continuing credibility of the Hong Kong authorities' commitment to the fixed peg of the exchange rate.

26. See Lal (1993), Chap. 6.

27. The real exchange rate (er) is defined as the relative price of non-traded (pn) to traded goods (pt). As the nominal exchange rate (e) effects the price of traded goods given their foreign currency price (pf), the real and nominal exchange rate are linked by the relationship: er = pn / pt = pn / e.pf. An inappropriate nominal exchange rate (e) can lead to a misaligned real exchange rate (er).

28. The refusal of the IMF and the Group of Seven to bail out the foreign lenders in the most recent Russian crisis may however show that at last this danger is being recognized.

29. In a rearguard action, however, the OECD has just announced a task force that will study how to prevent tax competition between states, which is rightly feared to be eroding the ability of states to extract the maximum revenue from their citizens. But whether one should applaud this attempt to create a cartel of predatory states to maximize the exploitation of their prey depends upon whether one sides with the predator or the prey. But even if such a cartel could be

formed it would be subject to the form of cheating which undermined the OPEC cartel; for instance, some country or other would find it in its interest to attract mobile factors of production with the inducement of lower taxation. By so openly avowing the cause of the predatory states that control its purse strings the OECD would seem to have signed its death warrant in the eyes of economic liberals.

30. I may claim some foresight in seeing trends earlier than most others. See Chaps. 8 and 15 in Lal (1993).

31. I deal with some of these in my 1995 Ohlin lectures, Lal (1998c).

32. See Lal (1998c) for details and substantiation.

33. But see Lal (1998a, 1998c).

34. See Hayek (1979).

35. See Lal (1996b).

References

F. Aftalion (1990). *The French Revolution: An Economic Interpretation.* Cambridge: Cambridge University Press.

M. Feldstein and C. Horioka (1980). "Domestic Saving and International Capital Flows" *Economic Journal*, vol. 90, June, pp. 314–329.

M. Goldstein et. al (1993). *International Capital Markets.* Washington D.C.: International Monetary Fund.

F. A. Hayek (1954): *Capitalism and the Historians*, London: Routledge.

_____ (1976/78). *Denationalisation of Money.* London: Institute of Economic Affairs.

_____(1979). *Law, Legislation and Liberty.* Chicago: University of Chicago Press.

E. Hecksher (1955). *Mercantilism.* 2 vols., 2nd rev. ed. London: Allen and Unwin.

J. R. Hicks (1969). *A Theory of Economic History.* London: Oxford University Press.

D. Lal (1975). *Appraising Foreign Investment in Developing Countries.* London: Heinemann Educational Books.

_____ (1978). *Men or Machines.* Geneva: ILO.

_____ (1983/1985/1998). *The Poverty of 'Development Economics'*, Institute of Economic Affairs, London; Harvard University Press, Cambridge, Mass, 1985; 2nd revised and expanded ed., London: Institute of Economic Affairs.

_____ (1993). *The Repressed Economy*, Economists of the 20th century series. Aldershot, UK: Edward Elgar.

_____ (1994a). *Against Dirigisme.* San Francisco: ICS Press.

_____ (1994b)."In Praise of the Classics," in G, Meier, ed. from *Classical Economics to Development Economics.* London: Macmillan.

_____ (1996a). "Foreign Aid: An idea whose time has gone", *Economic Affairs*, Autumn 1996, pp. 9–13.

_____ (1996b). "Participation, Markets and Democracy." *New Directions in Development Economics.* M. Lundahl and B. J. Ndulu (eds.), London: Routledge.

_____ (1998a). *Renewing the Miracle: Economic Development and Asia.* Inaugural Harold Clough lecture, Institute of Public Affairs, Perth, July 1998.

_____ (1998b). "Taxation and regulation as barriers to international investment flows." Paper for Mont Pelerin Society Golden Anniversary meeting, Washington DC, Aug. 1998.

_____ (1998c). *Unintended Consequence: Factor Endowments, Culture and Politics: On Economic Performance in the Long Run.* Cambridge, Mass: MIT Press.

D. Lal and H. Myint (1996). *The Political Economy of Poverty, Equity and Growth.* Oxford: Clarendon Press.

A. Maddison (1991). "A long run perspective on saving." University of Groningen, Netherlands: mimeo.

_____ (1992). "A Long-run perspective on saving." *Scandinavian Journal of Economics*, vol. 94, no. 2, pp. 181–196.

K. Minogue (1993). *The Constitutional Mania.* Policy Studies No.134. London: Center for Policy Studies.

B. R. Mitchell (1992). *International Historical Statistics: Europe, 1750–1988.* New York: Stockton Press.

M. Oakeshott (1973). *On Human Conduct.* Oxford: Clarendon Press.

_____ (1993). *Morality and Politics in Modern Europe.* New Haven, Conn.: Yale University Press.

M. Obstfeld (1995). "International Capital Mobility in the 1990's" in P. B. Kenen (ed.). *Understanding Interdependence*, Princeton, N.J.: Princeton University Press, pp. 201–261.

K. H. O'Rourke, A. M. Taylor, and J. G. Williamson (1996). "Factor Price Convergence in the Late 19th century." *International Economic Review*, vol. 37, no. 3, pp. 499–530.

K. H. O'Rourke and J. G. Williamson (1994). "Late 19th century Anglo-American Factor Price Convergence: Were Hecksher and Ohlin Right?" *Journal of Economic History*, vol. 54, pp. 892–916.

D. Rodrik (1995). "Why Is There Multilateral Lending?" *Annual World Bank Conference on Development Economics.* Washington, D.C.: World Bank, pp. 167-193.

R. Rogowski (1989). *Commerce and Coalitions.* Princeton, N.J.: Princeton University Press.

R. Rosecrance (1986). *The Rise of the Trading State.* New York: Basic Books.

_____ (1999). *The Rise of the Virtual State.* New York: Basic Books.

A. K. Sen (1992). *Inequality Reexamined.* Cambridge, Mass.: Harvard University Press.

R. Sugden (1993). "A Review of Inequality Reexamined by Sen." *Journal of Economic Literature*, Dec.

A. M. Taylor (1996). "International Capital Mobility in History: The Savings-Investment Relationship." *NBER Working Paper*, No. 5743, Sept., mimeo.

J. G. Williamson (1995). "The Evolution of Global Labor Markets since 1830: Background Evidence and Hypotheses." *Explorations in Economic History*, vol. 32, pp. 141–196.

_____ (1996): "Globalization, Convergence and History." *The Journal of Economic History*, vol. 56, June, pp. 277–306.

M. Wolf (1994): *The Resistible Rise of Fortress Europe.* Rochester paper No. 1, Trade Policy Unit, Center for Policy Studies, London.

4

The Rise of the Politically Incorrect One-Handed Economist[1]

JOHN MUELLER

The world may well be on the verge of a massive expansion of economic growth.

Professor Lawrence Henderson of Harvard University once suggested that by 1912, for the first time in human history, "a random patient with a random disease consulting a doctor chosen at random stood better than a fifty-fifty chance of benefiting from the encounter."[2] This vivid observation suggests how recent the coherent rise of medical science has been and, further, it points out that, not so long ago, physicians, while perhaps generally dedicated and well meaning, often did more harm than good. After all, a doctor who doesn't understand germ theory may innocently carry a disease from one patient to the next, making matters far worse than if the patients had instead consulted a priest, a shaman, or a snake oil salesman, or if they had simply stayed quietly at home in bed.

In this chapter, I would like to propose that economics is now about where medicine was a century ago. Essentially, I suggest, economics has probably reached the point where the random government official or business executive consulting the random economist is likely to benefit from the encounter. That is, economists have now substantially come to a workable and essentially valid basic consensus about how economies function. Because of this, they generally know what they are doing, their pills and palliatives are more likely than not to work, and the policies they prescribe have a good chance of enhancing an economy's ability to grow.

And there is another change. In the past, the advice of economists was very often politically unattractive because policymakers have given noneconomic values higher priority, because other advisers seem to have more intuitively plausible palliatives, or because acceptance of the advice would clearly cause short-term political pain. Now, however, the economists' advice is increasingly being accepted by decisionmakers.

This chapter explores the rise of economic science, its increasing acceptance, and the consequent prospects for a vast worldwide economic expansion.

In the process, I suggest that economists and like-minded idea entrepreneurs seem substantially to have managed to get across four highly consequential and enormously controversial ideas: the growth of economic well-being should be a dominant goal, wealth is best achieved through exchange rather than through conquest, international trade should be free, and economies do best when the government leaves them substantially free.

The chapter also muses over the curious fact that advances in economic well-being do not necessarily cause people to profess that they have become happier. Rather, each improvement seems quickly to be taken in stride, and standards are continually raised to compensate. However, this phenomenon seems to help stimulate further economic development, and it may have a kind of intellectually invigorating quality of its own.

One-Handedness

Fifty-years ago, Harry Truman often became frustrated with economic advisers who kept telling him on the one hand that a certain consequence could be expected from an action while on the other hand that the opposite consequence might come about. He frequently expressed a yearning for what he called "a one-handed economist."

It seems to me that over the twentieth century, economists, through trial and error, through experiment and experience, through abstraction and empirical test, have developed a substantial consensus about broad economic principles, if not always about nuance and detail. And thus we seem to be approaching the age Truman yearned for—the age of the one-handed economist.

I need to stress that I am applying a standard here that is significant but not terribly exalted. By present standards, after all, medicine was woefully inadequate at the turn of the century, and physicians were still misguidedly killing a fair number of their patients. But, as Figure 4.1 demonstrates, over the course of this century medicine has advanced from a base that has turned out to be essentially sound, and the result has been a spectacular and historically unprecedented increase in life expectancy, first in developed countries, and then more recently in the less

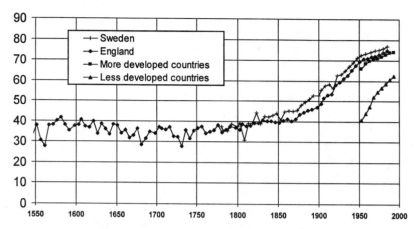

FIGURE 4.1   Life Expectancy at Birth, 1550–1990

developed world.[3] In like manner, although economics is hardly an exact science, if economists have at last essentially gotten the basics correct, this accomplishment is potentially of enormous importance to the advancement of economic well-being.

The "economists" I am referring to might perhaps be better designated "policy economists"—people whose business it is to derive coherent and practical policy prescriptions from what they take to be the central notions of economic science. Included in this group would be not only many academics in economics departments and business schools, but also policy and financial analysts working for or running think tanks, private businesses, and investment firms as well as those hanging out at policy agencies like the Federal Reserve, the Congressional Budget Office, the International Monetary Fund (IMF), and the World Bank. It would also include those seeking to develop technical tools for analyzing and assessing the real world—as, of course, modern medicine has been dependent for much of its success on the development and proliferation of a raft of probing, measuring, and analyzing methods and tools.[4]

I do not propose that these economists now have an all-embracing theory of the economy: after all, physicians were correctly convinced that aspirin relieves pain and that smoking causes cancer before much of an explanation was developed for why these things are so. Nor, certainly, do I mean to suggest that economists never disagree or err. For a very long time physicians ordered parents to warm formula milk before feeding it to their infants presumably under the plausible assumption that bottled milk should be the same temperature as breast milk; eventually, however, someone determined that babies were generally quite capable of digesting cold milk, and the conventional advice was accordingly abandoned after causing great inconvenience to parents and occasional danger to their babies when sleepy parents inadvertently fed them scalding milk.

But I propose that, in general, economists now are substantially on top of their topic, that they are amassing knowledge in a manner generally progressive and cumulative, and that the advice they render is likely—or more likely than not—to be sound.

An impressive indication of this came in the early 1990s when economists were confronted with a new and quite astounding problem. For various reasons, some two dozen countries with highly controlled (and underproductive) economies, including some of the biggest in the world, were suddenly freed of economy-stifling ideological controls and wished to become rich. As Lawrence Summers observes, the death of Communism caught the economics profession unprepared: Although there had been quite a few studies at that point about the transition of market economies to controlled or command economies, "there was not a single book or article on the problem of transforming an economy from the communist to a market system." Indeed, the word *privatization* had only been recently developed in connection with Margaret Thatcher's relatively modest efforts in the 1980s to denationalize comparatively small portions of the British economy.[5]

Economists were called in to sort out this novel problem. Even though their ideas about how to encourage economic well-being and growth had been principally derived from analysis of economies that were relatively free, it is impressive testimony to the fundamental soundness of these ideas that the advice so generated proved to be substantially (though not invariably) sound even when applied under these unprecedented and unstudied circumstances. In case after case, countries that generally followed the advice have been able to achieve considerable (though certainly not painless) success in transforming their economies and in achieving meaningful growth, often in an astoundingly short time. Similar success, following similar advice, seems to have recently been achieved in many places in southern, eastern, and southeastern Asia and in much of Latin America.[6]

Political Incorrectness

Economists may give sound advice, but, as the variable post-Communist experience shows, the politicians and administrators who are their advisees may reject it because they find it politically incorrect.

They may find it so, first, because they disagree with the value or the goal the economists advocate. For the most part, this has not been a problem for medicine: The physician's goal—better health for the patient—is readily accepted. By contrast, the economist's goal of economic growth and well-being has often been rejected—been found to be politically incorrect—because people hold other, often conflicting, values, like honor or class differentiation or traditional justice or piety, to be more important. Accordingly, for economic science to triumph, it has been necessary for economic goals to become dominant.

Second, modern economists, like modern physicians, have had to convince their advisees that they know what they are talking about and that their proposed remedies will function. This has not been an easy task because, as modern economics has advanced, it has developed a perspective that often runs counter to some competing notions about how economies ought to work. Many of these alternative notions are morally appealing and alluringly commonsensical—and hence politically correct—like the still-popular views that the best way to protect domestic employment is to restrict competitive imports or that the best way to beat inflation is for the government to dictate prices.

Finally, the advice of economists, even when accepted as valid, may be rejected because politicians and administrators find it to be politically painful to carry out. In this case, the analogy with medicine works quite well. As it has burgeoned, the science of medicine unfortunately did not discover that such agreeable remedies as eating chocolate could cure maladies. Rather, it kept coming up with remedies that involved cutting patients open, encasing them with plaster, drilling into their aching teeth, consigning them to passive inactivity, giving them bad-tasting tonics, denying them the tasty foods they most want to eat, mandating boring exercises, and puncturing them with long needles.[7] People had to become convinced that physicians and dentists knew what they were doing before they would follow advice like that. And they also had to become willing to swallow the medicine—that is, to suffer short-range pain for the promise of long-term benefit—particularly when priests and palmreaders regularly arrived at palliatives that were less painful and more convenient.

In like manner, many—perhaps most—of the remedies modern economics has advanced have turned out to be politically painful, particularly in the short run. As Michael Weinstein puts it, economists "compulsively remind people to eat their spinach."[8] For example, if economists could discover that subsidies to politically active dairy farmers would not only help the farmers but also importantly benefit the economy as a whole, politicians would be hanging on their every word—the advice would be pure political chocolate. Unfortunately, economists have generally prescribed political spinach: Cutting the dairy farmers from the public dole—no matter how deserving they may be as people, no matter how bucolic their farms, no matter how well groomed their cows—and letting them descend quietly into ignominious bankruptcy and then perhaps to seek other, unsubsidized, work. Moreover, there is very often political dilemma in that the people who will benefit in the long term from the economists' advice don't know who they are while those who will be disadvantaged in the short term know this only too well and are quick to scream.

Four Economic Propositions
That Have Become Increasingly Accepted

For the economists' politically incorrect perspectives and prescriptions to prevail, then, populations and policymakers have had to become convinced that economists know what they are talking about and also to accept their dominant goal—achieving a healthy, growing economy—as well as their often-painful devices for achieving that goal. It has been a long, uphill struggle, but as the century changes, economists and their allies seem substantially to have been successful in this endeavor.

Four propositions seem central to this process, and each has been mightily contested over the last century or two. In my view, it has been essential for economists and like-minded idea entrepreneurs to get these propositions accepted to be effective.

Moreover, if these four elemental propositions have become substantially accepted, the ancillary consequences are enormous. Not only do they seem to hold the formula for a huge expansion of economic well-being, but in combination they suggest the demise of such central human institutions as empire and war.

The Growth of Economic Well Being Should Be a Dominant Goal

As central goals, economists often stress, or effectively stress, advances in economic well-being, a concept usually including considerations of economic growth as well as assessments of how the wealth generated by that growth is distributed, particularly insofar as it brings people out of poverty. To develop this perspective, they frequently assume, model, and essentially favor people who are acquisitive: People who are centrally, indeed entirely, occupied with advancing their own long-term economic well-being.

This perspective has traditionally rankled with people who treasure such values and goals as honor, heroism, empathy, altruism, sacrifice, selflessness, generosity, piety, patriotism, racism, self-respect, spirituality, nationalism, and compassion. They often condemn the economic motives as crass, materialistic, cowardly, vulgar, debased, hedonistic, uncaring, selfish, immoral, decadent, and self-indulgent.

Religion has been one such opponent. As George Stigler observes, "a dislike for profit seeking is one of the few specific attitudes shared by the major religions." Thus, the Pope rails in a 1991 encyclical against "consumerism" in which "people are ensnared in a web of false and superficial gratifications rather than being helped to experience their personhood in an authentic and concrete way."[9] Similar rejections of economic well being and growth as dominant goals in favor of authentic and concrete personhood have routinely been fostered by such religious or moral leaders as Gandhi and Khomeini.

Intellectuals too, including even Adam Smith, have held that the "commercial spirit . . . confines the views of men" with the result that the "minds of men are contracted, and rendered incapable of elevation."[10] And such thinkers as Alexis de Tocqueville, Thomas Jefferson, and Montesquieu professed great concern that rampant commercialism would lead to a timid and indifferent citizenry, leaving a country ripe for despotism.[11] In Stigler's understatement, "The intellectual has been contemptuous of commercial activity for several thousand years."[12]

In addition, as Albert Hirschman has observed, throughout the ages people who exalt the aristocratic and martial virtues—chivalry, honor, nobility, glory, valor, and martial heroism—have opposed wealth seeking as a dominant goal. After quoting Benjamin Franklin on the economic value of hard work, honesty, punctuality, and frugality, Max Weber notes that such sentiments "would both in ancient times and in the Middle Ages have been proscribed as the lowest sort of avarice and as an attitude entirely lacking in self-respect."[13] Indeed, appropriately greedy economic actors will routinely grovel: They will have no sense of honor or self-respect or dignity as they seek to satisfy the whims of the consumer who, they feign to believe, is "always right" even when patently wrong. As long as they profit financially, they should be quite happy to let others walk all over them.[14]

From such behavior, Adam Smith concluded that commerce could render a man "incapable of defending his country in war. The uniformity of his stationary life naturally corrupts the courage of his mind, and makes him regard with abhorrence the irregular, uncertain, and adventurous life of a soldier." Thus, he argued that commerce "sinks the courage of mankind" with the result that "the heroic spirit is almost utterly extinguished," and the "bulk of the people" grow "effeminate and dastardly" by "having their minds constantly employed on the arts of luxury."[15] Tocqueville was so alarmed at the prospect of the decadence of plenitude that he advocated the occasional war to wrench people from their lethargy.[16] Similarly, in Japan the code of the Bushido held the pursuit of (material) gain to be dishonorable and accordingly held the economic pursuit of profit in contempt. And Immanuel Kant at one point contended that the "commercial spirit" fosters "a debasing self-interest, cowardice, and effeminacy, and tends to degrade the character of the nation."[17]

Many economists are, or at any rate act like, economic determinists and, to be sure, when anything notable takes place there is almost always someone somewhere who is profiting financially. Agile economic determinists (working on the principle, "follow the money") can usually ferret out the profiters (or "profiteers") and triumphantly proclaim them to be the essential cause of the event. (The fact that there are also often many important and influential people *losing* money on the event rarely troubles them very much.)

But, clearly, noneconomic values have often been deemed more worthy than economic ones. For example, Simon Kuznets has pointed out that the quest for otherworldly eternity and the quest to maintain inborn differences as expressed in class structure have frequently been taken to be far superior to economic advancement. And, as Nathan Rosenberg and L. E. Birdzell observe, a number of business innovations that clearly have been successful economically—such as joint-stock companies, department stores, mail-order houses, chain stores, trusts, branch banks, and multinational corporations—have inspired great efforts to make them unlawful by those who prefer to maintain traditional, even folksy, ways of doing things even if this means slower economic development. At the same time, sentimental, economically dubious preference has often been shown for cooperatives, small farms, and mom-and-pop stores.[18]

An important area in which noneconomic values have usually dominated is war. Like murder, war rarely makes all that much economic sense even though it would be difficult to find a war in which no one has profited financially. For the most part, in fact, economic motivations often seem like a rationale for impulses that are actually more nearly moral, aesthetic, emotional, or psychological. As Quincy Wright observed after a lifetime of study of the matter: "Studies of both the direct and the indirect influence of economic factors on the causation of war indicate that they have been much less important than political ambitions, ideological convictions, technological change, legal claims, irrational psychological complexes, ignorance, and unwillingness to maintain conditions of peace in a changing world."[19]

Thus, Hitler's invasions were linked to a sort of crackpot economic theory about "living space," but to see his goals as primarily economic is to give short shrift to his egomania and to his much more motivating notions about race and the value of war in nation building.[20] Elsewhere and at the same time, Japan's catastrophic refusal to abandon its hugely—even absurdly—costly effort to conquer China when the United States so demanded made little economic sense. And, on the other side, the main reason the United States became involved in Asia in opposition to Japan in the late 1930s was an aesthetic, sentimental, or moral impulse to keep the heroic, persecuted Chinese from being dominated by a vicious foreign regime: as Bruce Russett notes, "by embargoing Japan in 1941 the United States was giving up an export trade at least four times that with China."[21]

The Cold War and its various damaging hot wars in places like Korea and Vietnam were mainly impelled by a Communist expansionary ideology that stemmed not so much from economics as from an elaborate theory about social class warfare that was profoundly romantic and sentimental (and misguided). The Cold War abruptly evaporated not out of economic necessity, but because the Communists abandoned their threatening theory.[22]

Likewise, although the Gulf War of 1991 is often considered to have been primarily about petroleum, if economic considerations of that sort had indeed been dominant, Saddam Hussein would have quickly retreated after his economy was destroyed and it became clear he would be unable actually to sell the oil he had just conquered in Kuwait. Moreover, George Bush (motivated, it appears, mainly by aesthetic or humanitarian repulsion and by personal pique) would never have invaded because any problem of oil supplies had already been solved by the quite cheerful willingness of Saudi Arabia and other countries to pump additional supplies—indeed, the only thing keeping oil prices high at the time was Bush's threat to start a war.[23]

It seems likely, then, that, if people with business motivations had actually been running the world, its history would have been quite a bit different (and generally better). Economists and their like-minded allies have made an important contribution by helping to teach the world to value economic well being above passions that are often economically absurd.[24]

As Bush and Hussein demonstrated in 1990, the pursuit of wealth is hardly the only motivating factor today. The desires in China for reintegrating Taiwan or in South Korea for reunification with the impoverished north are essentially romantic and sentimental, and tempestuous and violent disagreement over the fate of Jerusalem scarcely makes much economic sense either.

However, the single-minded pursuit of wealth has come generally to be unashamedly accepted as behavior that is desirable, beneficial, and even honorable, and we seem now be reaching the point where business motivations have become much more important than they have been in the past. Thus in formulating his policy toward China in the 1990s, U.S. President Bill Clinton decided that economic considerations should substantially dominate ones about human rights—a conclusion that, however dismaying to some rights groups, generally went down well politically.

In this regard, it may be useful to review the association proposed by Kant between the "commercial spirit" and "self-interest, cowardice, and effeminacy." Maybe he had it right, and maybe that's not such a bad thing.

After all, under the free systems advocated by economists, people can service their long-term economic self-interest only if they are able to provide a good or a service other people freely find of value. And in the process of producing this good or service, acquisitive providers have generally discovered that they can profit better when their business practices are honest, fair, civil, and compassionate.[25]

Moreover, although it may be cowardly by the standards of those who exalt the martial virtues to turn one's back when insulted, it is possible, by other standards, to suggest that lethal battles fought over the cut of one's coat or over the color of one's sneakers or over "spheres of influence" or over a chunk of land not big enough to bury the slain are not only economically foolish, but quite childish.[26] Perhaps a world where a form of cowardice is rampant might be better than one where people are routinely running around looking for fights to prove, or test, their manhood—constantly seeking the bubble reputation even in the cannon's mouth, as Shakespeare's Jaques puts it.

And it may be effeminate to avoid unnecessary conflict, to temper anger, and to be guided by the not entirely unreasonable notion that other people do, in fact, sometimes have feelings. But such gentle, accommodating behavior is, in general, economically beneficial—that is, it enhances the general prosperity. And a world where that quality is in abundance may not, after all, be all that undesirable even if it sometimes comes laden with a degree of treacly sentimentality.

Thus, a society dominated by "self-interest, cowardice, and effeminacy" might, under some circumstances, prove to be entirely bearable. And, in part through the insidious efforts of generations of economists, societies in the most advanced portions of the world have increasingly moved in that direction.

Wealth Is Best Achieved Through Exchange, Not Through Conquest: The Demise of Empire and War

The nineteenth-century British historian, Henry Thomas Buckle, hailed Adam Smith's *Wealth of Nations* as "probably the most important book that has ever been written" because it convincingly demonstrated that gold and silver are not wealth but are merely its representatives, and because it shows that true wealth comes not from diminishing the wealth of others, but rather that "the benefits of trade are of necessity reciprocal."[27] Smith's insights are elemental and profound, and, as Buckle suggests, they had once been counterintuitive—that is, Smith and others had to discover them and point them out. Thanks in part to the promotional efforts of legions of economists and other like-minded idea entrepreneurs, they have now substantially infused the world.

The gradual acceptance over the course of the twentieth century of propositions 1 (wealth-enhancement should be a dominant goal) and 2 (wealth is best achieved through exchange rather than conquest) has helped lead to one of the most remarkable changes in world history: the virtual eradication of the ancient and once vital notion of empire.

For millennia, the size of a country's empire was accepted as one of the chief indicators of its greatness. Although, the quest for empire was often impelled by such noneconomic factors as the appeal of adventure or the need to "civilize" or convert the unenlightened, it was often partly based—or rationalized—as well on economic or pseudo-economic reasoning. Over the last century, economists and allied idea entrepreneurs like the best-selling English journalist and economic writer, Norman Angell, have successfully undercut the appeal of empire by convincing people more and more that economic well being, not the vague sense of "owning" distant lands, should be the dominant goal and that trade, not conquest, is the best way to accumulate wealth.[28]

Another combined effect—not necessarily intended—of agreement with propositions 1 and 2 is that war becomes unacceptable.

In 1795, reflecting a view of Montesquieu and others, Immanuel Kant argued that the "spirit of commerce" is "incompatible with war" and that, as commerce inevitably gains the "upper hand," states would seek "to promote honorable peace and by mediation to prevent war." However, this notion is incomplete because, as Buckle pointed out, "the commercial spirit" can be "warlike."[29] Thus, commerce truly becomes "incompatible with war" only when *both* propositions 1 and 2 are accepted.

Angell also understood this. His critics, such as the prominent American naval historian, Admiral A. T. Mahan, argued that even if it were true that war is economically unprofitable, nations mainly fight for motives other than economic ones such as "ambition, self-respect, resentment of injustice, sympathy with the oppressed." Angell replied by continuing to stress, reflecting proposition 2, that the inescapable economic chaos of war "makes economic benefit from victory impossible." But he also argued, in line with proposition 1, that nations should come to realize that "bread and a decent livelihood" are of paramount concern, not such vague and elastic goals as honor, power, and influence.[30]

Angell helped to crystallize a line of reasoning that has been gaining in acceptability ever since. It is the central contention of Richard Rosecrance's important book, *The Rise of the Trading State*, for example, that over the course of the last few centuries more and more countries have come to the conclusion that the path to wealth is through trade rather than through conquest, and he cites the striking and important examples of two recent converts: "Today West Germany and Japan use international trade to acquire the very raw materials and oil that they aimed to conquer by military force in the 1930s. They have prospered in peaceful consequence." Among trading states, Rosecrance observes, "the incentive to wage war is absent."[31] Put another way, free trade furnishes the economic advantages of conquest without the unpleasantness of invasion and the sticky responsibility of imperial control.

Thus war is unlikely if countries take prosperity as their chief goal *and* if they come to believe that trade is the best way to achieve that goal. Thanks in part to the success of economists, both propositions have now gained wide currency.

Furthermore, although war has hardly evaporated from the planet, it is worth noting that the nations of the developed world have avoided war with each other for the longest period of time since the days of the Roman Empire, a remarkable development partly (though certainly not entirely) caused by the increasing joint acceptance of propositions 1 and 2. Thomas Jefferson once referred to Europe as "an arena of gladiators," and countries like France and Germany once seemed to spend almost all their time either preparing for wars against each other or fighting them. But they have now lived—and prospered—side by side for over half a century without even a glimmer of war talk. Whether this will set the pattern for the rest of the world remains to be seen, but it is certainly of interest, and may be of consequence, that areas like Latin America and east and southeast Asia, where wars were endemic for decades after World War II, have now opted for peace and, not unrelatedly, for the banal pleasures of economic development.[32]

International Trade Should Be Free: From Adam Smith to Bill Clinton

One may accept economic development as a primary motivation and agree that exchange is a better way to prosper than conquest, but one could still conclude that prosperity is best achieved by restricting imports to favor and protect local enterprises—the once-dominant mercantilist view. Free trade, in fact, has been a hard sell, but at the end of the twentieth century it seems to have emerged triumphant, and the active proselytizing of the economics profession has probably been especially crucial in this important development.[33]

In 1993, President Bill Clinton committed one of the greatest acts of political heroism in the nation's history: energetic (and successful) support for approval of the North American Free Trade Agreement (NAFTA). He was well positioned politically to finesse and evade the issue and was urged to do so by many of his political advisers. Nevertheless, he decided to counter not only this recommendation but also the adamant desires of one of his party's most important supporters, organized labor, as well as those of many of his party's major figures including the leader in the House of Representatives.[34] As far as I can see, he took up this painful and difficult task for no good reason except that he had come to the conclusion that NAFTA—and, more generally, free trade—was good for the country in the long term.[35]

From this remarkable achievement Clinton (predictably) gained no notable electoral advantage. Indeed, his advocacy chiefly inspired the (temporary) hostility of labor, which seems to have been inclined to sit on its hands in the 1994 elections, something that may have helped with the losses Clinton's Democrats sustained in that contest. However, by his actions Clinton strongly put the Democratic imprimatur on the notion of free trade, got the world off its decades-long delay on advancing the General Agreement on Tariffs and Trade (GATT), and essentially put a consensual cap on a notion that economists had gradually come to accept over the two centuries since the publication in 1776 of Adam Smith's *Wealth of Nations.*

Thus, by the end of the twentieth century the world has come substantially to embrace the idea, not only that wealth is enhanced by exchange rather than by conquest as in proposition 2, but that unfettered trade between countries is the best way for everyone to prosper. There will, of course, be countless bobbings and weavings, and even some notable setbacks, on this principle in specific application as countries jockey to obtain the best deal in a rapidly changing world. But what is important is that the basic idea seems substantially to have been accepted.

In many ways, the increasing acceptance of free trade is quite remarkable because political logic is notably on the side of protectionists and mercantilists. After all, domestic businesses (and labor organizations) have great clout in a country's politics while foreign businesses generally have little, and the locals should be able to use their advantageous position to keep foreign competition out.[36] In addition, the businesses and workers who will be hurt by cheaper or better foreign products are likely to know who they are, while those who will gain from exports are less likely to be aware of their advantage since the benefits are likely to materialize only in the long term. Moreover, even if a firm does find a market abroad and thus has an incentive to lobby for free trade, the firm is often likely to soon discover that entrepreneurs in the nation to which is it exporting espy its success, set up local competition, and then pressure their government to close out the hapless innovative foreigner. Finally, free traders are up against the sentimental and intuitive appeal of autarky or self-sufficiency, concepts that go back at least to Aristotle and have been dominant for millennia.[37]

Deeply awed by such obstacles, George Stigler suggested gloomily in 1975 that free trade was "unattainable without a fundamental restructuring of the political system."[38] No such restructuring has taken place. Yet, although Clinton was surely well aware that free trade was a politically incorrect venture, he still went ahead with it. It seems to me that the chief reason he and other sensible politicians have been willing to bear that pain is that they have finally—and, understandably, rather reluctantly— bought the free trade line that has been consensually touted by economists for decades. As a certifiable policy wonk, Clinton has undoubtedly heard and ingested the arguments economists make about why free trade is a good idea, but he is not an economist himself, has never made a systematic analysis of the idea on his own, and has probably never even read a technical study of the issue. Chiefly, I suspect, he favors free trade (even to the point of risking his political life on the issue) because, like the patient who dutifully swallows the distasteful medicine prescribed by the authoritative physician, he trusts the expert consensus.

Friedman observed in 1984 that "no subject has so united economists since Adam Smith's *Wealth of Nations* was published in 1776 as belief in the virtues of free trade. Unfortunately, with a few exceptions during the nineteenth century, that professional consensus has not prevented one country after another from imposing trade barriers."[39] But now, in considerable part because of Clinton's (and Friedman's) efforts, a substantial international consensus by policymakers on this issue does seem finally to have been achieved. Whatever waffling and backsliding there may be on the details of implementation, the general thrust and trend seem clear.

The relation between peace and trade. Although Kant and many others have proposed that trade enhances the prospects for peace, history does not suggest that this notion has much validity: Most wars, after all, are civil conflicts, waged between groups that know each other only too well and trade with each other only too much.

But a good case could be made for the opposite causal proposition: Peace often leads to, or at any rate facilitates, trade. That is, peace ought to be seen not as a dependent, but rather as an independent, variable in the relationship.

For example, the long and historically unprecedented absence of war among the nations of Western Europe since 1945, has not been caused by their increasing economic harmony. Rather, their economic harmony has been caused, or at least expedited, by the peace they have enjoyed. Similarly, the rise of the multi-national corporation and the building of the long-envisioned channel tunnel between France and Great Britain are the consequences of peace, not its cause.

Put the other way, international tensions and the prospect of international war have a strong dampening effect on trade. Each threatened nation has an incentive to cut itself off from the rest of the world economically to ensure that it can survive if international exchange is stifled by military conflict. Therefore, policies variously known as autarky, self-reliance, and self-sufficiency are likely to be very appealing. In the peaceful modern trading world, however, such once seductive notions have come to seem quaint.

Similarly, the Cold War could be seen in part as a huge trade barrier as Edward Yardeni points out elsewhere in this volume. With the demise of that politically derived and economically foolish construct, trade will be liberated. But it is peace that will have facilitated trade, not the opposite.

Economies Do Best When the Government Leaves Them Substantially Free

As the experience in places like Japan and South Korea has shown, it is possible to accept free trade between nations while maintaining that the domestic economy should still be kept under major governmental controls. But, as the notion that international trade should be free and open has become increasingly accepted, so has the proposition that the domestic economy should also be free.

This is a fairly recent development. It has not been that long since Joseph Schumpeter famously and repeatedly declared "centralist socialism" to be the "heir apparent" to capitalism. In 1976, Fred Hirsch published a book about why the twentieth century had "seen a universal predominant trend toward collective provision and state regulation in economic areas," and around the same time Milton Friedman presented a paper (a very depressing one from his point of view) seeking to explain why collectivist beliefs flourish in the world of ideas.[40]

However, things have changed markedly since then. As economist Robert Heilbroner, not usually known as an ardent free-marketeer, noted only a few years ago: "There is today widespread agreement, including among most socialist economists, that whatever form advanced societies may take in the twenty-first century, a market system of some kind will constitute their principal means of coordination. That is a remarkable turnabout from the situation only a generation ago, when the majority of economists believed that the future of economic coordination lay in a diminution of the scope of the market, and an increase in some form of centralized planning." Or, in the words of an economist who *has* been a consistent free-marketeer, R. M. Hartwell, "The intellectual agenda about the role of the government has changed from one determined by the desirability of intervention to one determined by the desirability of market economy." The big question, he observes happily, is no longer "Why not more government, more public ownership, and more control and regulation of the market," but rather "Why not less government, more privatization, and less interference with the market?"[41]

Applying the language Henderson used when he assessed the state of medicine as it was in 1912, Heilbroner and Hartwell are saying that, by the present state of economic knowledge, the random politician or governmental official consulting the random economist only a generation ago was likely to get the wrong advice: It would perhaps have been better, on average, to consult a reader of tea leaves or an astrologer.

Much of the most widely accepted economic thinking of the time derived from the work of John Maynard Keynes whose central theme, according to his biographer, was "the state is wise and the market is stupid." Working from that sort of perspective, India's top economists for a generation supported policies of regulation and central control that failed abysmally—leading one of them to lament recently, "India's misfortune was to have brilliant economists." And Latin American economies were misdirected for decades by antimarket *dependencia* theory as forcefully and confidently advocated by well regarded economists in the United Nations Economic Commission on Latin America.[42]

In many respects the economic consensus Heilbroner and Hartwell note has burgeoned only recently, particularly after the abject and pathetic collapse of command and heavily planned economies in the late 1980s and early 1990s. As a top Indian economist put it recently, "Between the fall of the Berlin Wall in 1989 and the collapse of the Soviet Union in 1991, I felt as though I were awakening from a thirty-five-year dream. Everything I had believed about economic systems and tried to implement was wrong."[43]

The economic advice decisionmakers around the world are hearing, and increasingly are accepting, is to rely on the market rather than forcing on it externally derived and politically comfortable concepts of fairness and justice. And with this acceptance, a set of alternative propositions about the virtues of revolution and of the justice possible through a command or heavily manipulated economy have effectively been scrapped as romantic, unrealistic, unproductive, and increasingly irrelevant.[44] In practice, all capitalist, or market capitalist, states may not end up looking a great deal like each other, any more than all democracies do. In particular, the degree to which the government intervenes in the economy with tax and welfare policy, regulation, trade restrictions, price supports, and direct control over certain individual enterprises varies considerably. But the trend seems clear.

The new consensual approach can probably be summed up in one short phrase: "trust the market." And, like the rise in international trade, this advice has been facilitated by a decline of war fears: as a prominent Italian economist has put it, "A state company has to do with war, national interest, and self-defense," whereas privatization "is driven by the absence of war, and by the opening of the international system that makes raw materials, money, and technology available to everyone."[45]

One of the principles that inform that advice, that international trade should be free has already been discussed. Among the others seem to be the following:

Wages and Prices Should Be Allowed Freely to Find Their Own Ranges and Limits. It would be difficult to underestimate the economically pernicious effects of efforts to determine the "just wage" and the "just price" by non-market judgments. Yet for millennia prices were substantially set by custom, government, or the church, and the progressive abandonment of this intuitively appealing and hence politically correct approach has been one of the major achievements of modern economics—it is quite possibly the economic equivalent of the germ theory. And it has been a tough struggle. Rationing has enjoyed quite a bit of political appeal even in peacetime, and many politicians, like Harry Truman, have had a deep and abiding belief in wage and price controls, while a Republican president, Richard Nixon, suddenly re-instituted them as late as the 1970s.[46] The quest for the "just price" is still popular in some areas—over cable television rates, for example, and rent control lingers in a declining number of places. But, substantially, the battle has been won.

Government Regulation Is Often Unwise and Can Be Counterproductive. For the most part, the quest for optimal regulation or for full-bore economic planning has been changed to a preference for reducing or even ending regulation and planning in many areas. Government may still sometimes play a helpful economic role by maintaining a viable justice system to enforce contracts and property rights and to police fraud and violent coercion, and it may also usefully seek to regulate matters of health and safety and to control socially undesirable side effects or externalities like air pollution—though even here regulations designed to shape parameters to allow the market do the hard work may well prove to be sounder than efforts to plan. But, as Yergin and Stanislaw put it, the idea would be to move the state away from being the "producer, controller, and intervenor" to being the "referee, setting the rules of the game to ensure, among other things, competition."[47]

The Government Should Abandon Enterprises That Can Be Handled by the Private Sector. "Privatization" is a word that came into notable use only in the last decades of the twentieth century, intended to be used in pointed distinction to an older word, "nationalization." The realization has taken hold that private enterprise simply does much better than the state at providing a whole series of goods and services—from communications to transportation to education to utilities to mail service to ship building—that many once felt could be provided better, and more justly, by the state. Privatization has been a key development in the post-Communist states, and even the highly entrenched welfare states of Western Europe have sold off over $100 billion in state assets since 1985.[48]

High Taxes, Especially at the Top, Can Be Economically Counterproductive, and Capricious or Discretionary Ones Almost Always Are. Confiscatory and discretionary expropriation was once standard practice by rulers around the world. The campaign against it has been a long and arduous one even though tax restraint has almost always been to the long-term economic advantage of the confiscators.[49]

A Considerable Amount of Economic Inequality Is Inevitable and Essentially Desirable. Government may sometimes play a useful social or safety net role by cushioning pain through the judicious transfer of some degree of wealth from the economically successful to the unsuccessful.[50] But the Communist experience suggests that efforts to induce true economic equality are likely to fail and, to the degree they are successful, to exact a cost—often a very considerable one—in economic growth.

Uncompetitive Enterprises Should Not Be Subsidized and Should Be Allowed to Fail. This notion is, of course, extremely painful politically, but the disastrous experiences in the Soviet Union and elsewhere (in India a major state fertilizer company with 1200 employees, completed in 1979, had by 1991 yet to produce any fertilizer for sale) have helped economists to underscore its wisdom.[51]

Government Spending Should Be Kept Reasonably Low, and Government Deficits Should Be Kept Under Control. A form of the welfare state remains in place in all developed countries, but the belief that such spending can detrimentally get out of hand seems increasingly to be accepted, and some of the most entrenched welfare states are judiciously trimming back.[52]

Principles like these centrally informed the successful advice given to the post-Communist states and to others seeking economic growth, and such principles have often been considered counterintuitive, immoral, or unjust. But however politically painful, they seem increasingly to be accepted by policy-makers and politicians around the world.[53]

Of course, the gathering—indeed, gathered—consensus among economists does not mean there is no room for debate. There may be controversy, for example, over the desirable tradeoffs between growth and the distribution of wealth, or over whether it is better to go for maximum growth or to sacrifice some development to reduce the amplitude of the boom and bust cycles around an upward path, or over how high a government's deficit can rise without stifling the economy, or over the degree to which a regulation will hurt more than it will help, or over what rate of inflation is most desirable. But, substantially and increasingly, the debate is likely to be more nearly a matter of degree than of fundamental principles.

The Prospects for Massive Economic Growth

If it is true that economists now generally know what they are talking about and if it is true that policymakers are now substantially and increasingly willing, however reluctantly, to accept and act on their often counterintuitive and politically painful advice, the prospects for major economic advances in all—or virtually all—corners of the globe are highly favorable.

Perhaps the most important single fact about economics, economic history, and economic development—and, indeed, about human material well being—is tidily conveyed in Figure 4.2.[54] Over the last two centuries or so an enormous and accelerating expansion of economic wealth and well being has taken place in the developed world—an expansion that has been utterly unprecedented in the history of the human race. The figure also suggests that this growth has begun to come to many places in the less developed world, particularly in the last half or third of the twentieth century.

Explanations for this development have placed an emphasis on technological and organizational innovation and development, and on an expansion of knowledge, science, and education—this together with the important fact that government and religion, advertently or inadvertently, somehow happened to afford people the freedom to exploit and pursue economic opportunities.[55] In addition, in my view, an important, even crucial, contributor to this historic process may well have been the gradual acceptance by people in business of the virtues of honesty, fairness, civility, and compassion as innovative capitalists discovered the economic value of these virtues.[56]

This remarkable economic expansion has taken place substantially by accident or default. It was not notably guided by government policy—indeed, it frequently took place *despite* government policy—because it occurred when economists often didn't know what they were talking about or fundamentally disagreed over policy, or, when they could agree, were often ignored by decisionmakers who were pursuing divergent agendas, were mesmerized by faulty economic folk-wisdom or ideology, or were paralyzed by political cowardice.

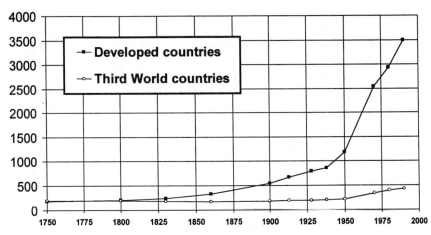

FIGURE 4.2   Real GNP Per Capita, 1750–1982

The rather uniform anticipation among economic historians is that this economic expansion will continue, broaden, and even escalate in the future.[57] This cheery prediction may prove pessimistic, however, because it leaves out the enhancing benefits that will derive from the efforts of the economics profession itself. As the state of medical knowledge at the turn of the current century portended major health improvements in the century to come, we may now be on the verge of similar advances in the area of economic growth as we enter the next one.

Of course, there is no way to be sure that economists really know what they are talking about any more than one could have been certain a century ago about the state of contemporary medical science. It is, I suppose, possible that the economists' current affinity for markets will prove as faddish and unsound as the bias many of them once showed toward planning, regulation, and trade restrictions. If so, we are in big trouble to the extent that their advice is increasingly being accepted by decision-makers. However, judging from the depth of the emerging consensus and, in particular, from the frequent successes of economic analysis and advice in recent years, I find it reasonable to suggest that this time, at long last, they may very well have gotten it right and that the consequent benefits to the well being of the planet's population could be enormous.

Economic Development, Professed Happiness, and the Catastrophe Quota

A considerable expansion of economic well-being does not mean people will feel—or at any rate say they feel—happier, however.

Aristotle once argued that "The happy man is one whose activity accords with perfect virtue and who is adequately furnished with external goods." Or in the words of a Slovak filmmaker, "It is better to be rich and healthy than poor and sick." Or, as Pearl Bailey put it even more succinctly, "I've been rich, and I've been poor, and rich is better."[58]

If people will be furnished with external goods in the next century to a degree scarcely imaginable even by our present standards of affluence, it might seem to follow that, as long as virtue at least holds its own, people should become much happier. The evidence suggests, however, that this will not occur.

Three Conclusions About Happiness

Happiness, or a sense of well-being, is a rather elusive quality, but insofar as it can be specified and measured in public opinion surveys, there seem to be three reasonably clear conclusions.

People Profess to Hold Economic Considerations Important When They Assess the Degree to Which They Are Happy. When people in various countries are asked about happiness and their personal concerns, economic matters—including such issues as the standard of living and housing—tend to be the most often mentioned. Not surprisingly, health also scores highly as do family and personal relationships.[59]

Moreover, Wealthier People Are More Likely to Profess Being Happy Than Poorer Ones in the Same Society. One survey of the happiness literature describes as "overwhelming" the amount of evidence showing that there is a positive—though sometimes not a very high—correlation between income on the one hand and happiness and other measures of subjective well-being on the other. This relationship holds even when other variables such as education are controlled.[60]

However, When a Country Grows Economically, the Assertions of Its People As to Their State of Happiness Do Not Similarly Grow. The very considerable economic growth the United States experienced in the postwar era was not associated with a corresponding increase in professions of happiness in public opinion surveys. Data from Western Europe from the 1970s and 1980s suggest much the same thing.[61]

One study, however, argues that these results are not surprising because they deal with economic improvement in areas that were already comparatively affluent. It contends that a notable rise in happiness in England, France, the Netherlands, and West Germany took place between the terrible immediate post-war years and the 1960s or 1970s. Thus, it is concluded, the wealth-happiness connection is subject "to the law of diminishing returns": once a person is adequately furnished with external goods, in Aristotle's phraseology, further increases in happiness do not take place.[62]

At best, of course, this suggests that happiness will increase only when a country moves from misery to some degree of economic security and that little additional gain is to be expected thereafter. But, as Richard Easterlin notes, even this conclusion is questionable when one looks at data from Japan. By 1958, that country had substantially recovered from the war, but it sported an income level lower than or equal to ones found in many developing countries today. During the next 30 years, Japan experienced a spectacular economic resurgence in which real per capita income multiplied five-fold and in which the benefits of economic growth were quite widely spread throughout the population. Yet there was little or no increase in Japanese happiness ratings.[63]

Four Explanations for the Remarkable Inability of Economic Growth to Inspire Assertions of Happiness

If economic growth is what it is all about, then, the world is likely soon to experience massive improvement. But if happiness (or at any rate professions thereof) is what it is all about, it won't.

There seem to be several possible explanations for this curiously unpleasant state of affairs about happiness.

It Is Relative Wealth, Not Absolute Wealth, That Matters.   In exploring this explanation, Easterlin has ferreted out a crisp observation by Karl Marx: "A house may be large or small; as long as the surrounding houses are equally small it satisfies all social demands for a dwelling. But if a palace rises beside the little house, the little house shrinks to a hut." Thus, the argument runs, people may use a relative standard, not an absolute one, when assessing their well-being. If everybody's wealth increases at more or less the same rate, accordingly, relative incomes remain the same, and so does happiness. There exists a "consumption norm," suggests Easterlin, and one gauges one's happiness relative to this norm, not to the norm's absolute placement.[64]

But this cannot be the full explanation. After all, health is also an important component in happiness self-evaluations, and while people may think of wealth in relative terms, they are unlikely to think of health in the same way. That is, people simply do or do not feel healthy, and the health of others is likely to be quite irrelevant to their judgment on this issue. Since health has been improving at least as impressively as income in places like the United States, happiness should be going up even if people adopt a relative standard with respect to the wealth component of the happiness calculation. But it isn't.

There is a difference, of course, between the two issues in that one can imagine a maximum, satiated condition of health but not necessarily of wealth (moreover, sick people are obviously less likely than poor ones to be interviewed on surveys). However, concerns about the future must also play a role in health considerations just as they do for ones about wealth. Thus, healthy people in, say, the 1940s should have found their happiness tainted a bit by fears that they or their children could at any moment come down with polio. When medical science cured that problem, people should, to that degree, have become happier; but they didn't.

Nonmaterial Concerns Dominate Perceptions of Happiness. The observation that happiness does not increase when material well-being increases has logically led to the conclusion that material well-being is not very important to people's sense of happiness. Angus Campbell adopts such a point of view and concludes that happiness is positively related to status and marriage and to having family, friends, and a satisfying job.[65]

But economic and health considerations are clearly of considerable importance in personal assessments of happiness and well-being, as noted above. And, since there have been enormous improvements in wealth and health in the United States and other surveyed countries, the failure of happiness to rise cannot be caused by other factors unless it can be shown that these have greatly deteriorated over the same period of time—something Campbell does not find.[66]

Material Accumulation Leads Not to Satisfaction, but to Boredom and Discontent. Tibor Scitovsky argues that prosperity, particularly in the United States, is simply not very satisfying—that it has led not to contentment and pleasure, but to leisure-induced boredom and then to rebellion, drug-taking, violence, and environmental deterioration. People, he suggests, seek "satisfaction in the wrong things, or in the wrong way, and then are dissatisfied with the outcome."[67]

This perspective distrusts prosperity—a process in which people are bountifully and indiscriminately supplied at an attractive price with the things they happen to think they want. The concern is that, in a world that lacks danger and stimulating challenge, people will come to wallow in luxury and to give in to hedonism. In the process, not only do their minds rot, but also they wallow in malaise, ennui, and Weltschmerz and become dissatisfied and essentially unhappy.

It is an old fear for successful capitalism, a fear voiced even by some of its champions. Adam Smith anticipated that as workers came to concentrate on repetitive tasks they would "become as stupid and ignorant as it is possible for a human creature to become" and be rendered incapable of exercising "invention" or "of conceiving any generous, noble, or tender sentiment." Similarly, Alexis de Tocqueville was concerned that, when "the love of property" becomes sufficiently "ardent," people will come to regard "every innovation as an irksome toil," "mankind will be stopped and circumscribed," the mind "will swing backwards and forwards forever without begetting fresh ideas," "man will waste his strength in bootless and solitary trifling," and, though in continual motion, "humanity will cease to advance." In this century Joseph Schumpeter famously opined that managers would lose vigor and initiative as they became embedded in huge bureaucracies.[68]

There may be something to such concerns, but they would lead one to anticipate that happiness should actually decline in affluent areas, something that hasn't happened.[69] In addition, they tend to square poorly with indications that the world's economy is becoming increasingly, not decreasingly, competitive and that human capital—drive, intelligence, innovation, and risk-taking initiative—is fast becoming the quality in greatest demand. Intellectuals who consider business to be boring, mindlessly repetitive, unsatisfying, or lacking in daring, courage, and imagination have never tried to run—much less start—one.

Improvements in Well Being Are Effectively Unappreciated: The Catastrophe Quota.   I have yet to run into an American over the age of 47 who regularly observes, "You know, if I had been born in the nineteenth century, I'd very probably be dead by now." Nobody really thinks in such terms, yet the statement is completely true—and, of course, I don't mean in the sense that just about everybody who happened to be born in the last century is no longer with us, but that life expectancy in the United States as late as 1900 was 47.

It is often observed that people don't appreciate their health until they get sick, their freedom until they lose it, their wealth until it is threatened, their teeth until they ache. In other words, when things get better, we quickly come to take the improvements for granted after a brief period of assimilation: They become ingested and seem part of our due, our place in life.

Occasionally, people in affluent societies might pause to wonder how they, or anyone, ever got along without air conditioning, credit cards, faxes, EKGs, jet transportation, frozen pizza, VCRs, garbage disposals, cable television, automatic money machines, flu shots, Vanna White, laser surgery, thermal underwear, telephone answering machines, or quilted toilet paper, but on those rare occasions, the pause is brief, the observation is generally something of a joke, and few are willing seriously to concede that at least some of these eagerly accepted additions to their lives might somehow have made them happier. As Ludwig von Mises puts it philosophically: "Under capitalism the common man enjoys amenities which in ages past gone by were unknown and therefore inaccessible even to the richest people. But, of course, these motorcars, television sets and refrigerators do not make a man happy. In the instant in which he acquires them, he may feel happier than he did before. But as soon as some of his wishes are satisfied, new wishes spring up. Such is human nature."[70]

Lebergott proposes that if every economically significant good added since 1900 were to disappear, and if the remaining items—like salt pork, lard, and houses without running water—were marked down to 1900 prices, few would judge their economic welfare to have improved. Yet nostalgic images of, say, 1900 American life rarely remember rotten teeth or note that each day at least three billion flies were created in cities by horse manure. Instead there is a tendency to look back at the past myopically, forgetting its complexities, horrors, and inconveniences, and often bathing it in a golden glow.[71] As part of this, we like to view the past as a simpler time, though the plays of Shakespeare and Aeschylus rather tend to suggest that people in olden times really did have some pretty complicated problems.[72]

A systematic, if quiet, process of standard raising also takes place. A caption poised above an old carpet sweeper on display in an exhibit in the Strong Museum in Rochester, New York, observes, "Labor-saving devices like carpet sweepers helped middle-class people satisfy their desire for cleanliness within the home." Lest one conclude that this was an improvement however, the caption writer quickly adds, "Unfortunately, each new development raised standards and expectations for cleanliness, making the ideal as hard as ever to achieve."[73]

The media may play something of a role in all this. Good news often doesn't sell well. For example, life expectancy at birth for Americans rose in 1993 to a record 75.5 years, a fact the *New York Times* found so boring that it simply reprinted an Associated Press dispatch on the issue and buried it on the thirteenth page of its September 1 issue. The *Atlantic* seems addicted to articles like "The Crisis of Public Order," "The Drift Toward Disaster," "The Coming Anarchy," and "The Coming Plague," and the editors will only be truly happy, some suggest, when they come across an authoritative article entitled, "World Ends, Experts Say." Sensitive to such proclivities, a *New Yorker* wag once proposed as the first line of a poem: "Harm's bordello is the op-ed page."[74] In part because of such press proclivities, the remarkable long-term trends documented in Figures 4.1 and 4.2 often surprise people.

The political process is also essentially devoted to bringing out the bad news. Incumbents may often like to stress the positive, but challengers can't—they must work very hard to ferret out things that are wrong and that, at the same time, concern a fair number of voters. If they are successful in this, it would be impolitic for the incumbents simply to dismiss the voters' concern. They must agree, or appear to agree, that the problem is genuine and then propose a solution that seems superior to the one proposed by the challenger. The process leads to nice anomalies: air quality in the United States has improved markedly over the last decades. Yet most people think (and many people seem to *want* to think) that the opposite is true.[75]

Moreover, although some advances, like the end of the Cold War, can come about with dazzling speed and drama, many improvements of the human condition are quite gradual and therefore difficult to notice. Rosenberg and Birdzell observe that the remarkable transformation of the West from a condition in which 90 percent lived in poverty to one in which the incidence of poverty was reduced to 20 or 30 percent of the population or less took a very long time: "Over a year, or even over a decade, the economic gains, after allowing for the rise in population, were so little noticeable that it was widely believed that the gains were experienced only by the rich, and not by the poor. Only as the West's compounded growth continued through the twentieth century did its breadth become clear."[76] Clearly, the same can be said for the massive improvements in life expectancy over the last century that have proved to be so easy to ignore.

The result of all this, is that the catastrophe quota always seems to remain comfortably full. When a major problem is resolved or eliminated or eased substantially, or when a major improvement is made, there may be a brief period of reflective comment, but then problems previously considered small are quickly elevated in perceived importance.

Nowhere is this clearer than in international affairs where the Cold War and the threat of nuclear holocaust have evaporated in recent years to the distinct inconvenience of doomsayers everywhere. But with scarcely a pause for breath they have adroitly come up with a list of new problems to plague us in our "new world disorder."[77]

For example, one enumerator of "new" problems lists "the proliferation of weapons of mass destruction and the ballistic missiles to carry them; ethnic and national hatreds that can metastasize across large portions of the globe; the international narcotics trade; terrorism; the dangers inherent in the West's dependence on Mideast oil; new economic and environmental challenges."[78] That none of these problems is new and that some of them are actually of less urgent concern than they were during the Cold War is of little concern. Wars deriving from ethnic and national hatreds are neither new nor increasing in frequency in the world, and nuclear proliferation is no more a new problem—in fact, may well be less of a problem—than it was in 1960 when John Kennedy repeatedly pointed out with alarm that there might be 10, 15, or 20 nations with a nuclear capacity by 1964.[79] And the international drug trade has obviously been around for quite some time, while the West's supposedly dangerous dependence on Mideast oil has been a matter of pointed concern at least since 1973. The effect of terrorism has often been more in the exaggerated hysteria it generates than in its actual physical effects—fewer Americans are killed by international terrorists than are killed by lightning.[80]

Economic and environmental challenges are hardly new either, but new alarms can be raised. In a pessimistic best seller in 1993, historian Paul Kennedy was able to work up quite a bit of concern over pollution, immigration, and robotics. Interestingly enough, war, a central preoccupation of his pessimistic best seller of 1987, had apparently vanished from his worries: the word, "war," does not even appear in the index of the later book. Or, like Zbigniew Brzezinski, one can focus on such enduring, if vaporous, problems as "turmoil."[81]

And, if these concerns don't seem alarming enough, we can always hark back to the time when we could ventilate about the government's budget deficit, a problem chiefly caused by the fact that people were living too long. Happily, in the course of the century improved medical care not only generated a wonderful new problem to complain about (for a while at least), but supplied the average American with nearly 30 additional years of lifetime in which to do so (and with his or her original teeth, to boot).

As capitalist prosperity expands, we will also be nicely poised to become concerned that people will become overwhelmed, even paralyzed by the array of choices confronting them in the marketplace. One pundit asserts that "As social scientists, we know that with an increase in choices, people tend to become more anxious"; a sociologist points out that "If you have infinite choice, people are reduced to passivity"; and a futurist ominously worries about "overchoice—the point at which the advantage of diversity and individualization are canceled by the complexity of the buyer's decision-making process." Clearly, if Hamlet was faced by only two alternatives and found himself agonizing over it for five full acts, we must be far, far worse off today. This conundrum seems to be an updated version of the classic philosophic puzzle known as "Buridan's ass" in which the animal is placed at an equal distance from two bundles of hay and eventually starves to death in terminal indecision.[82] There seems to be no evidence any ass ever actually underwent this agony, but the information thus far is merely anecdotal, and this might well be one of those many issues crying out for well-funded systematic research.[83]

Development and the Quest for Happiness

In the end, however, there may be benefits to the endless and endlessly successful quest to raise standards and to fabricate new desires to satisfy and new issues to worry about. Not only does this quest keep the mind active, but it probably importantly drives, and has driven, economic development as well. Rosenberg and Birdzell find it unlikely that a "self-satisfied people could move from poverty to wealth in the first place," and David Hume observes that commerce "rouses men from their indolence" as it presents them with "objects of luxury, which they never before dreamed of," raising in them a desire for "a more splendid way of life than what their ancestors enjoyed."[84]

By contrast, Easterlin puts a rather negative spin on all this when he applies the phrase, "hedonic treadmill," to the process and concludes "each step upward on the ladder of economic development merely stimulates new economic desires that lead the chase ever onward." The word "treadmill" suggests an enveloping tedium as well as a lack of substantive progress. However, the "chase" not only enhances economic development, but has invigorating appeals of its own. As Hume notes, when industry flourishes people "enjoy, as their reward, the occupation itself, as well as those pleasures which are the fruit of their labour." As part of this process, "the mind acquires more vigour" and "enlarges its power and faculties."[85]

Moreover, there is no evidence that economic development exhausts the treaders, lowers their happiness, or inspires many effective efforts to turn back the clock. Professions of happiness may not soar, but, despite the anguished protests of some intellectuals, people do not seem to have much difficulty enduring a condition of ever-increasing life expectancy and ever-expanding material prosperity.

Terminal Conclusions

All this suggests, then, two modest predictions about the next century:

1. The world is likely to experience a massive increase in economic growth and well being, and

2. Nobody will be particularly impressed.

Notes

1. For helpful information and pointed commentary, I would like to thank Stanley Engerman.

2. Quoted, Alan Gregg, *Challenges to Contemporary Medicine* (New York: Columbia University Press, 1956), p. 13.

3. For discussions, see Stanley Lebergott, *Pursuing Happiness: American Consumers in the Twentieth Century* (Princeton, NJ: Princeton University Press, 1993); Julian L. Simon, ed., *The State of Humanity* (Cambridge, MA: Blackwell, 1995); Richard A. Easterlin, *Growth Triumphant: The Twenty-First Century in Historical Perspective*. (Ann Arbor, MI: University of Michigan Press, 1996). Data in Figure 1: Sweden and England data from Samuel H. Preston, "Human Mortality Throughout History and Prehistory," in Julian L. Simon, ed., *The State of Humanity* (Cambridge, MA: Blackwell, 1995), pp. 30–36; and from correspondence with Preston. More developed and less developed data from Ronald Bailey, ed., *The True State of the Planet* (New York: Free Press, 1995), p. 403.

4. See, for example, Stanley L. Engerman, "The Standard of Living Debate in International Perspective: Measures and Indicators," in Richard Steckel and Roderick Flood, eds., *Health and Welfare During Industrialization* (Chicago: University of Chicago Press, 1997).

5. Lawrence H. Summers, "The Next Chapter," *International Economic Insights*, May/June 1992, 12. Privatization: Daniel Yergin and Joseph Stanislaw, *The Commanding Heights: The Battle Between Government and the Marketplace That Is Remaking the Modern World* (New York: Simon & Schuster, 1998), pp. 114–115.

6. Yergin and Stanislaw 1998; Joel S. Hellman, "Winners Take All: The Politics of Partial Reform in Postcommunist Transition," *World Politics* 50 (January 1998):203–234.

7. Though, lately, beneficial health effects have happily been found in the moderate, but regular, ingestion of red wine, liquor, and pizza: Jane E. Brody, "Personal Health: The nutrient that reddens tomatoes appears to have health benefits," *New York Times*, 12 March 1997. Maybe things are beginning to turn around.

8. Michael Weinstein, "Dr. Doom Becomes Dr. Pangloss," *New York Times*, 18 August 1997, A18.

9. George J. Stigler, *The Intellectual and the Marketplace* (Cambridge, MA: Harvard University Press, 1984), p. 150. Pope: *New York Times*, 3 May 1991, A10.

10. Adam Smith, *Lectures on Justice, Police, Revenue and Arms* (Oxford: Clarendon, 1896), pp. 257, 259.

11. Roger Boesche, "Why Did Tocqueville Fear Abundance? or The Tension "Between Commerce and Citizenship," *History of European Ideas* 9 (1988):25–45.

12. George J. Stigler, *The Economist as Preacher and Other Essays* (Chicago: University of Chicago Press, 1982), p. 32.

13. Albert O. Hirschman, *The Passions and the Interests: Political Arguments for Capitalism Before Its Triumph* (Princeton, NJ: Princeton University Press, 1977). Max Weber, *The Protestant Ethic and the Spirit of Capitalism* (New York: Scribner's, 1958), p. 56.

14. This is neatly illustrated in a story related by P. T. Barnum:

One of the ushers in my Museum once told me he intended to whip a man who was in the lecture room as soon as he came out.

"What for?" I inquired.

"Because he said I was no gentleman," replied the usher.

"Never mind," I replied, "he pays for that, and you will not convince him you are a gentleman by whipping him. I cannot afford to lose a customer. If you whip him, he will never visit the Museum again, and he will induce friends to go with him to other places of amusement instead of this, and thus, you see, I should be a serious loser."

"But he insulted me," muttered the usher.

"Exactly," I replied, "and if he owned the Museum, and you had paid him for the privilege of visiting it, and he had then insulted you, there might be some reason in your resenting it, but in this instance he is the man who pays, while we receive, and you must, therefore, put up with his bad manners."

My usher laughingly remarked, that this was undoubtedly the true policy, but he added that he should not object to an increase of salary if he was expected to be abused in order to promote my interests.

P. T. Barnum, *Struggles and Triumphs: or, Forty Years' Recollections of P. T. Barnum, Written by Himself* (New York: American News Company, 1871), p. 496.

15. Adam Smith, *An Inquiry into the Nature and Causes of the Wealth of Nations* (Oxford: Oxford University Press, 1976), p. 782 (V.i.f). Smith 1896, 257–259. By contrast, he held the "art of war" to be "certainly the noblest of all arts" (1976, 697: V.i.a). In 1914, German general Friedrich Bernhardi was of the opinion that "all petty and personal interests force their way to the front during a long period of peace. Selfishness and intrigue run riot, and luxury obliterates idealism. Money acquires an excessive and unjustifiable power, and character does not obtain due respect." *Germany and the Next War* (New York: Longmans, Green, 1914), p. 26.

16. Boesche 1988, p. 39.

17. Immanuel Kant, *The Critique of Judgement* (London: Oxford University Press, 1952), p. 113.

18. Simon Kuznets, *Modern Economic Growth: Rate, Structure, and Spread* (New Haven, CT: Yale University Press, 1966), pp. 12–14. Nathan Rosenberg and L. E. Birdzell, *How the West Grew Rich: The Economic Transformation of the Industrial World* (New York: Basic Books, 1986), p. 309.

19. Quincy Wright, "War: The Study of War, " in David L. Sills, ed., *International Encyclopedia of the Social Sciences*, vol. 16, (New York: Macmillan–Free Press, 1968), p. 463. For an extensive discussion of the varying role of economics as a motivation, or excuse, for war, see Evan Luard, *War in International Society* (New Haven, CT: Yale University Press, 1986).

20. Eberhard Jäckel, *Hitler's World View: A Blueprint for Power* (Cambridge, MA: Harvard University Press, 1981).

21. *No Clear and Present Danger: A Skeptical View of the United States' Entry into World War II* (New York: Harper and Row, 1972). As Samuel Eliot Morison points out, "The fundamental reason for America's going to war with Japan was our insistence on the integrity of China": *The Two-Ocean War: A Short History of the United States Navy in the Second World War* (Boston: Little, Brown, 1963), p. 45. Melvin Small notes that "the defense of China was an unquestioned axiom of American policy taken in along with mother's milk and the Monroe Doctrine. . . . One looks in vain through the official papers of the 1930s for some prominent leader to say, 'Wait a second, just why is China so essential to our security?'": *Was War Necessary? National Security and U.S. Entry into War* (Beverly Hills, CA: Sage, 1980), pp. 238–239. And Warner Schilling observes crisply, "At the summit of foreign policy one always finds simplicity and spook," and he suggests that "the

American opposition to Japan rested on the dubious proposition that the loss of Southeast Asia could prove disastrous for Britain's war effort and for the commitment to maintain the territorial integrity of China—a commitment as mysterious in its logic as anything the Japanese ever conceived." "Surprise Attack, Death, and War," *Journal of Conflict Resolution* 9 (September 1965):389. See also John Mueller, *Quiet Cataclysm: Reflections on the Recent Transformation of World Politics* (New York: HarperCollins, 1995), pp. 103–108; Paul W. Schroeder, *The Axis Alliance and Japanese-American Relations, 1941* (Ithaca, NY: Cornell University Press, 1958), p. 209.

22. See John Mueller, "The Impact of Ideas on Grand Strategy," in Richard Rosecrance and Arthur A. Stein, eds., *The Domestic Bases of Grand Strategy* (Ithaca, N Y: Cornell University Press, 1993), pp. 48–62; Mueller 1995, chap. 2; Myron Rush, "Fortune and Fate," *National Interest* (Spring 1993):19–25.

23. John Mueller, *Policy and Opinion in the Gulf War* (Chicago: University of Chicago Press, 1994), chap. 8.

24. See also Hirschman 1977; Donald McCloskey, "Bourgeois Virtue," *American Scholar* 63 (Spring 1997):180–182.

25. On this issue, see John Mueller, *Capitalism, Democracy, and Ralph's Pretty Good Grocery* (Princeton, NJ: Princeton University Press, 1999), chaps. 3–4.

26. For A. A. Milne's perspective on such thinking, see his *Peace with Honour* (New York: Dutton, 1935), pp. 4, 222–223.

27. *History of Civilization in England* (New York: Appleton, 1862), pp. 154, 157. See also Milton and Rose Friedman, *Free to Choose: A Personal Statement* (New York: Harcourt Brace Jovanovich, 1980), pp. 1–2; Smith 1976, pp. 429–451 (IV.i).

28. On this issue, see also Neta C. Crawford, "Decolonization as an International Norm: The Evolution of Practices, Arguments, and Beliefs," in Laura W. Reed and Carl Kaysen, eds., *Emerging Norms of Justified Intervention* (Cambridge, MA: American Academy of Arts and Sciences, 1993), pp. 37–61; Ethan A. Nadelmann, "Global Prohibition Regimes: The Evolution of Norms in International Society," *International Organization* 44 (Autumn 1990):479–526; Rosenberg and Birdzell 1986, p. 17. Beginning in 1908, Angell argued that "It is a logical fallacy to regard a nation as increasing its wealth when it increases its territory." Britain, he pointed out, "owned" Canada and Australia in some sense, yet it certainly did not get the products of those countries for nothing—it had to pay for them just as though they came "from the lesser tribes in Argentina or the USA." The British, in fact, could not get those products any cheaper than the Germans. Thus, he asked, "If Germany conquered Canada, could the Germans get the wheat for nothing? Would the Germans have to pay for it just as they do now? Would conquest make economically any real difference?" He also argued that the popular notion that there were limited supplies in the world and that countries had to fight to get their share was nonsense: "The great danger of the modern world is not absolute shortage, but dislocation of the process of exchange, by which alone the fruits of the earth can be made available for human consumption." *The Great Illusion: A Study of the Relation of Military Power to National Advantage* (London: Heinemann, 1914), p. 31; *The Great Illusion 1933* (New York: Putnam's, 1933), pp. 108, 175.

29. Immanuel Kant, *Perpetual Peace* (Indianapolis, IN: Bobbs-Merrill, 1957), p. 24; see also Hirschman 1977, 79–80, 134–135; Buckle 1862, 157. Peace activists of

the nineteenth century were quick to take up Kant's argument, and often with a similar sense of optimism. Particularly prominent were two Englishmen, Richard Cobden and a Quaker, John Bright, who saw international peace as one of the benefits of free and unfettered trade; and in 1848 John Stuart Mill concurred: "It is commerce which is rapidly rendering war obsolete." Michael Howard, *War and the Liberal Conscience* (New Brunswick, NJ: Rutgers University Press, 1978), p. 37. On booty as an important, though usually not primary, motive for medieval war, see Richard W. Kaeuper, *War, Justice, and Public Order: England and France in the Later Middle Ages* (New York: Oxford University Press, 1988).

30. A. T. Mahan, *Armaments and Arbitration: The Place of Force in the International Relations of States* (New York: Harper, 1912), p. 131. A nation's "wealth, prosperity, and well-being . . . depend in no way upon its military power," Angell argued, noting that the citizens of such war-avoiding countries as Switzerland, Belgium, or Holland were as well off as the Germans, and much better off than the Austrians or Russians. *After All: An Autobiography* (New York: Farrar, Straus and Young, 1951), p. 165; Angell 1933, 89–92, 230; Angell 1914, 36.

31. Richard Rosecrance, *The Rise of the Trading State: Conquest and Commerce in the Modern World* (New York: Basic Books, 1986), pp. 16, 24. For a discussion of the mechanism by which attitudes toward war have been reshaped, and particularly of the crucial role of World War I in this process, see John Mueller, *Retreat from Doomsday: The Obsolescence of Major War* (New York: Basic Books, 1989), and especially Mueller 1995, chap. 9.

32. Thomas Jefferson, *Democracy* (New York: Appleton-Century, 1939), p. 263. Since Roman Empire: Paul W. Schroeder, "Does Murphy's Law Apply to History?" *Wilson Quarterly* 9 (New Year's 1985): 88. These developments might also affect religion. Modern science and medicine have been destructive of two of religion's once popular appeals: its ability to explain the physical universe and its ability to heal. And the notion, at one time accepted even by atheists, that religion is vital because it supplies a moral code, is being undercut when, apparently for the first time in history, formerly pious Europe has developed societies that are orderly, moral, and generally admirable even though religion, particularly organized religion, plays little effective part. Now, the newly emerging unselfconscious acceptance of material gain as a dominant goal may tend to devalue another of the church's appeals. Religion attained prominence in human life in part because it can sometimes supply spiritual uplift as a sort of relief from material woes and fates and because it seeks to give higher meaning to a dreary and difficult life. But if people become primarily materialistic and rich, they may come to feel they need religion less. Of course, in other areas, such as portions of the Islamic world, religiosity may have actually been heightened in recent years, and it certainly retains a considerable degree of force in the United States. Thus, whether Europe constitutes a true harbinger remains to be seen. For the argument that it is not, see Peter L. Berger, "Secularism in Retreat," *National Interest*, Winter 1996/97, pp. 3–12. For the argument that religion is weakest where it is state dominated and strongest where there is a vigorous competitive market for religion, see Laurence R. Iannaconne, Roger Finke, and Rodney Stark, "Deregulating Religion: The Economics of Church and State," *Economic Inquiry* 35 (April 1997): 350–364.

33. Actually, to be complete about this, there may be something of a clash between propositions 2 and 3. Logically, an ardent free trader should favor conquest—at least ones where damage is minimal and where long-term resentments are not stirred up—since this would expand the free-trade zone to the general benefit. For example, free traders would presumably hold that North Americans would generally benefit if Canada were painlessly and benevolently to conquer the United States, making it, perhaps, its eleventh province.

34. Elizabeth Drew, *On the Edge: The Clinton Presidency* (New York: Simon & Schuster, 1994), pp. 338–346.

35. It is not true that "only Nixon could have gone to China"—the Democratic presidents before him tried several times to improve relations with that country, only to find the door closed (see Mueller 1989, 184–185). But it seems likely that no Republican could have amassed the necessary (mainly Democratic) votes in Congress to pass NAFTA.

36. Legal restrictions forbidding foreign countries or interests from contributing to political campaigns are, to that degree, unwise policy. See Peter Passell, "Economic Scene: Salmon eaters salute a victory against the protectionists," *New York Times*, 22 January 1998, C2.

37. F. A. Hayek, *The Fatal Conceit: The Errors of Socialism* (Chicago: University of Chicago Press, 1988), p. 45. On the once central, but now abandoned, quest in India for "self-sufficiency" and in Latin America for freedom from "dependency," see Yergin and Stanislaw 1989, chaps. 3, 9.

38. George J. Stigler, *The Citizen and the State: Essays on Regulation* (Chicago: University of Chicago Press, 1975), p. xi; see also James Buchanan, "Socialism Is Dead; Leviathan Lives," *Wall Street Journal*, 18 July 1990, A8.

39. Milton Friedman, *Tyranny of the Status Quo* (San Diego, CA: Harcourt Brace Jovanovich, 1984), p. 129. However, in the 1930s Keynes advised against the "economic entanglements" of trade. Jeffrey Sachs, "International Economics: Unlocking the Mysteries of Globalization," *Foreign Policy*, Spring 1998, pp. 102–103, 110.

40. Joseph A. Schumpeter, *Capitalism, Socialism and Democracy.* 3rd ed. (New York: Harper & Row, 1950), p. 417. Fred Hirsch, *The Social Limits to Growth* (Cambridge, MA: Harvard University Press, 1976), p. 1. Friedman: R. M. Hartwell, *A History of the Mont Pelerin Society* (Indianapolis, IN: Liberty Fund, 1995), p. 165. See also Yergin and Stanislaw 1998, 22; Seymour Martin Lipset, "Reflections on Capitalism, Socialism & Democracy," *Journal of Democracy*, 4 (April 1993):43–55.

41. Robert Heilbroner, *21st Century Capitalism* (New York: Norton, 1993), p. 97. Hartwell 1995, 191. On this issue, see George J. Stigler, "The Politics of Political Economists," *Quarterly Journal of Economics* 73 (November 1959):522–532; Yergin and Stanislaw 1998.

42. Keynes: Robert Skidelsky, *Keynes* (New York: Oxford University Press, 1996), p. 117. India and Latin America: Yergin and Stanislaw 1998, pp. 215, 234; see also Sachs 1998, p. 101.

43. Yergin and Stanislaw 1998, p. 138.

44. See Robert Heilbroner, "Economics by the Book," *Nation*, 20 October 1997, pp. 16-19; Yergin and Stanislaw 1998.

45. Yergin and Stanislaw 1998, p. 137.

46. On the once dominant notion of the "just price" and the "just wage," see Rosenberg and Birdzell 1986, p. 38. Nixon: Yergin and Stanislaw 1998, p. 62.

47. There also seems to be an increasing belief that it may be wise judiciously to regulate the financial system itself, because, as one economist has put it, "There's more of a stake in keeping the financial sector honest than there is, for instance, in cosmetics." Yergin and Stanislaw 1998, 373, 349. See also Charlotte Denny, "World Bank in surprise policy U-turn," *Guardian Weekly*, 6 July 1997. On the successes of governmental efforts to deal with environmental concerns in the last few decades, see Gregg Easterbrook, *A Moment on the Earth: The Coming Age of Environmental Optimism* (New York: Viking, 1995). See also Peter Passell, "Economic Scene: A new project will measure the cost and effect of regulation," *New York Times*, 30 July 1998, C2.

48. Yergin and Stanislaw 1998, p. 317.

49. See Rosenberg and Birdzell 1986, pp. 119–123; E. L. Jones, *The European Miracle: Environments, economies, and geopolitics in the history of Europe and Asia*, 2nd ed. (Cambridge, UK: Cambridge University Press, 1987); Barry R. Weingast, "The Political Foundations of Limited Government: Parliament and Sovereign Debt in 17th- and 18th-Century England," in John N. Drobak and John V. C. Nye, eds., *The Frontiers of the New Institutional Economics* (San Diego, CA: Academic Press, 1997), pp. 213–246; Martin McGuire and Mancur Olson, "The Economics of Autocracy and Majority Rule: The Invisible Hand and the Use of Force," *Journal of Economic Literature* 34 (March 1996):72–96; Bradford De Long and Andrei Shleifer, "Princes and Merchants: European City Growth Before the Industrial Revolution," *Journal of Law and Economics* 36 (October 1993):671–702; Douglass C. North and Barry R. Weingast, "Constitutions and Commitment: The Evolution of Institutions Governing Public Choice in Seventeenth-Century England," *Journal of Economic History* 49 (December 1989):803–832.

50. For Margaret Thatcher's ready acceptance of this role, see Yergin and Stanislaw 1998, p. 124.

51. Yergin and Stanislaw 1998, p. 216.

52. Marlise Simons, "Dutch Take 'Third Way' to Prosperity," *New York Times*, 16 June 1997, A6. Roger Cohen, "The Cries of Welfare States Under the Knife," *New York Times*, 19 September 1997, A1.

53. It is common to calculate government spending as a percentage of gross domestic product and to conclude that, since this figure has risen in the last decades in most developed countries, governmental "control" over the economy has risen. But most government spending in these countries has not been in consumption but rather in subsidies and transfers, items that do not enter the GDP calculation (Clive Crook, "The Future of the State," *Economist*, 20 September 1997, 5–48). What purports to be a "percentage," therefore, is actually a ratio. Moreover, in assessing "control" of the economy, the rise of transfers may well be far less significant than the declines in regulation, in confiscatory taxation, and in once popular wage and price controls. On this issue, see John V. C. Nye, "Thinking About the State: Property Rights, Trade, and Changing Contractual Arrangements in a World with Coercion," in John N. Drobak and John V. C. Nye, eds., *The Frontiers of the New Institutional Economics* (San Diego, CA: Academic Press, 1997), pp. 138–141.

54. Data from Paul Bairoch, *Economics and World History* (Chicago: University of Chicago Press, 1993): p. 95.

55. See, in particular, Rosenberg and Birdzell 1986. See also David S. Landes, *The Unbound Prometheus: Technological change and industrial development in Western Europe from 1750 to the present* (Cambridge, UK: Cambridge University Press, 1969); David S. Landes, *The Wealth and Poverty of Nations: Why Some Are So Rich and Some So Poor* (New York: Norton, 1998); Jones 1987.

56. On this point, see Mueller 1999, chaps. 3–4.

57. See, for example, Simon 1995; Easterlin 1996, p. 84, 153; Lebergott 1993; Rosenberg and Birdzell 1986, p. 333; Landes 1998, chap. 29; Jones 1987; E. L. Jones, *Growth Recurring: Economic Change in World History* (Oxford: Oxford University Press, 1988); Ben Wattenberg, "Going ga-ga over the Golden Age," *Washington Times*, 20 March 1997, A17; Steven E. Landsburg, *Fair Play: What Your Child Can Teach You About Economics, Value, and the Meaning of Life* (New York: Free Press, 1997).

58. Aristotle: quoted, Angus Campbell, *The Sense of Well-Being in America: Recent Patterns and Trends* (New York: McGraw-Hill, 1981), p. 56. Slovak film: "Je Lepšie Byt' Bohatý a Zdravý, Ako Chodobný a Chorý" by Juraj Jakubisko. Pearl Bailey: quoted, Stephen Kunitz and Stanley L. Engerman, "The Ranks of Death: Secular Trends in Income and Mortality," *Health Transition Review* 2 (Supplementary Issue, 1992), 29; Charles Murray attributes this pithy observation to Sophie Tucker: *In Pursuit: Of Happiness and Good Government* (New York: Simon & Schuster, 1988), p. 68.

59. Richard A. Easterlin, "Does Economic Growth Improve the Human Lot? Some Empirical Evidence," in Paul A. David and Melvin W. Reder, eds., *Nations and Households in Economic Growth: Essays in Honor of Moses Abramovitz* (New York: Academic Press, 1974), 90–96, mostly using data and analyses from Hadley Cantril, *The Pattern of Human Concerns* (New Brunswick, NJ: Rutgers University Press, 1965). On this issue, see also Murray 1988, chap. 4.

60. Ed Diener, "Subjective Well-Being," *Psychological Bulletin* 95 (May 1983):553. See also Campbell 1981, 241; Easterlin 1974, 99–104; Easterlin 1996, 133–135; Murray 1988, 66–68; Ronald Inglehart and Jacques-Rene Rabier, "Aspirations Adopt to Situations—But Why Are the Belgians So Much Happier Than the French?" in Frank M. Andrews, ed., *Research on the Quality of Life* (Ann Arbor, MI: Institute for Social Research, University of Michigan, 1986), 22–23. People in wealthy countries may be happier on average than those in poorer ones, but the association is often weak and inconclusive. See Inglehart and Rabier 1986, pp. 40, 44–50; Easterlin 1974, pp. 104–108; Easterlin 1996, p. 138; but see also Ruut Veenhoven, "Is Happiness Relative?" *Social Indicators Research* 24 (February 1991):9–12.

61. Easterlin 1995, pp. 136, 138; Campbell 1981, pp. 27–30; Tom W. Smith, "Happiness: Time Trends, Seasonal Variations, Intersurvey Differences, and Other Mysteries," *Social Psychological Quarterly* 42 (March 1979):18–30.

62. Veenhoven 1991, p. 19. Data for Britain and France: Ruut Veenhoven, *Happiness in Nations: Subjective appreciation of life in 56 nations 1946–1992* (Rotterdam, Netherlands: Erasmus University of Rotterdam Department of Social Sciences, 1993), pp. 146–147. See also Murray 1988, chap. 4.

63. Easterlin 1995, pp. 136–140; using data from Veenhoven 1993, pp. 176–177. See also Inglehart and Rabier 1986, p. 44.

64. Easterlin 1974, pp. 111–116.

65. Campbell 1981. See also Murray 1988, chap. 4.

66. In seeking to explain why professions of happiness did not rise between 1946 and 1977 in the United States, Stanley Lebergott points to a different consideration: the ominous simultaneous expansion in nuclear megatonnage. The considerable increases in measured real incomes during that time, he suggests, cannot offset fears of "collective suicide" or of concerns over "poverty, civil rights, nuclear plant explosions, the environment" (1993, p. 14). The problem with this explanation is that people seem to respond in very personal terms when they are asked about happiness; political considerations like those suggested by Lebergott scarcely enter the happiness calculus unless the question specifically asks about concerns for the nation itself (see Easterlin 1996, p. 134). Moreover, at the same time the problems Lebergott mentions were rising in the United States, others were dissipating—concerns about food shortages or labor disputes, for example. Even more pointedly, there was actually a considerable decline in fears of atomic war with the relaxation of international tensions that began with the signing of the test ban treaty of 1963: See John Mueller, "Changes in American Public Attitudes toward International Involvement," in Ellen Stern, ed., *The Limits of Military Intervention* (Beverly Hills, CA: Sage, 1977), pp. 326–328.

67. *The Joyless Economy: The Psychology of Human Satisfaction* (New York: Oxford University Press, revised edition, 1992), pp. vi–viii, 4. In like spirit, a letter sent to the *New York Times* from Latvia worries that youth is being "worn down by grinding affluence" (5 January 1998, A24). On the "horrors of prosperity," see Auberon Waugh, *Brideshead Benighted* (Boston: Little, Brown, 1986), pp. 49–51.

68. Smith 1976, p. 782 (V.i.f). Alexis de Tocqueville, *Democracy in America* (New York: Vintage, 1990), p. 263. Schumpeter 1950; see also Neil McInnes, "Wrong for Superior Reasons," *National Interest*, Spring 1995, pp. 85–97.

69. Charles Murray, in line with this proposition, argues that job satisfaction has declined in the United States (1988, pp. 134–135). But poll data do not support this conclusion: See, for example, Richard G. Niemi, John Mueller, and Tom W. Smith, eds., *Trends in Public Opinion: A Compendium of Survey Data* (Westport, CT: Greenwood, 1989), p. 238.

70. Ludwig von Mises, *The Anticapitalistic Mentality* (Grove City, PA: Libertarian Press, 1972), p. 3. See also Murray 1988, pp. 68–69.

71. Lebergott 1993, p. 15; and, for his authoritative calculation on flies and horse manure, p. 24n. For a rare exception to myopic recollection, see Otto L. Bettmann, *The Good Old Days—They Were Terrible!* (New York: Random House, 1974).

72. Today successful people in the post-Communist countries often complain that they now spend so much time accumulating wealth that they are no longer able to spend long evenings with friends drinking cheap vodka and talking and laughing: Alessandra Stanley, "A Toast! To the Good Things About Bad Times," *New York Times*, 1 January 1995, 4–1. Complaints like this arise even though economic development generally increases options; it does not close them off. As the Amish have shown, it would still be entirely possible to reject economic change.

Opportunities may increase, but that doesn't mean one has necessarily to reject the old ones.

73. For a discussion of ever rising standards of cleanliness and personal hygiene (at one time people routinely went around encrusted in dirt, rarely washed, and, well, smelled), see Juliet B. Schor, *The Overworked American: The Unexpected Decline of Leisure* (New York: Basic Books, 1991), pp. 89–91.

74. Nicholson Baker, "From the Index of First Lines," *New Yorker*, 26 December 1994–2 January 1995, 83. See also David Whitman, *The Optimism Gap* (New York: Walker, 1998), chap. 7; Gregg Easterbrook, "America the O.K." *New Republic*, 4 and 11 January 1999.

75. Air quality: Easterbrook 1995; Hugh W. Ellsaesser, "Trends in Air Pollution in the United States," in Julian Simon, ed., *The State of Humanity* (Cambridge, MA: Blackwell, 1995), pp. 491–502. People think: *Washington Post*/Kaiser Family Foundation/Harvard University Survey Project, "Why Don't Americans Trust the Government?" 1996.

76. Rosenberg and Birdzell 1986, p. 6, also p. 265. However, improvement was evident to economist Alfred Marshall when he published the first edition of his classic textbook in 1890: *Principles of Economics* (London: Macmillan, 1890), pp. 3–4.

77. For an extended critique, see John Mueller, "The Catastrophe Quota: Trouble After the Cold War," *Journal of Conflict Resolution* 38 (September 1994):355–375.

78. R. James Woolsey, Jr., Testimony before the Senate Intelligence Committee, 2 February 1993.

79. Sidney Kraus, ed., *The Great Debates: Kennedy vs. Nixon, 1960* (Bloomington, IN: University of Indiana Press, 1962), p. 394.

80. Data: Mueller 1995, p. 23.

81. Paul Kennedy, *The Rise and Fall of the Great Powers* (New York: Random House, 1987); Paul Kennedy, *Preparing for the Twenty-First Century* (New York: Random House, 1993). Zbigniew Brzezinski, *Out of Control: Global Turmoil on the Eve of the 21st Century* (New York: Scribner's, 1993).

82. Overchoice: Lena Williams, "Free Choice: When Too Much Is Too Much," *New York Times*, 14 February 1990, C1. Buridan's ass comparison suggested by Stanley Engerman.

83. Such research, however, might find that the problem sometimes solves itself. If customers in supermarkets become paralyzed with anxious indecision in front of, for example, the corn flakes, they will block the aisles. This will reduce the profits of the store owner, who will then logically be forced to increase the aisle space, reducing in turn the choice angst confronting the previously hapless customers.

84. Rosenberg and Birdzell 1986, p. 5. David Hume, *David Hume: Writings on Economics* (Madison, WI: University of Wisconsin Press, 1955), p. 14.

85. Easterlin 1996, p. 153. Hume 1955, p. 21; see also Murray 1988, chap. 7.

5

The Economic Consequences of the Peace

EDWARD YARDENI

I. Introduction

The end of the Cold War in 1989 was undoubtedly one of the most important events in world history.[1] The monumental political importance of the end of the superpowers' military and ideological rivalry was obvious and immediately recognized by everyone transfixed by the television coverage of the populist demolition of the Berlin Wall during November 1989. The end of the Cold War marked the beginning of a new era, not only for international political relations, but also for the global economy. Ten years later, there is still more agreement than disagreement about the political consequences of the end of the Cold War. Yet, even today in 1999, the *economic* consequences of the end of the Cold War are either not fully recognized, or are hotly debated:

Deflation

History shows that peace times are usually periods of deflation (i.e., falling prices). Since the start of the 1990s, inflation rates in the major industrial economies have declined significantly and are near zero as the decade ends. Yet, most economists continue to believe that history will not be repeated because central banks will avert deflation with reflationary monetary policies. Easy money should eliminate excess supply—the cause of deflation—by boosting demand, thus closing the gap with supply.

   I think they are wrong. The forces of deflation have not been defeated, and they are likely to prevail over the next few years.[2] Perversely, easier credit might prop up supply more than boost demand. In the long run, the most effective way to eliminate excess supply is to allow market forces to put insolvent producers out of business. In the short run, of course, this is the most painful path, and often triggers political intervention, that worsens the long-term deflation problem.

Globalization

"Globalization" and "restructuring" have become part of the vocabulary of the new era. The definitions are vague and may explain why there is so much controversy about whether these are good or bad trends. Protectionists decry the economic and financial turmoil caused by globalization and restructuring. In their opinion, the Asian contagion and the Long-Term Capital Management crisis are recent examples of the downside of global capitalism. They advocate government protection from these "cruel and unfair" market forces, and more government regulation of "crony capitalism."[3]

I am for regulated free-market capitalism. I hope this will be the choice of Asians, Russians, Latins, and other peoples who have experienced recent reversals of fortune. Whether we like it or not, markets always become more global during peacetime, forcing companies to restructure the way they were doing business during the preceding wartime. We can resist these changes, or else we can adapt, and learn to prosper in competitive markets. Recent problems in Asia were not caused by unregulated crony capitalism, but rather by crony corruption. Capitalism may have defeated Communism, but it has yet to completely triumph over another adversarial economic system, namely, corruption. Capitalism is, first and foremost, a legal system that protects property rights and enforces contracts. I advocate government regulation (not protection)—especially in banking and securities markets—to eliminate corrupt practices, thus fostering a legal climate that is conducive to capitalism.

New Economy

In the United States, during the second half of the 1990s, economists debated whether the business cycle was still relevant in the new era. The so-called "New Paradigm" or "New Economy" camp argued that inflation could remain low even if strong economic growth continued to push the unemployment rate to the lowest level in decades. The high-tech revolution is just one of several new developments that have weakened the traditional trade-off between unemployment and price inflation. The counter-revolutionaries sought to debunk the new era, and to defend the old order: Strong growth would lead to inflation. Higher inflation would force the Federal Reserve to boost interest rates. Tight credit would then cause a recession. The old-era business cycle is alive and well.

I believe that the traditional business cycle model is no longer relevant. However, I am not promoting a new paradigm. Rather, I believe that a very old paradigm (i.e., perfect competition) has never been more relevant. If so, then inflation is probably dead, and a "Fed-led" recession is, therefore, very unlikely. But recessions can occur in the new era. For the first 10 years, the new era was a golden era for much of the global economy, especially in the United States. New eras are rarely golden all the time. Bad things can happen even in new eras.[4]

Yahoo Economy

Contributing to the sense that we are in a golden era is the high-tech revolution. In the stock market, the technology sector has been the strongest of the 11 sectors of the Standard and Poors (S&P) 500 composite of companies since 1993. More recently, Internet stocks have soared beyond any traditional relationship with actual and prospective earnings. Some argue that the new economy is morphing into the "Yahoo Economy." Technology has the potential to create extraordinary prosperity for everyone around the world.

I am sympathetic to this happy notion. But there are some clouds that come with the silver lining. For example, the Internet is not good for everyone. It is bad for intermediaries between producers and consumers. In many ways, it is fundamentally deflationary.[5]

Over the past 10 years, I have promoted the notion that the end of the Cold War—the triumph of Capitalism over Communism—was wildly bullish for stocks.[6] I argued that it would lead to lower interest rates and inflation rates around the world. I was one of the first to predict that the aging of the Baby Boomers would be very bullish for stocks.[7] I was an early proponent of the bullish implications of the high-tech revolution. I have been one of the strongest advocates of the new economy view claiming that a secular rebound in productivity would allow strong growth and low inflation.

War and Peace and Prices

The collapse of the Berlin Wall marked the end of the 50-Year Modern Day War—which includes World War II, the Cold War, and numerous regional wars from Korea to Vietnam to Central America to Southern

Africa and several other hot spots around the world. This war, which lasted half a century, was in its effect an unprecedented trade barrier. Americans were prohibited from trading with Communist countries. The Iron Curtain was a major obstacle to trade between all countries on opposite sides of the curtain. The lifting of the curtain, the destruction of the Berlin Wall, the collapse of Soviet imperial communism all simultaneously heralded the elimination of the world's greatest barrier to trade. Coincidentally, trade among "Free World" countries was liberalized further by 1) the Europe 1992 movement, 2) the Uruguay Round of trade talks under the General Agreement on Tariffs and Trade (GATT) completed during 1993, and 3) the North American Free Trade Agreement (NAFTA) of 1994. China remains in communist hands, but trade between China and the rest of the world, especially the United States, has expanded significantly in the 1990s.

There has been a dramatic expansion of global trade, capital flows, and direct investment since 1989:

1. According to data compiled by the International Monetary Fund, total world exports at an annual rate rose to $5.6 trillion during the first half of 1998, up 86% since 1989.
2. Cross-border loans of international banks soared 98% from $4.6 trillion during the second quarter of 1989 to $9.1 trillion in mid–1998, according to the Bank for International Settlements.
3. International banks increased their loans to Asia, (excluding Japan, Hong Kong, and Singapore) by 251%, from $137 billion to $481 billion, between the second quarter of 1989 and the second quarter of 1997, just before the start of the Asian crisis. Other lenders and investors poured money into Asia and other emerging economic regions with equal enthusiasm, expecting that the new era would produce golden returns.
4. The sum of U.S. direct investment abroad and foreign direct investment in the United States swelled from $94 billion at the start of the decade to a record $224 billion in 1998, according to Flow of Funds data compiled by the Federal Reserve. U.S. direct investment abroad hovered between $10 billion and $30 billion per year during the 1980s, then soared to a record $130 billion in 1998.

All wars are trade barriers. They divide the world into camps of allies and enemies. They create geographic obstacles to trade, as well as military ones. They stifle competition. Economists mostly agree that the fewer restrictions on trade and the bigger the market, the lower the prices paid by consumers and the better the quality of the goods and services offered by producers. These beneficial results occur thanks to the powerful forces unleashed by competition. Peace times tend to be deflationary because freer trade in an expanding global marketplace increases competition among producers. Domestic producers are no longer protected by wartime restrictions on domestic and foreign competitors. There are fewer geographic limits to trade, and no serious military dangers. As more consumers become accessible around the world, more producers around the world seek them out by offering them competitively priced goods and services that offer high-quality standards compared to the competition. Entrepreneurs have a greater incentive to research and develop new technologies in big markets than in small. Big markets permit a greater division of labor and more specialization, which is also conducive to technological innovation.

History shows that prices tend to rise rapidly during war times and then to fall during peace times. War is inflationary; peace is deflationary. In the United States, for example:

— During the War of 1812, the Consumer Price Index (CPI) rose 47%. It fell 48% after the war.
— During the Civil War, the CPI rose 81%. It fell 40% after the war.
— During World War I, the CPI rose 140%. It fell 35% after the war.
— From 1939 through 1947, during World War II and the start of the Cold War, the CPI rose about 50%.
— Then prices soared about 500% during the Cold War from 1947 to 1989.

During peace times, prices fell sharply for many years following all the wars listed above, except for the peace so far in the 1990s. Prices are still rising in the United States and in Europe, though at a significantly slower pace than during the previous two decades, when the Cold War was most intense. Japan is the one major industrial economy experiencing some deflation. If peace has been deflationary in the past, then why are prices still rising in the 1990s, albeit at a subdued pace? Is deflation still possible as we enter the next century? If peace prevails into the next millennium, will deflation prevail? Or is history mostly irrelevant, so inflation will persist and even rebound?

The "war and peace" model of inflation is simple and seems to account for the major price waves of the past. However, monetarists have plausibly argued that monetary policy and central bankers are also important contributors to the inflation process. I think some monetarists overstate their case when they claim that inflation is always a monetary phenomenon. *I believe that the competitive structure of markets is also a very important variable in understanding inflation.* But I also believe that money matters.

So far, in the peace of the 1990s, easy money has succeeded in offsetting the natural, peacetime forces of deflation. In the present situation, the central banks of the major industrial economies have eased credit conditions significantly in an effort to offset the forces of deflation. Of course, central bankers existed in the past when deflation prevailed, but monetary theory and operating procedures were primitive.

Gauging whether monetary policy is restrictive or stimulative can be controversial. Orthodox monetarists focus on the growth of the money supply. More eclectic observers might prefer inflation-adjusted interest rates (i.e., real interest rates). I'm content to look at the unweighted average of three-month Euro deposit rates to gauge the direction of monetary policy in the Group of Seven (G7) countries. My approach is admittedly unscientific and casual, but the conclusion is obvious and robust: The G7 central bankers have lowered interest rates sharply to avoid deflation. The G7 short-term rate plunged from about 10% in November 1989, when the Berlin Wall was dismantled, to 3.7% at the end of 1998. Nevertheless, inflation rates have continued to fall and are now very close to zero (i.e., literally on the edge of deflation). Why? Is deflation inevitable?

The End of Macroeconomics

Have the central bankers defeated or just delayed the forces of deflation? This is one of the big questions for economic forecasters looking into the next century. If the risk of deflation is minimal, then the downtrend in interest rates during the 1990s may be over and could possibly be reversed by the start of the new century. In this case, the major economic legacy of the end of the Cold War was short lived and much less significant than I believed it would be. Time will tell, of course. My hypothesis is that the forces of deflation have not been defeated, and they will soon prevail.

Francis Fukuyama wrote a controversial article in the summer 1989 issue of *The National Interest* titled, "The End of History?" He argued that the ideological battle between capitalism and communism was over. The clear winner was capitalism. The clear loser was communism. To the extent that history consists mostly of epic struggles between opposing forces, the triumph of capitalism also marked the end of history. In the same spirit, I would like to propose a simple notion: Macroeconomics is dead. The triumph of capitalism also marked the triumph of *micro*economics over *macro*economics. This is an unfortunate division in the economics profession. As a result, macroeconomists often fail to understand the effect of changes in market structure and industrial organization on the overall economy. They tend to promote an elitist (Keynesian) notion that they can fine-tune the economy from on high, while the little people go about their daily business.

My major premise is that our economic present is better understood, and our economic future is more accurately predicted, by a model from the microeconomics textbooks than from the macroeconomics textbooks. The new "in" model is Perfect Competition. Out are Keynesian, monetarist, and other macro models. The perfectly competitive marketplace has the following characteristics:

- The goal of firms is to maximize their profits.
- There are no barriers to entry for new firms.
- The factors of production are mobile.
- The number of competing firms can be as numerous as the market can profitably sustain.
- There is no protection from failure. There are no government support programs or self-perpetuating monopolies, oligopolies, or cartels.
- The goal of consumers is to maximize their utility given their budget constraints.
- Consumers are free to purchase the best products at the lowest price from any producer. They have cheap and readily available information available to them to make their choices.

This model of perfect competition predicts that the market price will be equal to the marginal cost of production. No one firm, or group of firms, can set the price. Profits are minimized to the lowest level that provides just enough incentive for a sufficient number of suppliers to stay in business to satisfy demand at the going market price. Consumer welfare is maximized. This simple model is fairly static and needs to be combined with models of economic growth. It also needs to be more dynamic to reflect the effect of technological innovation. Despite these limitations, this textbook model of perfect competition has probably never been more relevant than it is today. Let's compare today's economy to the textbook model:

1. In capitalist societies, the pressure to maximize shareholder value is intense. Company managers are taking big risks to restructure their businesses with the goal of increasing profitability. In formerly communist countries and in newly emerging ones, governments are privatizing state-owned enterprises and permitting foreign ownership.
2. Globally, there are fewer barriers to entry as a consequence of the end of the Cold War. This is certainly true geographically. It is also

true in other ways. For example, a potential barrier to entry in some industries is the availability of financing. Technology is especially dependent on venture capital. Low interest rates and booming stock markets around the world during most of the 1990s provided plenty of cheap capital—too much in some cases.

3. Factors of production are becoming more mobile because companies are becoming more mobile. U.S. corporations have a long tradition of setting up operations overseas in local markets. Indeed, this accounts for the U.S. trade deficit, especially with countries like Japan and Germany that until recently had a more mercantilist business tradition of exporting to their foreign customers. But change is occurring. Japanese and German companies are globalizing their operations.

4. Foreign business ventures are attracted to emerging economies because government regulations are minimal and labor costs are very low. This trend is putting pressure on the governments of industrialized nations to deregulate their economies and to meddle less in disputes between workers and their employers.

5. Consumers and businesses are rapidly taking advantage of the Internet to obtain, at virtually no cost, the information they need to find the lowest prices for just about any product or service they desire.

6. Global firms are adopting price cutting as a new competitive business strategy. They are striving to cut costs and to boost productivity in an effort to be among the lowest, cost producers in the world. Profit margins evaporate quickly in competitive markets, so companies are under enormous pressure to innovate at a faster and faster pace. The simple goal is to sell as many units to as many consumers worldwide as possible at the lowest possible price in the shortest time.

If perfect competition is the "new" model that best explains aggregate economic activity, then inflation may be dead too. If inflation is dead, then the traditional business cycle may also be dead. In the new era, companies are under enormous pressure to reduce their marginal costs so that they can offer the lowest prices. In this scenario, deflation is more likely than reflation. If inflation remains low, central bankers won't need to tighten monetary policy in an effort to stop a cyclical rebound in inflation. Inflationary booms are less likely. Policy-engineered recessions are less likely as well.

Of course, not all recessions are policy engineered. For example, a recession caused by the bursting of the speculative bubble in the stock market is very likely, in my opinion. However, the standard tools of macroeconomic analysis, particularly business cycle indicators, may no longer accurately reflect the true nature of our economy. Similarly, forecasts based solely on the business cycle model may also miss the mark. Furthermore, the secular trends unleashed by the high-tech revolution could overwhelm the cyclical pattern of the low-tech economy. Again, this is not to say that the business cycle is dead. However, it may no longer dominate the course of economic growth as it did in the past.

Deflation and Corruption

In a perfectly competitive market, producers and consumers are "price takers." No one has enough clout in the market to dictate the price that everyone must receive or pay. The "invisible auctioneer," who equates total market demand to total supply at the market's equilibrium price, sets the price. Clearly, there can't be excessive returns to producers in a competitive market. If there are, they will be eliminated as new firms are attracted to enter the excessively profitable market. Firms that try to increase their profits by raising prices will simply attract more suppliers, or else lose market share to firms that hold the market price.

While the model predicts that no firm can set the market price, the reality is that any firm can lower the price. It will do so if management can find ways to lower costs and increase productivity. If it lowers the prices of its output below the market price, it will increase its unit sales and market share. This will be very profitable as long as unit sales increase more than prices are reduced. The problem is that competitors are bound to follow the path of the market leader. However, everyone can still profit as long as consumers respond to the industry's price cuts by buying more units. This is the *Good Deflation* scenario. Everyone benefits. Consumers enjoy lower prices, and they respond by purchasing more, as their real incomes improve thanks to productivity gains. Companies thrive because their earnings are boosted as they gain more unit sales growth than they lose on the pricing side.

Alternatively, *Bad Deflation* occurs when companies are forced to lower their prices, but unit sales don't increase enough to maintain profitability. In this scenario, companies respond to weaker profits by cutting employment and by reducing capital spending. The deflationary spiral starts curling as consumers become insecure about their jobs and reduce their spending. In the Good Deflation scenario, consumers view lower prices as a good reason to buy more. In the Bad Deflation scenario, they respond to lower prices by postponing purchases, figuring prices will be even lower tomorrow, when they might have less uncertainty about their job security. Americans in the 1930s and Japanese in the 1990s experienced the bad version of deflation.

But why wouldn't unprofitable firms simply go out of business, leaving healthy firms in a position to enjoy higher prices once the excess supply is shut down? More often than not, the answer is corruption. Theoretically, in a free market, there is no protection from failure. In reality, all too often, insolvent companies remain in business. They may have highly placed political and business friends in the government or in their major creditors. Insolvent businesses—a.k.a., "zombies" or "the living dead"— can only survive and thrive in an environment of political rot (a.k.a., corruption). This zombie problem means that healthy companies are forced to compete against firms that don't have to be profitable to survive. Obviously, if the situation is allowed to persist, then it is only a matter of time before solvent companies become insolvent too.[8] This is the *Ugly Deflation* scenario.

Corruption is not the only source of Bad Deflation. An excessive supply of financial capital can also be a problem. In peacetime, there is more money and credit available to finance private-sector business. The opportunities to prosper seem as big as the potential global market. Before long, there is too much money chasing too few good deals. Yet, prosperity tends to generate overconfidence and unrealistic expectations. Projected returns are overestimated, while risk is underestimated. As a consequence, supply tends to race ahead of demand. The resulting deflation depresses returns and, at some point, stops the free flow of financing. When this happens, even solvent companies may be forced to shut down if their sources of credit dry up. This is another version of the Ugly Deflation scenario, of course. What could be worse than to see well run companies go under and fire all their workers because of an indiscriminate flight-to-quality in the credit markets? This happened in Asia in 1997 and 1998 and almost became a global problem during the summer of 1998.

What can policy makers do to avert the unhappy deflation scenarios? Here are five obvious policy responses:

1. Let insolvent firms fail. This is a major problem in many countries where there is a tradition of using government resources to protect companies from failure.
2. Establish effective bankruptcy laws and courts. Companies must have an orderly mechanism to restructure their business activities.
3. Foster mergers and acquisitions of weak firms by strong ones. This is a major problem in many countries where there is resistance to letting strong foreign companies acquire weaker local ones.
4. Tighten and enforce bank regulation and supervision. Limit lending to insolvent companies. Require proper accounting for problem loans. The Bank for International Settlements compiled a list of sound banking practices last year.[9]

5. Require greater and more frequent corporate disclosure (i.e., transparency). Corporate laws and regulations should force directors to act in the best interest of their shareholders, who should receive the information they need to be assured that this is the case.[10]

The basic message is to allow market forces to reduce excess capacity quickly. Today, this is not happening quickly enough, in my opinion.[11] The reason is obvious: Such restructuring is painful. Initially, this approach worsens deflation by increasing unemployment and depressing spending. Instead, the preferred solution to the deflation problem is believed to be a painless easing of credit conditions through stimulative monetary policies. Central bankers hope that lower interest rates will revive demand enough to absorb all the supply. It is my view that this approach is bound to fail because it may very well prop up supply much more than it is likely to boost demand. Credit crunches are nature's way of cleaning out insolvent borrowers from the economy. Easier credit conditions may actually exacerbate the zombie problem.

Internet

In the idealized model of perfect competition, there are no barriers to entry, no protection from failure for unprofitable firms, and everyone (consumers and producers) has easy and free access to all information. These just happens to be the three main characteristics of Internet commerce. The Internet is fundamentally deflationary. While current Internet spending is still a small fraction of total consumer and business spending, it is having a very deflationary effect on pricing already. Increasingly, pricing is determined at the margin by Internet commerce, which is extremely competitive.

The Internet certainly has the potential to produce bad deflation by cutting out the middle persons in every transaction. The only sure winner is the household and business consumer. Cybercompetition will force producers to accept puny profit margins. The technological costs of staying one step ahead of the competition are likely to burn money at a ferocious pace. For example, Amazon.com's revenues have grown dramatically, but costs have increased even faster. While consumers win as consumers, they could lose as employees of companies that cannot compete in cyberspace.

The Internet lowers the cost of comparison shopping to zero. Increasingly, the consumer can easily and quickly find the lowest price for any good or service. In the cybereconomy, the low-cost producer will offer the lowest price and provide this information at no cost to any and all potential customers anywhere on the planet. In the low-tech economy, the cost of searching for the lowest price was relatively high, thereby limiting a customer's search process to local or well-established vendors. Now vendors anywhere in the world can bid for business anywhere in the world.[14]

The Internet is the "killer" application that will continue to boost the sales of computer hardware and software. It's the "got-to-have-it" tool and toy for the next century. Internet-driven sales of high-tech gear will generate the cash flow and attract the financial capital needed by the computer industry to develop even more powerful computers at constantly falling prices. More powerful computers permit software developers to create more powerful multimedia programs. These processing and memory hogs, in turn, force computer users to upgrade to the latest generation of hardware, which is required to run the latest versions of the operating systems and applications.

In Biblical terms, better computers beget better software applications beget more demand to upgrade to even better hardware and software. The Internet begets more upgraders and more newbies. One of the most unusual, and certainly most unique, attributes of the computer industry is that prices fall even as processing power soars and demand exceeds supply. In high-tech markets, falling prices are the reason why demand exceeds supply. But why do prices fall so rapidly in the face of booming demand? As soon as a computer chip is introduced, manufacturers are already developing the next generation. Innovators of generation "n" chips are forced to create "n+1" chips. If they don't, the competition soon will. This situation means that the most successful producers of technology must cannibalize their own products to remain successful. The high-tech industry literally eats its young.

The cost of high-tech research and development is so great these days that high-tech manufacturers must sell as many units as possible of their new products in as short a time as possible before the n+1 generation is introduced. That's why they tend to offer more power at a lower price with the introduction of each new generation. Also, the introduction of n+1 immediately reduces the demand for the n*th* chip and the n*th* computer. As the price of the old technology falls, it limits the upside of the price of the newest technology. As a result of these unique trends, the purchasers of high-tech hardware are constantly receiving more bang for their buck.

The plunge in the cost of computing power is probably the most extraordinary deflation in the history of this planet. In effect, the high-tech revolution has created a fourth factor of production—namely, information. The original three factors are land, labor, and capital. Factors of production are substitutable for each other. Until recently, information was hard to substitute for land, labor, or capital. It was very expensive to collect, process, and manage. There were usually long lags between the creation of the raw data and its conversion into useful information. The lags made the information less useful once it was available. It was old news by the time it was available to decisionmakers.

With the high-tech revolution, enormous quantities of information can be collected, processed, and managed on a real-time basis at lower and lower costs. The price of information is deflating. As it gets cheaper and cheaper, it also becomes more substitutable for the other factors of production. Increasingly, real-time information is replacing labor and capital in the production process. For example, insurance companies can eliminate warehouses of archived files and the associated support staff with scanners that can transfer information to optical disks. The automakers have slashed their inventories with real-time information systems that can automatically place orders with vendors, schedule just-in-time deliveries, and monitor the transportation progress of the orders. As a result, inventories-on-the-shelves can be replaced with "inventories-on-wheels." Information replaces working capital.

The American Challenge and The Euro

Of all the major industrial nations, the United States has responded best to the economic challenges of the post-Cold War world. That's mostly because 1) industrial deregulation has increased competition, and 2) labor markets have become more flexible in the United States. Labor markets remain relatively rigid in Europe, and very much so in Japan. American workers tend to be more mobile than their European counterparts. They are willing to move very far within the United States to find employment. They accept the fact that job security no longer exists. Instead of automatic raises each year, more of workers' pay is in the form of incentives and profit sharing.

Most American workers are probably working harder than they did five or ten years ago. With the unemployment rate below 4.5%, they seem to have more job security. However, American workers recognize that, in highly competitive markets, there is no business security. They seem to understand the importance of keeping costs down to keep their companies competitive and to keep their jobs.

They also seem to know that a large federal deficit, open-ended social welfare programs, and high taxes aren't good for the competitive position of the United States. They increasingly are inclined to set limits on the role of the government in the economy—real limits on the social welfare state before it becomes completely bankrupt, just in time for their retirement.

They made this quite clear during the November 1994 elections. The Democrats lost their stranglehold on Congress after the Republican's

1994 sweep. For the first time since 1948, Democrats held fewer than 200 seats in the House of Representatives. The results of the 1996 elections confirmed the sea change among American voters. The Republicans held onto both houses. Ross Perot's vote dropped from 19% to 8% of the popular presidential vote between 1992 and 1996. This was a clear sign that Americans had turned less protectionist. President Bill Clinton, a Democrat, shrewdly adopted the Republican agenda by pushing successfully for NAFTA and welfare reform.

As Americans continue to shrink the welfare state and reduce the role of government in the economy, then the competitive pressures on other industrial nations—especially in Western Europe—to do the same will intensify. Of course, the European nanny states are far bigger relative to their economies than is the American version. Moreover, European beneficiaries of social welfare seem to be much less willing to accept reductions in their benefits than are Americans. But, they don't have much choice. The end of the Cold War dramatically increased the global competitive pressures on the industrial social welfare state from newly emerging countries with much lower labor, tax, and welfare cost structures.

European leaders hope that a Europe united by a common currency will emerge as a more competitive economic force in the coming century. The European Monetary Union (EMU) is a daring economic experiment. The EMU has come to pass. It makes a great deal of sense by further pulling together a market of 292 million people. Indeed, it has already been a great success in Europe by lowering and converging inflation rates and interest rates at very low levels. The Euro is likely to force greater integration of Euroland's national economies by stimulating greater standardization, thus cutting the costs of doing business in the region and creating economies of scale. The unified European capital market will certainly be much more attractive to global investors who can now purchase the region's securities all in one currency. European entrepreneurs will have greater access to capital, boosting the number of new businesses and employment.

Europe could stumble because monetary unification can't work very well without labor market mobility and fiscal unification, which is an important missing ingredient. More likely, labor markets will become less rigid as European companies pressure their workers to be more flexible or lose their jobs to workers in Eastern Europe, China, and South Carolina.

Japan's Karaoke Capitalism

It certainly has been a new era in Japan since the stock market crashed at the start of the 1990s. It hasn't been a golden one so far. For all too long, Japan has been a rich country with poor consumers. The economic system has favored and enriched the producers, while the standard of living of average Japanese consumers has stagnated and certainly declined relative to their counterparts in other industrialized nations. Of course, there has been more job security in Japan than in other industrial economies. There is a greater respect for the well being of others, less crime, and more social cohesion. But, surely all these highly desirable traits of Japan's society can be maintained while providing a better life for the average worker.

In the 1980s, many observers of Japan both there and overseas began to believe that Japan had created a new and more successful form of capitalism. In America, we feared that it might be superior to our competitive system. We didn't understand their "keiretsu" system of cross-ownership and cooperation very well. Still, we were very impressed by the apparent successes of Keiretsu Capitalism.

With the benefit of hindsight, I believe that what appeared to be a new form of capitalism has really been mostly old-fashioned corruption. My impression is that few, if any, business and economic relationships are conducted on an arm's-length basis. There is too much colluding, conspiring, and rigging occurring among the business elite, the government bureaucrats, and even the mob. I prefer calling Japan's economic system "Karaoke Capitalism." The all-too-cozy cross-ownership relations among and between manufacturers, distributors, and the bankers worked well for all concerned when real estate values and stock prices were soaring and exports were strong. It must have been fun going to the karaoke bars to celebrate the boom during the 1980s.

But that was then, and this is now. Japan has only 3% of the world's landmass, yet it had 60% of the world's real estate value in 1989, by one estimate. It was the biggest speculative bubble of all times. It burst at the start of the decade and triggered a stock-market crash. The resulting bad loans created a horrendous banking crisis, which is proving harder to fix than was the savings and loan (S&L) debacle in the United States. Japan's policymakers not only failed to address this problem, they exacerbated it by propping up insolvent banks for almost a decade. Imagine how bad the economic and financial situation might be today in the United States if American banking regulators had propped up the S&L industry, instead of restructuring the industry.

Japan's leaders are once again promising to reform their political, economic, and financial systems. Many similar promises have been made before. They weren't kept.[13] The Liberal Democratic Party (LDP) deserves a great deal of credit for leading Japan's emergence as the second most powerful economic power on earth during the four decades following the end of World War II. However, in the 1990s, the LDP's policies have been disastrous.

The Japanese government, under the leadership of the LDP, has implemented several fiscal stimulus programs in the 1990s, presumably in an effort to revive economic growth. In reality, these expensive outlays have mostly enriched party members, their political cronies, and their supporters. The latest bank rescue plan and fiscal stimulus package are impressive in their size and scope. Over $500 billion in public funds will be used to restructure the banks. However, the risk is that huge sums of public funds will be used to temporarily ease the crisis without any meaningful reforms. In many ways, the banking problem has been socialized, without any clear plan to force better lending practices.

Emerging Economies:
Something Missing

In some ways, the emerging economies of today in Asia, Latin America, and Eastern Europe resemble the U.S. economy when it was emerging during the 1800s. The U.S. economy grew dramatically during that century. But there were lots of busts and panics along the way. There was plenty of corruption. Foreign investors lost huge sums of money on railroad deals that were either poorly conceived or just plain fraudulent. Long periods of inflation were followed by long periods of deflation. Despite all the turmoil and upheaval, the history of the U.S. economy is the history of one of the greatest emerging economies of all times.

There were at least two very important ingredients behind America's success story. The country had a dynamic legal system and a relatively egalitarian distribution of income. Capitalism is, first and foremost, a legal system. It requires laws that protect property rights. It depends on the enforceability of contracts. The legal system has to be anchored in a body of precedent, but it must be flexible enough to adapt to the changing requirements of a dynamic economy. The rulings of the Supreme Court during most of the 1800s consistently favored the advocates of economic progress.[14]

Many emerging markets today don't have legal and regulatory systems that can accommodate the needs of a rapidly growing economy. Without this legal infrastructure, economic activities become less and less efficient. Without well defined property rights and contracts, it becomes harder and harder to organize and execute the larger scale of transactions that are the milestones of growth.

Another major deficiency of many emerging economies is their income distribution. Fast economic growth requires a certain level of social stability and consensus. If, during periods of rapid growth, the rich get richer while the poor are left behind and see no prospects for sharing in some minimal way in the new bounty, then rebels will emerge. Insurrection is very unsettling to foreign investors.

Asian nations have some of the world's finest manufacturing plants and best workers, who are as productive as any in the industrialized capitalist economies of North America and Europe. Driven by the profit motive, Asians have prospered greatly over the past three decades. However, under the thin veneer of capitalism, there has been too much corruption. In the world's free markets for manufactured goods, Asians have been world-class competitors. But, at home, competition has been stifled. Asians have built the industrial and technological infrastructure necessary to sustain export growth. But, at home, there has been too little progress in establishing the legal, accounting, and regulatory infrastructure of capitalism necessary to sustain economic growth. Asia's prosperity has benefited mostly Asia's producing classes rather than the consumers. Asians have embraced free-market capitalism globally, while maintaining an antiquated culture of mercantilism and crony corruption at home.

This should all change for the better as a result of the Asian crisis as capitalism triumphs over corruption in the region.[15] Many Asian nations are implementing reforms in response to the region's financial and economic crisis. They are setting the stage for massive restructuring of Asian economies.

A significant milestone in reducing global corruption occurred during February 1999, when the Organization for Economic Development and Cooperation implemented a convention that makes the bribery of foreign public officials to win or retain business a criminal offense in more than a dozen industrialized nations.[16]

Conclusion

In 1919, John Maynard Keynes published a short book titled *The Economic Consequences of the Peace*. It was an emotional and vicious attack on the Treaty of Versailles, which he argued was imposing a Carthaginian peace on the Germans and would set the stage for years of economic suffering and political turmoil in Europe. As events unfolded, it was a remarkably accurate forecast. It was also a worldwide sensation. In fact, Paul Johnson suggests that the book turned U.S. public opinion against the Treaty and the League of Nations. The Senate voted against the Treaty, and the overwhelming defeat of the Democrats in the autumn of 1920 was seen as a repudiation of Wilson's European policy in its entirety.

After World War II, many economists predicted a depression, or at least stagnation. They expected a slower pace of business during the peace. The stock market ignored these dire predictions. The S&P 500 index soared 139% from April 1942 to May 1946. Industrial production did dip right after the war, but the revival of consumer spending fueled a long period of prosperity until the late 1950s.

Fortunately for us, the economic scenario of the current peacetime is following the prosperity script so far. The U.S. stock market is up a whopping 240% since the end of 1989. The end of the Cold War was a liberating event of historic proportions. The global economy was liberated from protectionism. The subsequent proliferation of free trade should continue to generate prosperity for Americans and all other humans on this planet who are willing to accept the competitive challenges.

Notes

1. This study is an update of my Topical Study #35, "The Economic Consequences of the Peace," May 7, 1997. I first started to forecast the economic and financial consequences of the end of the Cold War in Topical Study #17, "The Triumph of Capitalism," Aug. 1, 1989. These and other topical studies can be found on http://www.yardeni.com/topical.html.

2. See my Topical Study #32, "The Undefeated Forces of Deflation," Oct. 28, 1996.

3. In the progressive/populist tradition, William Greider critiques globalization in *One World, Ready or Not: The Manic Logic of Global Capitalism* (New York: Simon & Schuster, 1997). See also Robert Samuelson, "Global Capitalism, R.I.P.?" *Newsweek*, September 14, 1998. His main point is that "much of the world simply doesn't have the values needed for free markets."

4. I was the first proponent of the New Era view in Topical Study #15, "The New Wave Manifesto," Oct. 5, 1988, and Topical Study #25, "The High-Tech Revolution in the US of @," Mar. 20, 1995. *Business Week* coined the phrase, "New Economy." See Michael J. Mandel, "The Triumph of the New Economy," *Business Week*, Dec. 12, 1996, and "New Thinking About the New Economy," May 19, 1997. See also Stephen B. Shepard, "The New Economy: What It Really Means," *Business Week*, Nov. 17, 1997. "New Paradigm" was the paper tiger invented by Stephen Roach, the chief economist of Morgan Stanley and the leading defender of the Old Order on Wall Street. In academia, Professor Paul Krugman of MIT (www.mit.edu/krugman/) is the leading counterrevolutionary.

5. Topical Study #31, "Economic Consequences of the Internet," Oct. 22, 1996.

6. Topical Study #18, "Dow 5000," May 9, 1990, Topical Study #20, "The Collapse of Communism Is Bullish," Sep. 4, 1991, and Topical Study #23, "The End of the Cold War Is Bullish," Sep. 10, 1993.

7. Topical Study #12, "How the Baby Boomers Are Changing the Economy," Apr. 6, 1988.

8. John D. Rockefeller observed, "Often-times the most difficult competition comes, not from the strong, the intelligent, the conservative competitor, but from the man who is holding on by the eyelids and is ignorant of his costs, and anyway he's got to keep running or bust!" Quoted, Ron Chernow, *Titan: The Life of John D. Rockefeller, Sr.* (New York: Random House, 1998), p. 150.

9. Basle Committee on Banking Supervision, "Sound Practices for Loan Accounting, Credit Risk Disclosure and Related Matters," October 1998, (http://www.bis.org/publ/bcbs43.htm).

10. Countries that have the best legal protection for investors tend to have the biggest capital markets and the least concentration of share ownership. See Rafael La Porta, Florencio Lopez-de-Silanes, Andrei Shleifer, and Robert W. Vishny, "Law and Finance," National Bureau of Economic Research, Working Paper 5661, Jul. 1996. See also their Working Paper 5879, "Legal Determinants of External Finance," Jan. 1997.

11. See Sheryl WuDunn, "In Asia, Firms 'Fail' but Stay Open," *International Herald Tribune*, Sep. 9, 1998. Corporations are "failing" in record numbers, but many stay in business. "But governments and legal systems routinely protect tycoons from their own incompetence, setting the stage not for a Darwinian struggle but for the survival of the flimsiest." In many countries in Asia, the legal framework for bankruptcy is vague and loosely formed.

12. In Topical Study #31, "Economic Consequences of the Internet," Oct. 22, 1996, I observed, "The Internet is fast becoming a global auction market and could commoditize most markets for products and services." See also "Internet Is Opening Up a New Era of Pricing," *The Wall Street Journal*, June 8, 1998. The article notes that business-to-business commerce on the Internet is likely to dwarf the consumer sector.

13. "Earlier this year, it seemed that a sweeping corruption investigation might send a number of Japan's mighty philosopher-kings, the bureaucrats who largely run the country, to prison. But these days, despite a cabinet change, nearly the only government employee who has gone anywhere is Katsuhiko Kumazaki, the prosecutor who led a much-heralded investigation into scandals involving expensive free entertainment paid for by businessmen who wanted the bureaucrats' favors. Mr. Kumazaki, 56, was transferred in June to a remote coastal city, and the investigation seems to have fizzled out." Sheryl WuDunn, "Japan Corruption Investigation Fizzles," *International Herald Tribune*, Aug. 15–16, 1998.

14. According to Ron Chernow (op. cit., p. 297), "Standard Oil had taught the American public an important but paradoxical lesson: Free markets, if left completely to their own devices, can wind up terribly *un*free. Competitive capitalism did not exist in a state of nature but had to be defined or restrained by law. Unfettered markets tended frequently toward monopoly or, at least, toward unhealthy levels of concentration, and government sometimes needed to intervene to ensure the full benefits of competition. This was particularly true in the early stages of industrial development."

15. Transparency International (http://www.transparency.de), an international good-government advocacy group based in Berlin, annually ranks the world's governments from most to least corrupt. In its latest study, released Sep. 1998, the group found no improvement stemming from the World Bank and IMF efforts to reduce corruption by including anticorruption measures in their loan agreements. According to the group's latest Corruption Perceptions Index (1=least corrupt), of the 85 countries surveyed, Indonesia ranks 80, Russia ranks 76, Thailand ranks 61, Mexico ranks 55, China ranks 52, and Brazil ranks 46.

16. OECD, "Combating Bribery of Foreign Public Officials in International Business Transactions: Text of the Convention," http://www.oecd.org/daf/cmis/bribery/20nov1e.htm

6

Dancing with the Giant: The Transformation of North American Sovereignties Approaching the Twenty-First Century

ALAN S. ALEXANDROFF

The Consequences of Free Trade in North America

Trade policy at the end of the twentieth century is about a lot more than just trade. The North American Free Trade Agreement (NAFTA) adopted in 1994 by the three North American countries—the United States, Canada, and Mexico—is about trade, investment, and regulation just to name some of the areas included. But it's also a political story. Thus this chapter examines the loss of national sovereignty in America's closest neighbors. It also, more surprisingly, chronicles the loss of national sovereignty in the United States—the last remaining superpower. This story, then, represents an example of the rebalancing between markets and states in the quickening pace of globalization at the millennium.

In Mexico and Canada politicians successfully solved some issues with new free trade arrangements. Yet other consequences, unforeseen, or dismissed at the time of each national debate over free trade, have come to affect these societies as opponents argued at the time. The free-trade arrangements have accelerated the constraints on governmental action that advocates and opponents of globalization identified. The trade agreements have contributed to the ongoing reshaping of national sovereignties in North America. They reflect a new balance between the trading and territorial world, the terminology used by Richard Rosecrance in his path-breaking work on commerce and conquest in the modern world.[1] These regional trade arrangements have placed markets, not governments, in the center. Markets today create citizen opportunities, benefits, limits, and costs.

This story focuses primarily on America's neighbors—Canada and Mexico. This approach is a bit unusual, but it is designed to provide the American reader with a different "take" on the process of change in North America. However even this focus, as will become evident, is also a description of the United States. That is, to an extent seldom understood in the United States, the history and policy of Canada and Mexico is also the story of the United States.

North American free trade, then, reflects the unfolding story of the diminution and transformation of sovereignties across these three countries. Further though, it describes a model for the evolution of national sovereignty in sharp contrast to the other contemporary story of sovereignty's transformation—the European Union (EU). For some time now, Europe has presented the quintessential model for the evolution of developed nation-states in the face of globalization. Europe's development is built on administrative and political structures of evolving supranationalism and the broadening of markets. In contrast, the North American story is largely market driven within a framework of legal rules. There are, in dramatic contrast to the European Union, minimal administrative and political structures. It is a model where there is minimal institutional channeling of the forces of economic change.

The North American story is also a story of much sharper contrasts than in Europe. Canada and Mexico represent far smaller economies now tied through international treaties to the much larger economic neighbor. This very asymmetry highlights some of changes in sovereignty among the three countries.

The North American Players

The United States represents a history of contrast. American history chronicles a society and polity determined to act differently and achieve different ends than had been done in the old world. A great power, reluctant to exercise influence, but infused nevertheless with "exceptionalism,"[2] the United States claimed the mantle of a superpower following World War II. Its leaders sought to achieve with unmatched determination the triumph of democracy and capitalism. As part of this plan, the United States pressed relentlessly in the decades after the war for the liberalization of trade even while it constructed the cold war political and security structures around the globe. The United States pushed in the successive trade rounds for rapid trade liberalization under the General Agreement on Tariffs and Trade (GATT). It supported the regional integration of Europe notwithstanding the views expressed at the time that such integration could prove to be a competitive disadvantage to the United States. It protected Japan and encouraged its post-war economic growth.

By the 1980s, however, American zeal for multilateral liberalization began to wane. The growing success of the formerly vanquished, particularly Japan, but also Germany and the European Economic Community, and the increasing competition from a host of rapidly developing Asian economies, led to growing demands from American industry sectors and Congress for a level playing field.[3] Traditional American demands for free trade became increasingly demands for "free and fair trade." Reflecting recently on the effect of free trade, Michael Mandel in his study, "The High-Risk Society," describes the double-edged nature of trade liberalization: "Free trade, too, is a high stakes, high-return policy. Producers gain from fast-growing foreign markets, while consumers can buy lower-price imports. At the same time, however, foreign competition leaves a trail of devastated industries and workers."[4]

In the mid–1980s, the politics of trade in the United States reflected a growing sensitivity to the loss of American jobs, that could be argued, resulted from America's "open market" policies. The political debate took on an increasingly nationalist, even protectionist tone, recognizable more from American pronouncements in the military-political dimension and from pre-war trade positions.

The Canadian story is one of a vast country with a thin ribbon of population stretched across the continent "cheek-by-jowl" to its American neighbor. The country has defined itself as much by the fact it isn't the United States, and Canadians aren't Americans, as any positive definition of itself and its people. Canada is a country struggling to define its national identity under the burden of at least two societies—a majority French-speaking population in Quebec and an English-speaking majority in the rest of the country. The English Canadian political élite, particularly, has sought to define Canada's nature by focusing on measures of independence from its great southern neighbor.

Since World War II, trade and investment policy in Canada has alternated between Canadian desires and Canada's economic realities. A strong advocate for multilateralism,[5] Canada's trade and investment became, nevertheless, increasingly bilateral and focused on the United States. While a variety of initiatives were urged to moderate the growing continental pattern, the facts on the ground were, Canadians did an increasing volume of business with the United States.

Mexico is a populous developing society steeped in a rich culture and language, a long history, and a more recent revolutionary past. Mexico has been deeply marked by its relationship with the United States losing half its territory to the westward push of American settlers in the nineteenth century. In more recent times, Mexican politicians have sought to transform the nation into a prosperous developed society on a foundation of state control and anti-Americanism. While the strategy appeared increasingly successful, especially with the development of Mexican petroleum resources, it came crashing down in the 1980s.

The United States has been a country and society determined to protect national sovereignty, even as it urged the removal of barriers all around the world and the adoption of democracy. Canada and Mexico each in their own ways sought to protect their identities and defend national sovereignty often in reaction to the United States. Into this climate of nationalist rhetoric and the growth of protectionism nevertheless two free-trade arrangements were concluded that tightly tied together these three countries: the Canada-U.S. Free Trade Agreement (FTA) of 1989 and NAFTA of 1994. These arrangements motivate and reflect the diminution and transformation of sovereignty across the entire continent. The arrangements are a testament to the powerful forces at work in globalization. These forces, as made clear in North America, are reshaping nations, regions and indeed the international system.

Leap of Faith

Canada had danced the dance of free trade with the United States before. The last serious initiative to secure a "full" free-trade arrangement had occurred in 1947. Then, in secret, the Liberal government of Mackenzie King negotiated free trade with the Truman administration driven by Canada's imbalance of payments following World War II. These discussions continued for some six months but were abruptly ended by the Canadian Prime Minister who feared the consequences of trying to persuade the Canadian public of the advantages of a bilateral free-trade arrangement. Prime Minister King was worried that, as Michael Hart, a noted Canadian trade analyst wrote, "Canadian nationalists would once again confuse the reduction of custom duties and other trade barriers with the United States with patriotism."[6]

Canadian politicians turned, instead, to negotiate narrower sectoral arrangements with the United States. The classic example of this was the successfully concluded Canada-U.S. Auto Pact, that entered into force in 1965.[7] This sectoral approach underlined the apparent truism in Canadian politics that the Canadian public could not be persuaded to accept free trade with the United States: Free trade with the United States represented a national threat and therefore political folly. Or so it had become. From the days of the defeat of the Liberal Laurier government's efforts to secure free trade in 1911, this negative view of American free trade was expressed repeatedly in Canadian political circles.[8]

Much of the Canadian public was surprised in the mid-1980s when the Progressive Conservative Mulroney government announced its decision to seek a comprehensive free-trade agreement with the United States. The announcement came as an even more unfriendly shock to nationalist interests in the media, the political opposition, and a wide swath of cultural and social interests in Canada. All these groups, and others, viewed the United States with deep suspicion. Besides the antipathy that these interests held for the United States, part of the shock came from the dramatic turnaround taken by the new Conservative government. In the 1984 election campaign, the yet to be elected Prime Minister and his party had campaigned for improved relations with the United States. However, candidate Mulroney explicitly rejected a free-trade agreement with America.

In the seemingly endless alternation between bilateral Canadian initiatives and multilateral negotiation, Canada had completed a cycle not long before. Under the prior Liberal government, a discussion paper had been published proposing discussions with the United States in selected industries. While negotiations had been launched with the United States, they had failed.

The Conservative agenda of economic renewal and national reconciliation that had led the Conservatives to a majority government relied ultimately on securing assured access to Canada's biggest export market. Promotion of one obvious government trade strategy—a comprehensive free-trade agreement with the United States—was given a boost in November 1984, just a few months after the Government's election. At that time former Liberal Minister, and then current chairman of the Royal Commission on the Economic Union and Development Prospects for Canada, Donald Macdonald, announced the Commission's support for free trade. It was this former Liberal Minister who described this free-trade strategy with the United States in the now famous phrase—"leap of faith."

When the Macdonald Commission released its final report in 1985[9], the commissioners set out two principal reasons for recommending a comprehensive free-trade arrangement with the United States. First, they suggested, Canadians generally agreed that trade policy needed to "stimulate a stronger, more efficient, productive, competitive and growing economy." The branch plant structure of Canadian industry was not productive enough to compete successfully in the global economy. Second, Canadian producers needed, "better more stable and more secure access to a large market."[10] The rising chorus of protection in the United States threatened the main export market for most Canadian manufacturers.

This chorus in favor of U.S. trade protectionism in the 1980s, resulted, in part, from the macroeconomic policy of the Reagan administration and the overvalued American dollar. In 1985, the American trade deficit had reached $150 billion (US). For many Americans, and increasingly their congressional representatives, such a trade imbalance confirmed their belief that the United States had been unfairly taken advantage of by their allies who were also their economic competitors. These voices now demanded the United States take action to end unfair practices employed against American firms by these nations and their firms. The United States government needed to ensure a "level playing field."

With over 70 percent of its exports destined for the United States, Canada had a great deal to lose if the protectionist voices were heeded. Already Canadian decisionmakers were aware that there had been an increase in the number of investigations of Canadian export practices. In addition, specific legislation had been introduced in Congress to limit Canadian imports to the United States. In a final reflection recommending favorably a comprehensive bilateral arrangement with the United States, the Macdonald Commissioners concluded:

> A bilateral agreement constructed along these lines would make our manufacturing sector competitive by encouraging a process of restructuring and rationalization of Canadian industry to serve the North American market and, from that base, to penetrate overseas markets. It would also increase the security of access to our most important market, a condition essential for growth and new investment, given the relatively small domestic Canadian market. Finally, it would improve the access we now enjoy in the U.S. market and thus allow Canadian industries presently shut out of that market to grow and invest with renewed confidence.[11]

By the time of the release of the final report, the Mulroney government had moved dramatically to initiate a serious negotiation with the United States. Its purpose was clear: conclude a comprehensive free trade agreement with the U.S.

A Tough Slog but a Deal

The exercise of negotiating a comprehensive free-trade agreement with the United States proved to be an enormous frustration for the Canadian government and its negotiators. The beginning was far more upbeat. There were a series of positive statements of support from President Ronald Reagan. The Administration and Congressional officials released statements to the press that the United States sought a "big" free-trade agreement with Canada. There were warm statements by the two governments and their chief negotiators, Peter Murphy of the United States and Simon Reisman a long-time Canadian trade negotiator and head of the Trade Negotiations Office (TNO). Yet notwithstanding all these positive expressions of support, the two chief negotiators spent many fruit-less months in discussions with little progress to show for their efforts.

In reality the two countries, and their negotiators, approached the process and expected outcome dramatically differently. Canada saw the negotiation as an historic opportunity to create a comprehensive and broad trade arrangement with its chief trading partner. Such an arrangement would provide, by the end of the century, "an open and secure movement of all goods and services as well as better rules for the movement of investment and people between the two countries."[12] The key for the Canadian side—a new framework, which would deal with trade remedies such as countervailing duties, antidumping, and safeguard actions including actions against surges. Canada sought new procedures and rules to limit practices that gave rise to trade-remedy actions taken by American firms. In return, Canadian officials made clear Canada was prepared to entertain an agreement that would extend to services, government procurement, investment, and intellectual property, all areas the United States had suggested it wanted Canadian concessions in. But the "bottom line" for Canada and its negotiators was a new régime for trade in subsidies and trade remedy.

As noted above, American officials had joined in calls for a "big deal." America's chief negotiator apparently delighted in broadening the scope of the proposed agreement. So Peter Murphy at one point in the negotiations or another sought to include the Auto Pact, subsidies including such sensitive matters as cultural industries, social policies, and regional economic development policies. But the American negotiating position was quite different. The negotiation process revealed that the United States' negotiators saw the process as an opportunity merely to resolve outstanding irritants between the United States and Canada. There was no "big deal;" in fact there wasn't even a big picture.

In the end, the United States insisted on minor adjustments only in areas such as procurement and technical standards and in services. While there were some changes in intellectual property, investment, and subsidies, they were far more limited than the United States had urged early on in the negotiations. And, in the area of contingent protection, the agreement hit a brick wall. This refusal by the United States to conclude a new trade remedy régime almost destroyed the negotiation and the agreement. The United States proved unwilling to write precise rules defining acceptable and unacceptable practices in subsidies, countervailing duties, dumping and antidumping duties, and safeguard measures. It proved unwilling to subject these rules to bilateral administration and interpretation. Canadian negotiator, Simon Reisman in frustration, and in failure, suspended the negotiations in September 1987. Only an eleventh-hour compromise negotiated between Treasury Secretary James Baker and Canadian ministers saved the negotiation from complete collapse. As a result the final agreement in December, 1987 included this key compromise:

> Canadian and U.S. trade law would continue to apply and both sides would be free to change their laws, but they would have to specify that the changed law applied to the other and any such changes would be subject to bilateral review for consistency with the agreement and with the GATT;

> existing judicial review as to whether the law had been applied fairly and properly would be replaced by a binational panel on the basis of whatever standard would have prevailed in the domestic tribunal; and

> negotiations would continue for five years to negotiate a wholly new régime to replace the existing one.[13]

Although there were other compromises, the willingness of the U.S. Administration to accept a binding bilateral trade remedy process, made it possible for the Mulroney government to argue, somewhat disingenuously, that Canada had achieved its ultimate goal—assured access to Canada's most important export market.

The Mulroney government argued this point and many similar ones over and over again in its efforts to secure approval of the Canada-U.S. Free Trade Agreement. In the end the government was forced to fight an election that was dominated by whether Canadians should accept this comprehensive arrangement with the United States.

The electoral debate was fierce. Opposition spokesmen insisted that the agreement would threaten Canadian cultural policy, its tax-supported public health care system and other social policies, its water resources, and its control over energy. The condemnation was loud and persistent. At the core of the opposition, both the political opposition, especially the Liberal Party led by John Turner, and the social groups—unions, women, poverty organizations, health care advocates, and others was a view that free trade with the United States would lead first to economic and eventually political absorption. Some of the most articulate opposition pointed out that Canada was already too heavily dependent on the United States. Canada needed to find a policy approach that would redirect more trade to other trading partners. Without this, Canada, as a junior trading partner of the United States, would be unable to sustain an independent policy and would find itself unable to act in any way other than to support U.S. policy in the region and elsewhere. After a rancorous and often shrill election debate, the Mulroney Conservatives were returned with a second majority government. Canada entered into the FTA on January 1, 1989.

If the stakes, not to mention the volume of the debate over a comprehensive free-trade arrangement with the United States, were at the highest possible level when considering the FTA, almost the opposite presented itself to Canada in contemplating the extension of the agreement to include Mexico. Unlike the FTA, there was no compelling positive interest in Canada for an enlargement of the FTA. For the Canadian government the political costs were likely to be high; yet Canada-Mexico trade and investment was minuscule in comparison to the trade and investment relationship with the United States. Why then did Canada become a full player and proceed down this course to a trilateral free-trade arrangement? For the Canadian government this course of action just barely a year after the FTA was a matter of damage limitation. Canada could not allow the gains it had achieved in the FTA to be undone by a bilateral deal between Mexico and the United States. It could not stand by while the Americans redefined their economic relations in the Western Hemisphere starting with Mexico but conceivably extending to other players in the Hemisphere.

Just as the FTA had been concluded only with a national election, so the implementation of the North American Free Trade Agreement (NAFTA) was delayed until the Conservative government went again to the people for a mandate. But by 1993, Brian Mulroney was no longer Prime Minister and the election hardly could have represented more of a contrast. The heart of the Canadian election of 1993 was fought over the former Prime Minister himself. Trade was hardly discussed. The election and public opinion polls at the time made it clear that Canadians now accepted the reality of free trade with the United States. It was no longer a burning national question. Canadians believed that the country, particularly business in Canada, had adjusted to the new economic régime and there was no going back. The question that remained was who had been right about the consequences of a free-trade arrangement in North America.

Winning Prosperity, Threatening a Country?

For those Canadian negotiators who stuck it out to conclude the FTA, and then in 1991 went back to extend the deal to Mexico, there must be real satisfaction at the results of the agreement. If one looks at the trade measures, there is discernible trend that advocates of free trade would applaud. While the Canadian economy entered a severe recession in the early nineties, soon after the completion of the FTA, exports, principally to the United States, have been a bright spot in Canada's economic performance. Trade as a share of Gross Domestic Product (GDP) has grown since the 1960s but the share has accelerated since Canada entered into the FTA and NAFTA. Currently over 80 percent of Canada's exports and imports today are directed to the United States. In part because of the automobile and auto parts sector concentrated in Ontario, over 90 percent of Ontario's exports are targeted to the United States.

The trade picture that emerges for the period 1988–1995 is one where Canada's exports to the United States increased at a significantly faster rate than exports to other countries. Moreover, if you segment trade into liberalized and nonliberalized categories (liberalized meaning categories where tariffs have been reduced or eliminated as a result of provisions in the FTA), Canada's exports to the United States in liberalized sectors (14 out of 16 categories) grew considerably faster than both exports to the United States in sectors not liberalized and in comparison to the rest of the world.[14] There were similar tendencies for imports. And while data is far less reliable, it would appear that services also have increased, though the FTA made only a limited foray into the liberalization of services. More anecdotally, it appears that Canada's branch plant firms have made a painful passage to greater efficiency, corporate profitability, and competitiveness.

In 1975, Canada's exports of goods and services to the United States were equal to 15 percent of GDP. That had risen to 28 percent by 1995. With respect to merchandise trade, exports now represent almost 40 percent of Canada's GDP. This figure represents the largest percentage for any of the Group of Seven (G7) economies.

But it has come at a cost. It is a cost that opponents of the FTA had long feared. The economic union has begun to loosen, possibly disintegrate. Canadians, and Canadian business in particular, have reoriented activity to the United States. As Greg Ip, then of the *Globe and Mail*, wrote: "In the last 15 years, almost every province's economy has become more dependent on exports to other countries than on exports to other provinces. Within many companies themselves, the United States border and the 'Canadian market' have ceased to matter. The Canadian and U.S. markets for goods, capital, services and, increasingly, labour are becoming one." [15]

While the evidence is incomplete, since we do not have a handle on interprovincial trade in services, the Ontario example shows how significant a change the economic union has undergone. In 1981, interprovincial and international exports were about the same in this key, manufacturing province ($38 billion CDN); by 1995, international exports had risen to twice the value of interprovincial exports—$140 billion CDN versus $62 billion CDN. While not as dramatic as in Ontario, other major provincial markets, such as Quebec and British Columbia, have experienced the same changes. Surveying these changes in Canada, Ip concludes: "Free trade, it turns out has been about a lot more than trade, as many of its critics feared. It has acted as a spur to economic integration beyond the simple exchange of goods, going on to the harmonization of business standards and the creation of a single market for capital, services and perhaps, eventually, people."[16]

Using another measure, the acceleration of north-south trade can be underlined. In 1988–1989 the provinces exported twenty times more to other provinces than to states of the United States of comparable size and distance. John McCallum, the Chief Economist for the Royal Bank of Canada pointed out in a 1997 Report[17] that under the condition that there was no Canada-U.S. border, one could hypothesize, the province of Quebec, for example, should trade about ten times more with California than with British Columbia. In the example, the distances between Quebec and British Columbia and Quebec and California are about the same but the California market is ten times the size of the British Columbia market. Thus, the hypothesis that trade would be ten times larger with respect to California. However, actual trade in 1988–89 shows that the value of Quebec-BC trade was 2.6 times greater than Quebec-California trade. In other words the existence of the border promoted east-west trade. The actual pattern of trade reflects the border and the effect of the internal Canadian market.

Notwithstanding that, the trend over the last decade reflects the decline in the economic union. The data reveal that the provinces now only trade 14 times more wiht each other than with states of comparable size and distance, down from 20 times. While the data reveal still that it is not a world without national borders, the trend seems apparent. Canadians have fought for over 100 years to define economic exchange in an east-west direction to underpin this northern nation. But the economic bindings are being eroded. Canadian business and markets are being reoriented in north-south segments across the continent.

This reorientation of economic Canada is occurring even as the role of the national government is diminishing. Years of federal fiscal expansion left the government by the 1980s with a major federal debt and annual enormous federal deficits. First, slowly under the Mulroney government, and then in an accelerated fashion under the Liberal government of Jean Chrétien, the federal government began the painful task of reducing the deficit in part through the reduction by the federal government in transfer payments to the provinces. While successful, these steps reinforced a view that the federal government was increasingly less relevant to the lives of ordinary Canadians whether in Quebec, Ontario, or British Columbia. Some argued that the near-successful vote for sovereignty by Quebecers in October 1995, could be laid at the doorstep of these two trends: The perceived irrelevance of the federal government; and the loosening of the bonds of economic union in Canada as a result of free trade. Sovereigntists in Quebec were among the strongest supporters of the FTA and argued loudly that a sovereign Quebec could still rely on the free-trade arrangements under the FTA and NAFTA.

Leap of Fear

On August 21, 1990, President Carlos Salinas de Gortari of Mexico proposed initiating negotiations for a comprehensive free-trade agreement with the United States. On September 26, President Bush formally notified Congress of his intent to negotiate a free-trade agreement with Mexico. These public announcements followed a private proposal by President Salinas to George Bush to consider a free-trade agreement in a visit to Washington in June of the same year. What had caused Carlos Salinas de Gortari to propose such a "radical" step? As late as a State visit to Washington not a year earlier, President Salinas had dismissed the idea of a free-trade agreement. At that point, the Mexican President had argued that the "unevenness of the two economies made such an idea unrealistic."[18] What conditions changed so significantly to alter the President's mind?

It would appear that the President changed his mind after a series of foreign trips. Returning home from abroad he concluded that Mexico could not rely on either Europe or Japan to provide adequate foreign investment; nor could these countries absorb Mexico's anticipated exports.

Like Canada, Mexico had become a major trading partner with the United States in the decades following World War II. Canada was America's largest trading partner; Mexico followed right after Japan in third place. Mexico had undergone a debilitating revolution in the early twentieth century that took almost nineteen years to quiet. By the end of the revolutionary turmoil, Mexico had established a one party authoritarian government. It devised an economic development strategy that relied increasingly on the public sector and state-sponsored inward-oriented growth. One President after another of the *Partido Revolucionario Institucional* (PRI) sought to bring sufficient economic development to meet the rising population and manage the transformation of Mexico to a modern developed economy.

For some 40 years following 1940, Mexico experienced growth and the hope of change. From 1970 to 1981 the Mexican economy grew by on average 7 percent. However, Mexico found it necessary to rely on foreign loans to maintain growth and its expansionary fiscal policy. By 1976 because of a balance of payments crisis, Mexico was forced to devalue the peso, the first devaluation since 1953. Mexico, in turn began to rely on its petroleum resources. International banks were more than happy to loan Mexico money on the basis of its reserves and the rising price of oil.

In the summer of 1982, petrodollar recycling came to a dramatic halt. With increases in international interest rates and the sharp drop in petroleum prices, Mexico could no longer maintain the interest payments on the $100 billion (US) of external debt the Mexican government had built.[19]

By the time Carlos Salinas was elected President of Mexico, the country had suffered seven consecutive years of economic depression. Salinas surveyed a Mexican economy debilitated by macroeconomic instability, protectionism, and low international competitiveness. Average wages had declined some 40 percent and inflation had soared to triple digits. In 1987 inflation reached 160 percent.

The Salinas administration tackled the economic crisis. The President put together a team to solve or reduce the external economic crisis. That team negotiated a debt relief plan, the so-called "Brady Plan" that reduced the debt from $100 billion (US) to $86 billion (US) and in turn reduced debt-servicing costs. Salinas then raised revenues by enforcing tax laws and he began to cut public expenditures. As a result, the fiscal deficit shrank from 11.7 percent of GDP in 1988 to 5.8 percent in 1989 and inflation fell to 19.7 percent by 1989.[20]

In addition to these fiscal measures, Salinas began to dismantle the import substitution structure. The Salinas administration began privatizing the web of parastatal corporations as well as unilaterally lowering the tariff and nontariff barriers that had dramatically reduced the competitiveness of the Mexican economy. As a result of such actions, economic growth returned. Mexico's GDP grew 2.9 percent in 1989. Even capital began to flow back into Mexico after fleeing following the economic crisis and the nationalization of the banks during the De la Madrid government.

While the Salinas administration's efforts helped to restore a measure of confidence, it was apparent that more economic reform was needed. It was also apparent that the crisis was not purely economic. Because of the close integration of the PRI with the government and the government's ever-expanding role in the economy, Mexico's governance structure was also being challenged. There were ever more insistent calls inside and outside Mexico for democratization and the end of one-party rule. Critics urged that Mexico needed to open its economy and free itself from government's heavy hand. But additionally the opening up would require that Mexico break free of its authoritarian past. Yet after control of Mexico exceeding 40 years by the PRI, the political interests, local and national — the so-called "old guard" of the PRI, would not easily relinquish political and economic control.[21]

Salinas' direction was apparent. With his highly educated economic technocrats he intended to reform the economy through a series of liberalizing efforts and reform the political system more slowly. Salinas made it clear that political reform and democratization efforts would take a "back-seat" to economic reforms. Some critics argued that the Salinas efforts were designed to liberalize the economy without displacing the PRI from its central role in politics. Others insisted that the order of liberalization–economics and then politics—was bound to fail. The Salinas government could not reform the economy without first democratizing Mexico. One of the government's most articulate critics, Jorge Castañeda, offered this view of the need for reform:

> ". . . the absence of democracy in Mexico was not just a political drawback but one of the principal causes of the glaring social inequalities that plague Mexico; that cold-turkey, free-market policies would not solve Mexico's economic dilemmas; that only a combination of state and market, trade liberalization and protectionism, redistribution and integration with the United States could place Mexico back on the path of economic growth;"[22]

Rise and Fall in Mexico

Salinas began his *sexenio*, the single six-year term for Mexican Presidents, in difficult circumstances. He won election to the presidency with a bare majority of 50.4 percent the closest vote since the revolution. The opposition, and many observers, claimed that the PRI had stolen the election through vote fraud from the opposition. Having "won," however, the Salinas Administration undertook significant efforts to open the economy, as noted above. From one of the most protected markets with import licenses on most products including tariffs as high as a maximum 100 percent, the administration reduced the tariff régime to an average weighted tariff of 9.5 percent. As a result of these efforts, the economy began to grow again and manufacturing exports began to surge.

The dilemma facing Mexico's economic development was highlighted as a result of its economic reform policy. If Mexico chose to open its economy, then that economic reform course underlined Mexico's dependence on access to the United States market. Just as in the case of Canada, Mexico needed the security of market access to its largest trading partner to ensure growing exports.

While the Mexican economy began to respond to liberalization efforts, investment flows failed to increase rapidly enough to generate significant or sustainable growth. As noted above, trips to Europe and Japan had brought home to Salinas that Europe was too preoccupied with the fall of communism and the opening of Eastern Europe and Japan was far too hesitant to represent a source of expanded investment. While anti-Americanism had gone hand-in glove with the internal economic development model, the end of the statist approach, and the turn to liberalization, or *apertura*, enabled, in fact demanded, Salinas jettison some old "ideological baggage." In a liberalized Mexico, the United States became the major source of investment and trade and a key to job growth:

> More than a complement to the modernization policies embarked upon since 1985, NAFTA was seen as a silver bullet to neutralize the obstacles those policies engendered. When more capital than expected was needed and greater reluctance to invest was encountered, NAFTA would make up the difference. It would also relieve pressure from abroad to accelerate political reform, as U.S. supporters of NAFTA toned down their criticisms of human rights violations and electoral fraud in Mexico to avoid imperiling free trade.[23]

And the Mexican public largely approved this new revolution in Mexican politics. In a nation-wide poll in July 1990 it was found that 59.4 percent of the Mexican public favored a free-trade agreement and only 19.3 percent opposed it.[24] Interest and generally favorably ratings continued through the process of negotiation and then approval. Under such conditions the Salinas administration found it both logical, and politically possible, to set a course for free trade with the United States.

The early NAFTA period seemed to vindicate the actions of the Mexican government. Following the November 1993 U.S. Congressional approval of NAFTA, there was a significant inflow of capital into Mexico. In fact between 1991 and the end of 1993 foreign capital inflows grew from $23 billion (US) to $29 billion (US).[25] By early 1994, Mexican international reserves reached a record $30 billion (US). Consumer inflation dropped from 18.8 percent to 8.0 percent in 1993. From the late 1980s through 1992 the economy showed real dynamism growing on average 3.5 percent. Market capitalization grew enormously. From 1988 to 1993 capitalization went from $13 billion (US) to $132 billion (US), a ten-fold increase.

But there were signs that all was not well. The Salinas Administration, first because of the need to ensure American approval of NAFTA, and then because of political factors—most importantly the presidential election of 1994, failed to take critical corrective economic steps. By the second quarter of 1993, it was apparent that Mexican economic growth had all but disappeared. For all of 1993, the Mexican economy grew by a mere 0.6 percent. Meanwhile the trade imbalance continued to grow. By 1994 Mexico reached a record deficit of $18.5 billion (US). While inflows of capital continued, the key indicator—foreign direct investment (FDI)—failed to grow. FDI declined from $4.8 billion (US) in 1991 to $4.4 billion (US).

By 1994, influential voices were stressing the need for significant economic changes beginning with the overvalued peso. At a conference held by the Brookings Institution in Washington, Rudiger Dornbusch, a well known economist and longtime Mexico watcher, along with his colleague Alejandro Werner, warned that a significant departure from the then present peso exchange rate was required and recommended currency devaluation.[26] Subsequently, Dornbusch wrote in *Business Week* that the capital inflow to Mexico was substantially "hot money", likely to leave at the first hint of difficulty and only retained by high interest rates. Most commentators, however, and importantly Wall Street analysts, chose to ignore these warnings.

Meanwhile, political events kept chipping away at the stability of the administration. On January 1, 1994, the Zapatista rebels in Chiapas appeared out of the rain forests to make hemispheric headlines. Then on March 23, the PRI presidential candidate, Luis Donaldo Colosio was assassinated and there was panic in the Mexican financial markets. This assassination was followed by the assassination of PRI secretary general, José Francisco Ruiz Massieu. While the election of PRI candidate Ernesto Zedillo in August went easily, and without the controversy that accompanied his predecessor's narrow victory, the continuing uncertainty of the political environment kept the government off balance. The Mexican economic situation became ever more difficult particularly as interest rates began to climb in the United States.[27] As Mosés Naím suggested, by late 1994, the Zedillo administration faced "both political uncertainty and economic fragility."[28]

Once the government decided finally to attack the economic problem of capital outflows and the depletion of Mexican reserves, reactions were extreme. Following the unnerving report by the media on December 19 that the Zapatistas had broken through the military cordon in Chiapas, which in turn triggered a renewed capital flight, Mexican authorities decided to devalue the peso. Within two weeks of the initial devaluation, announced at 15 percent, the peso had lost more than 30 percent in U.S. dollar terms; the *Bolsa*, the Mexican financial market, had dropped almost 50 percent in dollar terms. By March 1995 almost 250,000 Mexicans had become unemployed as a result of the economic crisis that had been touched off by the initial government announcement. The crisis was clearly unwanted by those who had planned for and described rising prosperity as a result of NAFTA. Yet when it came, the way in which Mexico and the United States reacted showed the effect of NAFTA on how decisionmakers dealt with one another.

Constraining Sovereignty in North America

In January 1989, United States entry into the FTA with Canada passed with little notice in U.S. public opinion. Even in Congress there was little reaction. Other than the revolt in the Senate Finance Committee that almost defeated the administration's authority for "fast track" at the commencement of trade-treaty discussions, the negotiation, and then the approval of the treaty, occurred without serious opposition. This uneventful passage of the FTA contrasted sharply with the incorporation of Mexico in the NAFTA. While Canadians saw NAFTA as an expansion of the original FTA, the U.S. media, the public, and U.S. politicians treated it as a second and quite separate free-trade arrangement for the hemisphere. And whether it was Mexico's developing economic status, its history of conflict with the United States, "deep-seated" negative attitudes towards Mexico, or a growing concern about the border, drug trafficking, and illegal immigration, NAFTA received wide public attention and initiated a major debate by Congress and the U.S. public. In the fall of 1993 the prospect of NAFTA produced a classic debate in the United States. On one side was one of NAFTA's fiercest opponents, Ross Perot; on the other, administration booster, and the vice-president of the United States, Al Gore. In the end, President Clinton, and his administration, defended the agreement as one that would create jobs for Americans and increase its export trade. And while the vote in the House of Representatives was close, the Clinton administration was able to secure congressional approval.

With such a high-energy debate, it was not surprising to hear a variety of statements exaggerating the benefits and the costs of NAFTA. It came as something of shock, then, when the Mexican economic crisis suddenly emerged. It was with surprise that U.S. politicians, Wall Street investors, the media, and the U.S. public greeted this financial crisis. The administration's response suggested the deep effect of these comprehensive trade arrangements, though NAFTA had hardly been inked. Soon after the onset of the crisis, the Clinton administration sought approval from Congress for a $40 billion (US) package of loan guarantees. Republican Speaker of the House Newt Gingrich and Republican Senate Majority Leader Bob Dole supported the initiative, as did Allan Greenspan, Chairman of the Federal Reserve. Statements of support followed quickly from a variety of former presidents and cabinet ministers.

Notwithstanding all this political muscle, it became apparent that Congress would not easily, or in a timely manner, approve such a rescue package. In response to growing congressional questioning and opposition, President Clinton assembled an alternative package that did not require congressional approval relying instead on funds supplied by the U.S. Exchange Stabilization Fund and by the International Monetary Fund (IMF). These funds collateralized with Mexican oil receipts and including a stiff macroeconomic package to deal with structural problems in the Mexican economy highlight the importance of Mexico, and its continued economic health to policymakers in the United States. Against the backdrop of negative U.S. public opinion and the U.S. Congress, the Clinton administration pursued the rescue package. It represented a sharp contrast to U.S. actions in the Mexican debt crisis of the early 1980s.

If the U.S. administration felt impelled to act, then Mexico's actions represented equally the effect of the new régime in North America. As became apparent in the months following the first peso devaluation, the real cost fell on the Mexican people with tight money, a peso that fell from 3 pesos to the U.S. dollar to over 8 pesos, exorbitant lending and mortgage rates, and spiraling unemployment. Notwithstanding the calls from the political opposition outside and inside the PRI for protection from markets, Mexico did not resort to the kinds of measures that formed the basis of domestic reforms in the debt oil crisis. Mexico remained open to the hemisphere and international markets.

While the U.S. action shows a high degree of collaboration and sensitivity to the neighboring Mexican economy, resort to national action has not been eliminated as a result of NAFTA. Notwithstanding the agreed NAFTA timetable, the United States failed to begin licensing Mexican trucks to operate in the United States in 1996 citing safety concerns. And, Americans and U.S. politicians have not accepted without question the constraints on sovereignty that flow from these comprehensive arrangements.

For Canada, we noted, the heart of the FTA was the new restraint on the trade remedy régime in the U.S. And that constraint on American sovereignty has chaffed. In 1996, Republican Presidential candidate Bob Dole urged that the binational review régime be denied any future country acceding to NAFTA most immediately Chile. Twenty-one lobby groups organized as the American Coalition for Competitive Trade filed a complaint with the U.S. Court of Appeals. Their position, though not finally sustained in the courts, was that the binational panels organized under Chapter Nineteen of NAFTA are usurping the constitutional authority of the U.S. judiciary and that U.S. sovereignty cannot be fettered in these ways by international agreements.[29]

Yet the constraints are recognized and accommodated just as often as they are resisted. In November 1996, for instance, Mexico and the United States signed an agreement that gives both countries broad access to each other's rapidly growing direct-to-home television markets. Companies in both countries will be able to sign up subscribers in the other. While some restrictions are allowed, the agreement provides a significant opening of this market. For all practical purposes, "when it comes to satellite television transmission, the 2,000-mile border between the two countries should not be a barrier."[30] And the growing awareness of the "fading" of the border is apparent in the Mexican decision to recognize the right of Mexicans to hold U.S. citizenship without losing their rights as Mexican citizens. The reality of Hispanic influence in state and national races in the United States has gained Mexican legislative recognition.

North American Sovereignty As a Lumpy Cheese Melt

In the contemporary evolution of the international system, Europe, and particularly the EU, has taken center stage. The European Community, now Union, is the model of a more integrated state system—an emergent supranational organization of states in the international system. Most analysts describe a slow, even halting, but linear development in Europe. Underpinned by functionalist theory, analysts have chronicled the march to supranationalism in Europe. The contemporary cap to this march to a "United States of Europe" has been the Maastricht Treaty. Central to Maastricht is the current commitment by member states of the EU to the creation of a single monetary system. In turn, one presumes, Europe will march, or be led, to a common fiscal policy and then to further integrative steps. Yet, in fact, the painful building of this supranational Europe from the Treaty of Rome to Maastricht has more to do with the past than the future. It has more to do with old nationalism and the political effort to constrain elemental forces within these nations and ethnic communities of Europe.

European integration has relied fundamentally on the logic of economic integration overseen by institutional and bureaucratic structures that have tied together Western European societies and, increasingly, constrained national sovereignty. This growing web of linkages between and among the current states of the EU has a federalist impulse at its core. Designed to integrate Europe's great rivals—France and Germany, it now spreads to the greater part of Western Europe with the potential to reach into Eastern Europe in the post-Cold War environment. In the logic of functionalism, current linkages will lead to the extension of economic and societal activities from one field of activity to another and to an ever-widening roster of countries. There will be an ever tightening of economic and social activities that will feed the growing political and bureaucratic integration.

The product of this functional integration is the emergence of a supranational state. As Europe so starkly displays, the EU is built from the top down—from political and bureaucratic structures down to markets and civil society. Though at an uneven pace, the Europeans have tried to replicate, seemingly, the dynamism, economic integration, and material prosperity of the continental United States. It may also seek to approach the political integration of the United States. It is a doomed effort to create the structures of the nineteenth- and twentieth-century state in twenty-first century Europe. It suggests that the Europeans are trying to create a future out of the past.

Superficially, the regional-trade initiatives in North America appear to be copying the actions seen in European integration. Yet the logic in these regional agreements are distinct from that seen in Europe over recent decades. In North America policymakers are creating the past in the future. These regional-trade arrangements are notably distinct from Europe's efforts. They are not built on the foundation of political structures but primarily on markets. The creation of new free-trade arrangements in North America is devised absent any federalist impulse. Indeed, while there are institutional intergovernmental arrangements, including working groups and various secretariats, the structures are deliberately minimal and without political clout.

These comprehensive free-trade arrangements in North America are in marked contrast to the European administrative and bureaucratic behemoth that is today's EU. Common rules and the lowering of trade and non-trade barriers alike build the North American regional trade links. The focus in North America is the establishment of rules applicable across the NAFTA. These rules are set in place without the institutions and bureaucrats so dear to the EU.

Yet the constraints on sovereignty are real. Given the focus on common rule formation in the FTA, and then in NAFTA, in a formal institutional way national governments remain largely unconstrained. Nevertheless, the picture of national sovereignty that emerges in North America is one of a growing blurring of national barriers. I would liken the evolution of North America to a set of blocks of cheese that slowly melt. Governments remain though the blocks dissolve and flow slowly into one another. The national states remain and exert sovereignty to a greater or lesser extent dependent on continuing political pressure. Still the constraints on sovereignty are identifiable on a variety of substantive and physical aspects. The most evident blurring can be seen at the borders. There is a slow mixing without the evident reinforcement of institutional constraints.

It is, therefore, a slow melt of sovereignty as the balance between markets and government is altered. In North America the future is not a picture of states dissolving into a web of supranationalism, as we have seen in Europe. Instead it reflects a dynamic "goo"—a combination of markets, continuing governmental sovereignty, civil organizations private and not-for-profit entities, dissolving one into the other. The future is not just the trading state of Richard Rosecrance but the trading society as well. And it is being born, rather surprisingly, right here in North America at the beginning of the twenty-first century.

Notes

1. Richard Rosecrance, *The Rise of the Trading State: Commerce and Conquest in the Modern World* (New York: Basic Books, 1986).

2. The classic analysis of "exceptionalism" in American foreign policy can be found in Stanley Hoffmann, *Gulliver's Troubles, or the Setting of American Foreign Policy* (New York: McGraw-Hill Book Company, 1968).

3. Toronto University's Sylvia Ostry has written extensively on the creation of what she describes as the convergence club. In some detail she writes of the shrinking gap in per capita GNP between the United States and first Europe, then Japan, and finally East Asia and the contributing role that the United States played. See Sylvia Ostry, *The Post-Cold War Trading System: Who's On First?* (Chicago and London: The University of Chicago Press, 1997).

4. Michael Mandel, "The High-Risk Society," *Business Week,* October 28, 1996, p. 94.

5. For a description of Canada's successful multilateral diplomacy see the study by trade policy analyst and former trade official, Michael Hart. The study is entitled, *Fifty Years of Canadian Tradecraft: Canada at the GATT 1947–1997* (Ottawa: Centre for Trade Policy and Law, 1998).

6. Michael Hart with Bill Dymond and Colin Robertson, *Decision at Midnight: Inside the Canada-U.S. Free Trade Negotiations* (Vancouver: UBC Press, 1994), p. 57.

7. According to Canadian trade official and FTA negotiator, Gordon Ritchie, by the late 1960s, "a network of discriminatory special arrangements covering better than a quarter of our trade—autos and parts, oil and gas, and defence products" formed the basis of bilateral trade with the United States: Gordon Ritchie, *Wrestling with the Elephant: The Inside Story of the Canada-U.S. Trade Wars* (Toronto: Macfarlane Walter & Ross, 1997), p. 23.

8. Candidate Mulroney expressed this Canadian public's aversion to free trade in the 1984 election. He told Canada's *Maclean's Magazine,* "Canadians rejected free trade with the United States in 1911. They would do so again in 1983." Cited in Gordon Ritchie, p. 43.

9. *Report of the Royal Commission on the Economic Union and Development Prospects for Canada* (Ottawa, Minister of Supply and Services Canada, 1985), p. 269.

10. *Royal Commission,* Volume One, p. 269.

11. *Royal Commission,* Volume One, p. 375.

12. Hart et al., p. 300.

13. Hart et al., pp. 333–334.

14. These results are derived from the thorough analysis of trade economist Daniel Schwanen of the C. D. Howe Institute. The analysis not only examines trade but also investment and labor. His most up-to-date examination can be found in Daniel Schwanen, "Trading Up: The Impact of Increased Continental Integration on Trade, Investment and Jobs in Canada," *C. D. Howe Institute: Commentary No. 89* (Toronto: C. D. Howe Publications, March 1997).

15. Greg Ip, "The Borderless World," *The Globe and Mail,* Saturday, July 6, 1996, p. D1.

16. Ip, p. D5.

17. Royal Bank of Canada, "Has Canada Capitalized on Asian Growth?"(September,1997). In this section McCallum relies on previous work using gravity model measures from himself and Professor John Helliwell. See John McCallum, "National Borders Matter: Canada-US Regional Trade Patterns", *American Economic Review,* 85:3 (June, 1995), pp.615–619 and John F. Helliwell, "Do National Borders Matter for Quebec's Trade?" *Canadian Journal of Economics,* 29:3 (August, 1996), pp. 507–516.

18. Robert A. Pastor, "Post-Revolutionary Mexico: The Salinas Opening," *Journal of Interamerican Studies and World Affairs*, 32:3 (Fall, 1990), p. 16.

19. Thomas Legler, "Changes in the Neighbourhood: Reflections on Mexico in Transition," *Policy Staff Paper* (Ottawa, No. 96/02, February, 1996), p. 17.

20. Pastor, p. 4.

21. Nora Lustig, "Mexico: The Slippery Road to Stability," *The Brookings Review* (Spring, 1996), pp. 4–9.

22. Jorge Castañeda, *The Mexican Shock: Its Meaning for the U.S.* (New York: The New Press, 1995), p. 3

23. Castañeda, p. 55.

24. Pastor, p. 17.

25. The economic figures in the section are taken from tables prepared by Ecanal and presented by its President, Ramirez de la O.

26. Moisés Naím, "Mexico's Larger Story,", *Foreign Policy*, 99 (Summer, 1995), p. 119.

27. The opening of the Mexican economy led as well to the growing impact and influence of the U.S. economy on Mexico. And U.S. rates began to rise. As a result servicing the external debt grew, but Mexico also had to further raise its own internal rates to keep attracting foreign capital and to finance the current account deficit. For a general economic examination of this period see Sidney Weintraub, "Mexico's Foreign Economic Policy: From Admiration to Disappointment," in Laura Randall (ed.), *Changing Structure of Mexico: Political, Social, and Economic Prospects* (Armonk, N.Y.: M. E. Sharpe, 1996), pp. 43–54.

28. Naím, p. 118.

29. Financial Times of London, "NAFTA panels face legal challenge in the U.S.," *Financial Post*, Friday, January 17, 1997, p. 6.

30. Anthony DePalma, "U.S. and Mexico Reach Accord Over Satellite TV Transmission", *New York Times*, Saturday, November 9, 1996, p. 20.

7

Fifty Years of
Peace and Prosperity

CARL KAYSEN

Eric Hobsbawm has called the short twentieth century—1914–1991—the age of extremes. The century saw two world wars and two great revolutions reaching all over the world, bringing unprecedented suffering and slaughter. Toward its end it also saw a golden age of economic growth and increasing social equality—primarily—but not only for the west.[1]

What are the next fifty years likely to bring in world politics? How would a historian writing a 300-page overview of the first half of the twenty-first century (half of Hobsbawm's 600 pages for the twentieth) characterize the period?

A cautious person—say an assistant professor of international relations coming up for tenure in two years—would avoid answering the question, and expound, with full scholarly apparatus, the methodological impossibilities of scientific prediction in this area. And she would be right.[2] But a professor emeritus, unconstrained by membership in the guild of political scientists or international relations professors, feels no similar inhibitions, especially in response to an invitation to speculate in broad terms.

He can take full advantage of the difference between prediction, which demands a comprehensive and detailed theory of what governs the phenomena under study, and a means of estimating the values, or a range of values of the important parameters of the theory—for example the number and size distribution of independent sovereignties in realist theories of international relations, and historical explanation, which requires filling a plausible story consistent with the known facts as to why what happened, happened.

I do so, and answer the second of the two questions above: Fifty years of peace and prosperity.

If four sets of ongoing changes in the underlying forces shaping world politics continue, they will offer the explanation for this optimistic prediction for the next half-century: transformations in political organization, in ideology, in social organization, and military technology. And these changes are much more likely to continue than not.

Changes in Political Organization

In the long perspective, the most striking change in the world scene is the end of more than five centuries of European domination. This change began about the end of the last century and has accelerated in the last fifty years. In 1900, the major international actors were the four great European powers—the United Kingdom, France, Germany, Russia—and the emergent great power, the United States. Each was an imperial power, ruling over other peoples: Their Empires included a large share of the worlds' people. Italy and Austria-Hungary were of secondary importance; as was the Ottoman Empire; Japan was just emerging as an international actor. When the United Nations (UN) came into being in 1945, it enrolled 45 member states: 21 from Europe (including Belarus and Ukraine, then hardly independent states); 27 from Latin America; 7 from the Middle East; 4 from Asia and the Pacific; 3 from Africa; and 2 from North America. Today there are 184 member states: 48 from Africa; 49 from Asia-Pacific; 40 from Europe (including the now independent states of Belarus and Ukraine); 33 from Latin America and the Caribbean; 19 from the Middle East and the Caucasus; and 2 from North America.[3]

Except for their UN membership and their votes in the General Assembly, the states are highly unequal units, as measured in the three dimensions most widely used to assess the weight or power of states in the international order: population, income, and military power. Thirty-four of the 184 UN members are ministates with fewer than 1 million inhabitants; most of them are poor as well. At the other end of the scale are poor giants such as India and China with populations of nearly 1 billion and 1.3 billion respectively with per capita incomes of $300 and $500 respectively, and such very large states such as the United States and Japan, with populations of 265 and 130 million, and per capita incomes of about $30,000. Of the other six states with populations of more than 100 million, three are very poor, two are lower-middle income and one is upper-middle. Ten states have between 50 and 100 million population; four of them are rich; one is upper-middle; three are lower-middle; and two are poor.

TABLE 7.1   Number of States and Percent of World Population by Per Capita
Income Class

	Poor <$700	Lower-middle class $700–2785	Upper-middle class $2786–8625	Rich >$8626
# of states	56	47	25	24
Share of world population	54	18	13	14

For 152 member states (excluding ministates), there is information on
populations and income; their distribution by income classes is shown in
Table 7.1.[4]

Broadly speaking, the rich states are in Western and Central Europe,
North America, and the fringe of the Pacific, the poor in Africa, and Asia,
and the aspiring more widely distributed.

A state's military power is a function of three variables: population, income, and political decision to devote resources to the creation and maintenance of military power. At the present moment, military power is even
more unequally distributed than other aspects of state power. The United
States has a unique combination of substantial forces in being in all arms,
equipped with the most technologically sophisticated weapons and support systems now deployed anywhere, and manned by well-trained and
regularly-exercised troops. Its logistical capacities far surpass those of
any other nation and it can project substantial military power to almost
any part of the world. As a matter of budgetary choice, the level of U.S.
forces is significantly lower than it has been in the recent past, and well
below what the United States could support. Japan and Germany, both
large rich countries also have significant military capabilities, but in both
cases political constraints, now essentially self-imposed, limit their military power significantly below its potential strength. France and the
United Kingdom also possess well equipped, well trained forces of a similar size, again constrained by budgetary choices to a level well below
what their economies and populations could support.

The military power of Russia, only recently the core of the Soviet
Union's formidable armed forces, is now in disarray. China and India
maintain large military forces, but of uneven quality, and far short of the
technological level and training of those of the West and Japan.

The wealth and power of states will change over time. China appears
to be among the most rapidly growing economies; though India is not
growing as fast, its recent growth rate exceeds that of the larger rich
states. If Chinese per-capita income grew at an average rate of 7 percent

(about its current rate) for the next twenty-five years, it would be about five times its present level, reaching the current middle-income range. If China committed itself politically to do so over a substantial period, it could develop into a formidable military power, at the cost of a lower level of well being for its population, and, perhaps, a lower rate of economic growth than it might otherwise achieve with a different allocation of resources. For China to sustain so high a growth rate on average over a quarter century would be historically unprecedented, but it cannot be said to be impossible.

India, Brazil, possibly Indonesia, and Mexico might likewise be economically and technically capable of creating powerful military forces by the mid 2020s, if they choose to do so. The United States, Japan, and the European Union (EU) will continue to have that capacity, and even at their current rates of economic growth, will be able to devote more economic and scientific resources to the task at less relative cost to the well being of their citizens. However, the question of choice rather than capability is likely to be the decisive factor, as will be argued below. In any event, the disproportionate military power of the United States is almost certain to diminish over time.

New nations are not the only new actors on the international political scene. Both official and unofficial (non-governmental) organizations have multiplied in numbers and broadened their scope. The League of Nations was created in 1919 as a general-purpose political organization primarily but not exclusively concerned with security. It did not achieve the universal membership its creators envisioned. A year later, two related specialized bodies were organized in affiliation with the League: the International Court of Justice and the International Labor Organization. Five official intergovernmental organizations, in principle, universal, antedated the League. All were special purpose, one might say, technical organizations; the International Telecommunication Union (1865), the Universal Postal Union (1874), the World Intellectual Property Organization (1883), the International Institute of Agriculture, and the International Forestry Center (1904). The names of the first three organizations tell their purposes; within their narrow domains, they institutionalized international cooperation and created areas of international governance. The agricultural and forestry organizations functioned primarily to exchange information, and had no formal governance roles.[5]

Today the picture is much richer. The universal and broadly competent United Nations has associated with it 18 specialized agencies, ranging from the original International Labor Office (ILO), and International Telecommunications Union (ITU) to the World Health Organization (WHO), the World Meteorological Organization (WMO), the Food and Agricultural Organization (FAO), to the International Civil Aviation Organization (ICAO). Most function as transmitters of technical information. Some, like the old ITU and the ICAO have governance functions. There are 14 other UN Bodies, like the United Nations Children's Fund (UNICEF) and the United Nations High Commissioner for Refugees (UNHCR).[6] There is an equally multitudinous array of regional organizations, some with general political competence, most functionally specialized. Thus, Africa has the Organization for African Unity (OAU), in the former category, and the UN Economic Commission for Africa, in the latter, as well as more than two dozen more specialized functional organizations, ranging from health to water management. The Organization of American States (OAS), originally the Pan-American Union (1910), the oldest of the regional organizations, embraces all the countries of the Americas. The OAS originated at the initiative of the United States, as an instrument of American hegemony. It has grown into a more balanced forum, which the Latin American and Caribbean states frequently use to modify or oppose U.S. policies. Europe, the Arab countries of the Middle East and North Africa, Southeast Asia all have both general and specialized regional organizations.[7]

The growth in number and scope of nongovernmental international organizations (NGOs) beginning somewhat later has been even more rapid than that of formal intergovernmental ones. The UN gives recognition to NGOs by registering them. In 1985 the Economic and Social Council registered some 750 NGOs; eleven years later the number had doubled. In addition the UN Department of Public Information had registered 1400 other NGOs in 1996.[8] The organizations cover a wide spectrum of activities: disaster relief, health and medicine; human rights generally and rights of specific groups, women, children, aborigines; environmental concerns.

The typical NGO combines action in the field with political lobbying in national fora and in the United Nations system. Emblematic of this combined approach is Parliamentarians for Global Action, an NGO whose members are members of the legislatures in their respective states. The organization has been particularly active in arms control, advocating the Comprehensive Test Ban Treaty and the unlimited extension of the Non-Proliferation Treaty. The organization lobbies in the General Assembly; its members also lobby individually in their several legislatures, thus providing one example, among many, of the interpenetrating of national domestic and international politics.

It is a commonplace that the sovereignty of states in the economic sphere is greatly constrained by international forces. No state can individually order its macroeconomic monetary and fiscal politics with any wide range of choice independent of market constraints. Treaties and conventions set other constraints, whether on tariffs or fishing. Somewhat less frequently noticed is the increasing importance of substate political actors in the international realm. For example, the EU deals not only with its member states, but also directly with special regions within them in respect to subsidies for particular underdeveloped areas. American states now typically organize trade and investment missions in other countries, both promoting the exports of companies operating in them and seeking foreign investors within their jurisdictions. China's regions and large cities deal directly with foreign investors on a variety of issues, rather than through the central government. The national state is neither an exclusive nor a unitary actor on the international scene.

As the result of the multiplication of the number and kinds of international actors, states, substate political units, international organizations, and NGOs, all states, including large, rich, powerful ones, are involved in a continuous web of formal public and quasi-public international scrutiny and discussion of their activity in almost every sphere. The consequent need for states to justify themselves and the force of the international process and its echoes in the domestic political realm place significant constraints on the actions of individual states.

Changes in Ideology

Adam Smith has triumphed over Karl Marx worldwide. For 150 years, socialism and central planning offered a plausible alternative competing candidate as the basic organizing principle for a socioeconomic system. Their appeal was generated by the widely and deeply experienced shortcomings of the industrializing market economy of the nineteenth century: grinding labor, poverty, urban squalor, unemployment, geographical displacement, and the destruction of settled ways of life. These ills are still with us, now less widespread and less acute in the rich nations, but equally or more so among the poor majority of the world. But the collapse of the Soviet Union, which practiced what its ideologies and acolytes hailed as "real socialism" in the days of ascending Soviet appeal two and three decades ago, has all but swept Marxist socialism from the world ideological stage. Only the small states of North Korea and Cuba retain an official ideological commitment to Marxist socialism; both are in poor economic shape, and North Korea appears to be the most successful of the world's polities at isolating itself and its people from all interaction with the outside world. China talks socialism officially but has stopped practicing it. Communist parties elsewhere in the former socialist world, mostly rechristened and with, so to speak, new coats of exterior paint, remain strong, especially in Russia and some other republics of the former Soviet Union. Their strength lies in part in their continuing grip on an inherited organizational structure with deep penetration into their societies and in part in their promises to alleviate the pains of transition to a more market-directed economy by slowing down its pace.

The intellectual classes, the manufacturers of ideology, have been deeply affected by the change. From the Great Depression on, Marxist and Marxisant writers and thinkers almost everywhere, with the exception of North America and the United Kingdom, dominated these groups. The third-world intellectuals who came to the fore in the post-World War II wave of decolonization almost universally shared this orientation: their anti-imperialism was strongly entwined with anticapitalism, reflecting the Marxist understanding of imperialism. The collapse of the Soviet Union and its satellites reinforced the rightward shift of the ideological spectrum that was already underway in the rich countries of Western Europe, North America, and the Pacific Rim. It destroyed the symbolic appeal of an "actual socialism" the Soviets provided to the third world, as well as the Soviet role as a source of anti-imperialist, anticapitalist propaganda and material as well as symbolic resource for Marxist intellectuals. On the world stage, the ideological struggle over socioeconomic organization has become one in which the advocates of strong laissez-faire capitalism are advancing, their more social-democratic opponents are retreating, and Marxist anticapitalists are off in the wings, perhaps on the way out.

The ideological transformation coincides with the penetration of all corners of the world by the global market in goods, capital, and, to some degree, labor. The global market reaches into many areas that were mostly outside the reach of the earlier world market in the period from the 1870s to World War I.

Market capitalism is the carrier of two important wider ideological and cultural currents: instrumental rationalism, and individualistic hedonism. Instrumental rationalism, the culture of means-ends calculations, is embedded in the organization of business and its day-to-day management in the context of a market economy. The habits of rational calculation push organizations and the people manning them to universalism rather than particularism, efficacy rather than status, in respect to their workaday relations with others. The same habits and attitudes are embodied in the institutions that generate increases in the stock of knowledge on which improvements in the technology of production rest, and transmit it to the oncoming cohorts who staff the system. These forces are slow-acting, as the survival of many forms of social exclusion and domination in most modern countries shows, but they are persistent and, over time, powerful.

Individualism and hedonism are also strongly implicated in the market society. Individuals as both producers and consumers are taught to focus on their own (and their family's) achievements and satisfactions.

Occupational roles are increasingly the major source of social status, and income is a major index. The continued creation of new goods and services and the parallel creation of new wants for them are important drivers of economic growth.

A noteworthy aspect of individualism in the producers' role is the high social valuation market society places on successful entrepreneurship, the conception and realization in practice of something new: a new product, a new process, a new market, a new organization.[9]

The interrelated ideologies of democracy and human rights have spread in parallel with the ideology of the market, though not coextensively with it. Democracy and human rights are directly related, but analytically separate, connected in part by the idea of the rule of law. The central tenet of the democratic ideology is that only democratic governments are legitimate: namely those for which a broadly based electorate chooses its government in regular, frequent, and fair elections on a one-person-one-vote basis, and in which all are eligible to compete for office as well as vote. The ideology of human rights comprises two sets of elements: one set limiting the powers of governments over the lives of their citizens both substantively and procedurally; the other, specifying some minimum set of positive obligations of government to their citizens. There is much wider agreement on the first set—freedom of speech, press, assembly, and religious worship, due process of law in any deprivation by government of the liberty or property of its citizens—than on the second, which includes such matters as obligation to provide some minimum level of education for all children, or minimum subsistence for those who are unable to earn it in the marketplace.

Although there is a broad correlation between democratic government and respect for human rights, it is hardly a one-to-one correspondence: some oligarchical governments have been more respectful of human rights than many that are at least formally democratic.

The spread of ideologies of democracy and human rights is facilitated by the spread of the market economy and its ideology. Again, there is neither necessary connection, nor anything like one-to-one correspondence; one need only think of Singapore, Thailand, or Indonesia to make that point. Yet the changes over the last decade in South Korea and Taiwan also make a point. The connection between market society and democratic polity lies more in the ideological and cultural compatibility between the individualism that market-organized societies induce and reinforce, and the individualism that underlies democratic organization of the polity. To be sure, the egalitarian strand in democratic thought is not directly present in the individualism of the market, but the pressures of the culture of instrumental rationalism, pushing against ascriptive distinctions among persons, go in that direction. It is true that the market society tends to generate, and its ideology to justify, significant economic inequality, and in this respect it does not reinforce democracy. There is, however, another positive connection: The effective functioning of a market economy depends strongly on the rule of law with respect to property rights, and the limitations of the arbitrary exercise of power in economic matters by governments. Although, again, the rule of law in these respects does not directly promote democracy or human rights, it helps create a social climate favorable for them.

As well as being assisted in all these ways by the spread of the market as the primary means of socioeconomic organization, the ideologies of democracy and human rights are spreading on their own. They have wide appeal to the majorities of the world's population who live in polities where they are absent entirely or in part. The growth of a world society, discussed below, makes it easier for a wider and wider audience to be exposed to that appeal. Further, it makes the expression of direct opposition to these ideologies less legitimate. Governments are apt at least to invoke the labels to cover practices that are in part the opposite.

In an essay published in 1993, Ernest Haas discussed the distribution of states by the degree to which their citizens were free and their governments democratic.[10] He presented the compilation made by Freedom House shown in Table 7.2, which exhibits a significant increase in the percentage of states and their populations that are either "free" or "partly free."

His own more refined classification divides states into six classes as of mid-1992, as follows:

1. States with a relatively unbroken record of peaceful change of government by democratic means before and since 1975. **30%**
2. Formerly authoritarian or totalitarian states that have conducted a peaceful change of government by democratic means since 1985. **10%**
3. Formerly authoritarian or totalitarian states that now have regimes committed to democracy and that have conducted one peaceful and democratic election. **12%**
4. Authoritarian or totalitarian states committed to liberalization (regimes that have announced the intention of holding multiparty elections and allow freedom of advocacy and organization). **18%**
5. Authoritarian regimes under single-party dictatorship, or army rule, using selective repression without seeking forcible change in social and economic life. **19%**
6. Totalitarian regimes under single-party dictatorship, seeking forcible change in society and economy. **6%**
7. States whose situation is unclear because of unresolved civil war. **5%**

TABLE 7.2   Distribution of States and Populations by Extent of Political Freedom, 1973 and 1990

	Percent of States			Percent of Population		
	Free	Partly Free	Not Free	Free	Partly Free	Not Free
1973	29	25	46	32	21	47
1990	37	26	37	39	22	39

If one equates Haas's classes 1 and 2 with "Free," 3 and 4 with "Partly Free," and 5 and 6 with "Not Free" in the Freedom House classification, his classification shows a roughly similar pattern, and thus reinforces the judgment that democracy and human rights are spreading as practices and supports a stronger conclusion on the spread of the ideologies of democracy and human rights than the Freedom House data alone.

Changes in Social Organization

The ongoing and accelerating revolutions in technologies of transportation and communication, which have been central to the increasing global integration of national economies into a single world economy, are also creating a world society. The sense of a single world society is captured, if exaggerated, in Marshall McLuhan's phrase "the global village."[11] A world society can be defined as existing when important groups in most countries are in communication with each other and share ideas and interests, their shared ideas and interests constitute significant elements in their actions, especially as they impinge on the political sphere, and this impact is spread widely among nations.

The jet airplane has reduced the cost of international and particularly intercontinental travel to a level that has made mass tourism possible. The result is that increasing proportions of the middle classes of most countries have had some experience of societies other than their own.

More important is the joint effect of convenient, rapid, and cheap long-distance travel and cheap, reliable, and convenient long-distance communication by telephone, fax, and e-mail in uniting elites of various nations into international communities. Scientific elites have long been connected by interchanges of communication and international conferences and congresses, but the intensity and frequency of their interchanges and face-to-face meetings have greatly increased, and those meetings and interchanges have involved a larger fraction of working scientists than ever before. Social scientists and the social sciences are becoming as international as the natural sciences. The growing intellectual role of comparative studies in all the social sciences has played a role in accelerating the process. Other cultural elites—musicians, dancers, writers, scholars in the humanities, movie-makers, journalists—are having the same experiences. So are elites in some sports.

The globalization of the economy involves more and more businesses in activities in other than their home nations that go beyond the export of their products and include production, research, marketing, and service organizations that are staffed mostly by nationals of the countries in which they operate, but typically involving some expatriates, especially at higher management levels. Once such multinational corporations were largely American—with the exception of a few oil and other mineral producers. Today only fifteen of the fifty largest multinational corporations are American; nineteen are European; thirteen, Japanese; three are based in other countries.[12] As a consequence, business elites, including the engineers and applied scientists who work chiefly in a business framework, are becoming an international community too.

So are political elites. Here again, the tranche of top political leaders and professional diplomats has long had a certain community crossing national boundaries. In earlier centuries, it was to a substantial degree a kinship community, especially among monarchs and aristocrats. But now the interchanges encompass much wider groups and reach deeper, including members of legislatures and civil servants, as well as top political executives. Even military elites, in the past the symbolic bearers of national pride and identity, are creating communities across national and alliance lines.

Further, the internationalization of news and entertainment through CNN and the World Wide Web brings large parts of the nonelite world into virtual contact. It also spreads knowledge of what elites say and do, and thus narrows the distance between elites and nonelites.

Finally, the growing activity of NGOs of an international character also contributes to the formation of an international society. Some are focused directly on action, such as those concerned with disaster relief; some on political efforts to influence the actions of governments and formal international organizations, such as human rights agencies. All are in some sense political actors, mobilizing constituencies in many nations and acting in both the many domestic and the international political fora.

Perhaps the most important NGOs are the multinational corporations, though they usually are not thought of under this rubric. Like all businesses in a market economy, they are in continued interaction with governments that regulate, tax, and subsidize them, and are effortfully struggling to keep the terms of their relations favorable. A natural result of these interactions is the transmission of information and impulses originating on both sides of the transactions among jurisdictions. Furthermore, businesses can become involuntary transmissions agents for other forces, which originate in one or another of the societies in which they operate, and which are at best neutral and frequently hostile to their own immediate economic interests. American companies operating in South Africa in the '70s and '80s became an instrument for transmitting disapproval of apartheid on the part of many groups in the United States to the South African government in more effective ways than these groups could have achieved had the business connection not existed. Today, analogous pressures on U.S. producers of footwear and clothing with factories in South and East Asia may be causing changes in labor standards in those countries.

All these institutions and groups, some more, some less organized, that reach and function across national boundaries form the strands of the thickening web constituting an international society and permeating the boundaries between state and non-state actors and international and domestic politics.

Changes in Military Technology

The destructive power of organized military forces has increased vastly over the past half-century or so, greatly stimulated by the large investments in military technology during and after World War II. The most outstanding result of that impulse, the nuclear and ballistic missile revolution, is now virtually completed, having created the capability of delivering limitless destructive power to any place on the globe.

A second wave of innovations is now in course and will continue. It has two prime dimensions: the capability to deliver force in carefully graduated amounts with great precision even at great distances, and the capability to locate the assets of an opponent in a wide variety of circumstances—day or night, fair weather or foul, fixed or moving.

The new weapons produced by the first technological revolution may be too powerful and too indiscriminate to be used in actual fighting. So far, except for their first use, they have not been put into action, whatever their defensive value. The weapons issuing from the ongoing current wave of technological development are not under the same constraints. In early versions, the United States used them in the Gulf War, and they demonstrated some capacity to perform as hoped, though not living up to the ads, as newly developed weapons rarely do in their first use. Investment in improving them and developing new ones continues.

Logistic capacity to move forces from their home bases to remote areas is almost as important to a high-capability force as its weapons. This capacity depends more on organization and training and less on investments in technologies specialized to war. But it is expensive and requires large capital investments, especially in aircraft, ships, and communications equipment.

The gap between the power of a high-investment, high-technology, highly trained military force and that of ordinary forces is large and widening. Substantial continued investment is required to field, equip, train, and maintain such a force. Only rich and relatively large nations are able to create and maintain such forces, and it requires persistent political will to do so.

Not only wealth in general, but scientific and technical capacity is needed. Just how much capacity, over what domains of science and technology, depends in part on the degree to which advanced weapons are available in international trade. Nations have typically sought a high degree of self-sufficiency in the provision of crucial items of weaponry, and restricted the exports of their best and newest military products to close allies. More recently, treaties and international regimes have forbidden or restricted trade in particular suspect classes of weapons: weapons of mass destruction and ballistic missiles.[13]

If these practices continue, only nations commanding wide scientific and technical capacity in electronics, computers, telecommunications, optics, materials science, and aerospace would be able to maintain military forces at the forefront of capability. Further, a fairly large flow of recruits with at least good secondary education, as well as more highly educated officers in smaller numbers, would be needed to staff such a force. All these factors again point to the continuing disparities in military potential between the few large, rich nations and the rest. Whether those nations potentially capable of deploying and maintaining effective, wide-spectrum military forces at the frontiers of technical capability in fact do so, and at what scale, will remain, of course, a matter of political decision.

The proposition that the trends of change over the last half century sketched above—in political organization of the international world, in ideology, in the growth of a world society, and in military technologies and organization–will continue at a greater or lesser pace, or at least be maintained and not reversed over the next half century, is a much more likely forecast than the alternative proposition, that they will be reversed. If these trends do continue, how will they explain the half century of peace and prosperity that our imagined historian looking back from 2050 will have observed?

Why There Was Peace

The most salient international political issue at the beginning of the period was the gap in well-being between the minority of rich states and the majority of poor ones. This problem obviously could not be resolved or the gap diminished by a war of the poor against the rich (symbolically, South versus North). In terms of military power and the prospects of success, such a war was a nonstarter. Most of the poor nations, in fact, improved their lot over the period. Continued access to the markets and capital of the rich was the key for this result, as explained in the following section. This access was maintained and advanced by discussions in international fora, as well as by the balance of political forces in the domestic politics of the rich countries. While the impulse to protectionism was always present in the nations of the North in considerable strength, it was outweighed by the interests of those economic sectors which gained from imports, and saw investment and export opportunities in the South, reinforced by the political weight of organized groups focusing a widespread diffuse sentiment in the North that their countries had an obligation to help narrow the gap.

To be sure, the minority of rich nations in the North could have been indifferent to the majority of poor people and states in the South and could have sought to insulate themselves from their struggles, conflicts, and problems. At the beginning of the period, it was certainly the case that the bulk of international flows of trade and investment was among the rich and upper-middle-income nations, and some saw "letting the poor stew in their own juices" as a plausible policy path. But both economic and political pressures went in the opposite direction. The competition among business firms for access to markets, resources, and cheap labor drove the other way. So did the political pressure from the South in international fora, and their reflections and reverberations in the domestic politics of the North.

The rich states had no reasons to seek war, either with each other or elsewhere. They were mostly democratic, particularly the larger ones. Many of those that were not, were populist, in the sense that the welfare of the representative citizen was the central object of state policy, as, for example, in Singapore. The few who were exceptions at the outset of the period, such as Saudi Arabia or Kuwait, were too weak to consider war as a serious policy option.

For almost all the rich states, economic and social issues, rather than international ones, dominated domestic politics. The benefit/cost ratio for war in both economic and political terms was much more likely to fall short of one than exceed it. The continued increase in the destructive capabilities of conventional weapons weighed heavily in any such calculations, as did the existence of nuclear weapons. Further, the popular willingness in the rich countries of the North to support war, whatever a "realist" calculation might show, was very low. Only something that could plausibly be seen as a threat to the security and prosperity of their countries could justify political leaders in asking for public support for war.[14]

The middle-income states and the more successful among those initially poor were moving toward the rich in politics and ideology. Their prosperity was tied strongly to international markets and the attitudes of investors toward them. Market ties militated against war. At the beginning of the half century there were many conflicts between particular nations of the sort that had traditionally led to war, and had in fact erupted in war in the recent past. They included the conflicts between India and Pakistan over Kashmir; between Greece and Turkey involving Cyprus and the Aegean boundary between the two; between Israel and its Arab neighbors. The pressure of the international system organized through the Security Council and supported by most of the militarily powerful states finally resulted in the settlement of these conflicts by negotiation, although not without some further episodes of violence.

Two large states, Russia and China, were also engaged in conflicts with their neighbors that just bordered on violence at the beginning of the period. Both of them had the potential of becoming much wealthier and more militarily powerful; Russia was only newly and barely democratic, China was fully authoritarian. Arguably both had incentives to behave in a very different way from the other large, richer states. In fact, both discovered that their paths to prosperity, down which they had already started, lay through increasing integration into the capitalist world market and were inconsistent with seeking to dominate their neighbors by military force, either through intimidation or application. Over the course of time, they became more and more like other large, rich states in their international behavior and their domestic political structures. It might well have been different; possible alternative paths are discussed below.

In general, no state initiated a war or sought to settle an ongoing conflict by war because it would have united most of the rich and militarily powerful states against it. That initiating war would have this result became ever more likely as the delegitimization of war as an instrument of national policy proceeded in almost all democratic societies. The underlying commitment to the peaceful resolution of international disputes set forth in the UN Charter became the settled belief of the great majority.

The period had begun in an epidemic of internal conflict, chiefly in the poorer states, but in some middle-income ones too. Such conflicts seemed endemic in Africa, but took place in parts of South Asia and Latin America as well. They were caused by a mixture of elements: Simple struggles for power were often exacerbated by religious and ethnic conflict; ideological elements also played a role, partly reflecting class wars, partly the residue of Cold War struggles and the powerful mixture of anti-imperialism and anticapitalism. In many cases, the persistence of Cold War ideological conflict was reinforced by the continuing struggles for power between factions that had been supported if not organized by the United States or the Soviet Union, and, in Africa, by Cuba and China.

Over time these conflicts died out. Their most rapid end came in Latin America, where the change in U.S. behavior caused by the end of the Cold War and the replacement of dictatorial governments of the left and right by elected governments of a more democratic cast led to the resolution of many conflicts by compromise and conciliation: Nicaragua and El Salvador provided early examples. The Organization of American States and various NGOs played a facilitating role in these situations and others, providing political pressure on the parties to cease fighting and move to compromises and electoral resolutions of conflicts, and help in organizing elections and providing external observers of their fairness.

Many of these internal conflicts had external repercussions in the shape of refugee flows, weapons smuggling, and border crossings by armed bands that stimulated intervention by neighbors, by regional organizations, and by the United Nations seeking to dampen and ultimately resolve them. By 2010–2020, the middle of the half century, the organization of competent regional peacekeeping forces under the joint auspices of the United Nations Security Council and regional organizations such as the OAU and OAS, greatly assisted in halting armed conflicts at an early stage and substituting politics for civil wars.[15]

Peace Permitted Prosperity: How Did It Come About?

The absence of large and/or widespread wars permitted continued, if not uninterrupted, economic growth worldwide. The experience of the last several decades of this century taught nations what they had to do to take advantage of the natural dynamic of market capitalism to achieve sustained economic growth. The prime means were allowing and promoting the expansion of markets at home, and opening their economies to international trade and investment.[16] Domestic market expansion meant chiefly removing a variety of restrictions and obstacles to the growth of peasant agriculture and business, and also the provision of some indispensable public goods in a reasonably efficient manner, particularly education and public health, as well as the physical infrastructures that are needed for an urban society to function. These actions and the opening of the economies to international trade and investment were complementary—each set reinforced the other in a virtuous circle. The disappearance of the ideological conflict about the proper path to growth—market capitalism and international openness vs. socialism and self-sufficient development—that had marked the previous half-century made it much easier for the aspiring nations to learn and apply these lessons with reasonable persistence.

To learn and apply these lessons required governments of modest strength to behave in a modestly sensible way. They had to provide and maintain the legal framework for a market economy, enforcing property rights, restraining corruption within acceptable bounds, refraining from arbitrary confiscations. They had to have the legitimacy and strength to collect enough taxes to support these activities and to provide the physical and social infrastructure required—roads, education, public health. They had to engage in enough income redistribution and correction of egregious market failures to keep the social peace. The experience of the United Kingdom in the nineteenth century (1815–1914) shows that much economic inequality and social discord and conflict were consistent with vigorous economic growth and political stability.

Democratic and populist states, as most were, were always under pressure to avoid painful adaptation to economic change by protectionism and subsidization. These and other forces inclined them to promise more than they had resources to deliver and to cover the gap by inflation. They resisted these pressures with enough success to prevent inflation, overvalued currencies, and protectionism from choking the international flows of trade and investment that propelled growth.

These efforts of aspiring national governments were supported in a modest way by assistance from international organizations and the richer nations of the North. A modest amount of investment came through the World Bank and similar agencies; a greater amount of technical assistance, particularly in education, public health, and medicine came through a variety of international organizations and NGOs. But the major flows of both resources and technology came through the international market, the competitive efforts of business corporations seeking markets, labor, resources. The successful governments in the South grew increasingly skilled in using their control of access to their markets to bargain with international business over the conditions under which they operated. Increasingly over the period, the governments of the South were supported in these efforts by the development of international standards through the political activities in the North of NGOs and the publics they mobilized, as well as by their own political pressures in international fora. The result was something much less than mid-twentieth-century Western European social democracy, but also something more than mid-nineteenth-century laissez-faire.

A half-century historical conspectus that could be appropriately characterized as one of peace and prosperity by no means implies that both were uniform or continuous. Although these were no big wars, conflicts, both internal and international, episodically broke out, and some internal conflicts persisted. Most, but not all, countries followed the path of economic openness to growth. Some did so with more persistence than others; some failed entirely. But 2050 seemed as much better than 1995 in terms of peace and prosperity worldwide, as 1912 seemed than 1812 in Europe and North America.

Alternative Possibilities Dominated by Wars
and Preparation for Wars

The most plausible alternative possibilities that lead to a much bleaker outlook for the next half century involve Russia and China. Indeed many analysts writing today see them as not only plausible, but more likely than the optimistic scenario sketched above.

In this view, Russia today is "Weimar Russia," filled with unmanageable internal conflict, smarting with injured pride at a humiliating defeat in the Cold War and an equally humiliating postwar settlement, in which its former subservient allies became the allies of its conquerors, particularly the hated United States. The consequences are predicted to parallel those in Germany—an authoritarian nationalist Russia seeking to recreate the Soviet Empire that will at least re-ignite the Cold War in Europe, if not start a hot one.

This scenario is clearly possible. There are two reasons to deem it unlikely. The first, indicated above, is that it is inconsistent with the path to recovering its strength on which Russia has already started: converting from an almost isolated centrally planned socialist economy to a market economy integrated into the international market. Without a high degree of marketization and international integration, Russia will recover its economic strength only slowly, if at all. It would thus be hard put to build up its military strength, and without that strength it could neither attract its neighbors nor overawe them, especially if faced with an alliance of the rest of Europe against it. Second, and more fundamentally, without an ideological substitute for Communism, now dead beyond revival, Russia could not create a strong enough state to compel a majority of its people to commit themselves to this goal. Coercion and repression alone will not suffice.

The other threat, already on or just over the horizon, is an aggressive, expansive China, the world's most populous nation and with rapid economic growth, seeking hegemony over East Asia. It would do so as an authoritarian polity, allowing considerable scope for a market economy, and for the wealth and ease of its successful businessmen, so long as they accepted the political dominance of the state. It would attract considerable support from overseas Chinese throughout East Asia, and the respect, if not admiration, of other nearby nations where the traditions of democracy and human rights are shallow. The result would be, at best, a Pacific Cold War, with Japan either an uneasy neutral between North America and the Chinese-dominated continent, or joining the Chinese camp. At worst, there would be a Sino-American war arising from an American defense of the independence of Taiwan and the Philippines, necessary because of a Chinese failure to take seriously U.S. demonstrations of resolve in response to repeated aggressive moves by China.

The darkest view of the possible future sees the union of both these scenarios in a revived Sino-Russian alliance, this time with China as a more equal partner, but with Russia supplying the majority of the nuclear forces. The result: at best another fifty years of Cold War.

The reason for thinking these outcomes unlikely, even if not impossible, is the same for China as for Russia. China's prosperity is as dependent on international trade and investment as Russia's, perhaps more so. An overly aggressive path risks cutting back China's access to international markets severely and so ending its rapid growth along the capitalist road.

Another reason is that Chinese military capacity is still modest, especially relative to that of the United States and Japan. In the short run, aggressive behavior by China is much more likely to move Japan even closer to the United States, and their combined power far outweighs China's. Thus, even the narrowest calculation by the Chinese would not warrant the choice of an aggressive path in the near future. The possible reaction thereto, especially by the United States and Japan, would by combining economic and military pressure slow Chinese economic growth and could even halt it. The further into the future one looks, the more likely that the Chinese economic transformation will have produced a political transformation as the result of its continuing integration into the international economy and polity.

A third alternative scenario for a threatening rather than a promising future rests on the possible sustained failure of the rich states to deal with the social and political strains arising from rapid economic change, caused in part by globalization, in part by continuing changes in technology favoring highly skilled and educated workers over the less skilled. The current problems of job-displacement, unemployment, and increasing inequality in the distribution of income and wealth would be exacerbated. Political conflict within these countries would increase, and the response might be the support of more repressive government, implementing xenophobic and protectionist policies and tolerating or stimulating social aggression against minorities and immigrants. The increased social conflict and economic isolationism would have a negative impact on economic growth, leading to a vicious cycle of further social conflict and political repression. The same currents could feed anti-internationalism and hostility to aspiring industrializing countries in the third world. In the extreme, a new fascism, combining domestic repression with a nationalistic and aggressive external stance and seeking containment if not domination of nations populated by inferior peoples.

A currently fashionable variant of this scenario sees in the rise of religious fundamentalism, especially but not only in the Muslim world, a harbinger of a coming clash of civilizations—the Latin West, Orthodox

East and Southeast Europe, Islam, the Confucian, Hindu, and Buddhist worlds. This is a vision of a world of conflict, not cooperation, with endemic border wars and episodic outbursts of larger ones. In such a world, democracy and human rights would recede rather than flourish, and endemic war would make a poor environment for continued economic growth.[17]

Another gloomy possible future can be sketched centering on ecological catastrophe: climate change accelerated by continuing deforestation and increasing combustion of fossil fuel in China and other countries of the South; failure of population growth in the Middle East, South Asia, and Africa to slow down; soil erosion and water scarcity. This scenario reflects the proposition that markets will continue to fail to adapt by responding to scarcities through substitution and fostering new technologies and that national governments and international organizations will not adapt by supplementing and on occasion anticipating and leading market responses to changing constraints on resource use. Not impossible; but likely?[18]

Concluding Observations

Of course, the imagined historian, looking back from 2050, will be explaining what will have actually happened. This *jeu d'esprit* simply offers explanations for a set of plausible results seen as more likely than some possible alternatives.

No future, however plausible, is inevitable, hence our inability to predict it with any confidence. It is highly contingent, depending on choices to be made by political leaders, parties and other political organizations, businesses, investors, consumers, other kinds of social institutions, and ordinary people. These choices will be made by human beings in a variety of contexts under a variety of constraints. The faith that sustains the optimism of this essay is that there are available choices that can be made to lead to the favorable outcomes set out.

Notes

1. Eric Hobsbawn, *The Age of Extremes* (New York: Pantheon Books, 1994).

2. See Phillip E. Tetlock and Aaron Bellien, eds., *Counterfactual Thought Experiments in World Politics* (Princeton, NJ: Princeton University Press, 1996).

3. United Nations, *Divided World*, Adam Roberts and Benedict Kingsbury. eds., 2nd edition (Oxford: Clarendon Press, 1994), Appendix C.

4. World Bank, *World Development Report 1995* (New York: Oxford University Press, 1996), Tables 1 and 1a, pp. 162–163, 1a, p. 228.

5. George W. Barr, *International Organizations*, revised edition (Wilmington, DE: Scholarly Resources Inc., 1990).

6. Giuseppe Schiavone, *International Organization, A Dictionary and Directory,* 3rd edition (New York: St. Martin's Press, 1993).

7. Ibid.

8. United Nations, *Everyone's United Nations* (New York, 1996). For listings of individual organizations by function, see *The Times Guide to World Organizations* (London: Times Books, 1996).

9. Joseph A. Schumpeter was the first writer to give pride of place to entrepreneurship so defined in analyzing economic development. See his *Theory of Economic Development* (Cambridge, MA: Harvard University Press, 1936). This was an English translation of the work first published in Germany in 1911.

10. Ernest Haas, "Beware the Slippery Slope, Notes toward the Definition of Justifiable Intervention," in Laura W. Reed and Carl Kaysen, eds., *Emerging Norms of Justifiable Intervention* (Cambridge, MA: American Academy of Arts and Sciences, 1993).

11. Marshall McLuhan amd Quentin Fiore, *The Medium is the Massage* (New York: Random House, 1967).

12. Fortune, *Annual Fortune 500* issue, 1994.

13. Stockholm International Peace Research Institute, *SIPRI Yearbook* (Oxford: Oxford University Press, 1994), Part IV, Arms Control and Disarmament; also Chapters 11 and 14 in SIPRI Yearbook 1993.

14. See John Mueller, *Retreat from Doomsday, the Obsolescence of Major War* (New York: Basic Books, 1989); Carl Kaysen, "Is War Obsolete?" *International Security* 14 (Spring 1990); Bruce Russett, *Grasping the Democratic Peace* (Princeton, NJ: Princeton University Press, 1993).

15. See Carl Kaysen and George Rathjens, "Send in the Troops," *Washington Quarterly*, 20 (Winter 1997), for an analysis of the utility of UN and regional forces.

16. Deepak Lal and H. Myint, *The Political Economy of Poverty, Equity and Growth* (Oxford: Clarendon Press, 1996).

17. Samuel P. Huntington, *The Clash of Civilizations and the Remaking of the World Order* (New York: Simon and Schuster, 1996). For a skeptical review see Stephen M. Walt in *Foreign Policy*, no. 106 (Spring 1997), pp. 177–189.

18. See Carl Kaysen, "The Computer That Printed Out W.O.L.F.," *Foreign Affairs*, 50 (July 1972) for a discussion of the rigidities of earlier models of ecological catastrophe.

8

China, Japan, and Germany
in the New World Polity[1]

JOSEPH M. GRIECO

Why, despite being one of the great winners in the Post-Cold War international system, does China appear to be increasingly dissatisfied with the current world order? Why has it given evidence that it might be a revisionist state, one that is so deeply disenchanted with the East Asian political-territorial order that it might use force to alter that order? The discussion below seeks to address these questions through a comparison of recent changes in Chinese national strategy with those of two other key countries that have been major beneficiaries of the modern world order, Germany and Japan.

The Problem: Chinese Economic Success,
Chinese Political Dissatisfaction

China has been a major winner in the contemporary world system. With the collapse of the Soviet Union, China finds itself in a highly favorable security environment: For the first time in its modern history, no major state has an interest in trying or the capacity to undertake significant military operations against China.[2] Perhaps even more important, China has become one of the great economic growth machines of recent times. From the mid-1980s through the mid-1990s, its real gross domestic product per capita grew at a rate of 6.9 percent per year, a growth experience exceeded by only two countries during the same period (Thailand and the Republic of Korea). By 1994, China had the seventh largest economy in the world, surpassed only by the United States, Japan, Germany, France, the United Kingdom, and Italy.[3] China's future overall growth prospects by the early-to-mid-1990s were extraordinarily bright, and remained very favorable even in the face of the terrible economic crisis that swept through East and Southeast Asia and other emerging markets during 1997 and 1998. Projections from such sources as the CIA and the World Bank regarding China, that it might have the largest economy in the world (based on purchasing power parity estimates) by the year 2020, appeared to be still credible at the end of the 1990s.[4]

China's recent economic success can be traced to its structural reforms of the late 1970s, reforms that brought about the development of freer markets and substantial privatization of economic activity in the country by the mid-to-late 1980s. While the more purely domestic elements of the reform program have surely been the key to China's economic transformation, that transformation has also been due to China's decision to open its economy in large measure to the world and its subsequent enjoyment of increasingly beneficial economic relations during the 1980s and 1990s with its East Asian neighbors, the countries of Western Europe, and especially the United States. Between 1989 and 1995, for example, China's exports grew by 183 percent, from about $53 billion to about $148 billion, and by consequence China was the world's ninth largest exporter by the mid-1990s.[5]

Particularly profitable for China has been its trade with the United States. In 1994, for example, according to Chinese figures, China enjoyed a trade surplus with the United States in the range of $7.4 billion. China's success in the American market thus not only easily covered its imports of capital and other goods from the United States that year, it also generated a trade surplus capable of covering China's deficits with other important commercial partners—for example, Japan ($4.8 billion) and the European Union ($2.3 billion).[6]

The figures above suggest that, while it is not yet a member of the World Trade Organization (WTO), China has been in recent years one of the biggest beneficiaries of the opportunities for trade that are provided by that regime. China has also been a major beneficiary of the international regimes for international money and finance, the International Monetary Fund and the World Bank. It is a member of both arrangements, and as James Shinn has noted, China by the mid-1990s became the largest single national recipient of current World Bank loans.[7]

Given its tremendously successful economic performance and the important link between that superb performance and its external economic relations, one might expect that China would be essentially satisfied with the contemporary East Asian and international orders. Moreover, one might expect that China would want to do everything it could to ensure continued participation in the international political economy so as to maximize its prospects for future growth and even greater medium-term stature in world affairs. And yet, China has presented signs that it is dissatisfied with contemporary arrangements in East Asia, that it is pursuing a foreign policy toward the region that has revisionist elements, and that it may be willing to put into jeopardy its favorable global and political relationships in order to improve its position in East Asia.[8]

In particular, China is putting an increasing emphasis on the use of military instruments both in the region and, through arms sales, in other parts of the world. For example, China has threatened to use force to prevent the independence of Taiwan, and in 1996 undertook missile tests close to the island to make that threat credible. In addition, China has announced claims to the potentially oil-rich Spratly Islands region and indeed a large portion of the South China Sea, and has applied low levels of force in support of those claims.[9] Moreover, China has sold nuclear-weapons-related technology and nuclear-capable missiles to Pakistan and has come close to major sales of nuclear technology to Iran.[10]

China still lags far behind the United States in military capabilities, and it is quite possible that that gap will grow in favor of the United States in light of the information revolution in modern warfare. In addition, recent careful analyses of China's ability to project military force suggest that China cannot now use, and may not hope, for the foreseeable future, to use military force to compel Taiwan to accept control from the mainland, or to acquire the Spratly Islands.[11] Nevertheless, China has in recent years increased its allocation of national resources to the acquisition of military capabilities. According to the International Institute for Strategic Studies, for example, Chinese military expenditures, adjusted by International Monetary Fund (IMF) and World Bank estimates of purchasing power parities, may have increased by roughly 40 percent between 1990 and 1995.[12] Finally, as Alastair Johnston has recently demonstrated, China appears to be developing a war-fighting, as opposed to a deterrence-oriented, nuclear weapons doctrine.[13]

In light of these actions, China appears at a minimum to want to make it clear that it is a major power in Asia. Some evidence also suggests that it may want to bring about a significant change in the political and perhaps even the territorial status quo in that part of the world. Finally, China's recent actions in regard to Taiwan and, perhaps even more ominously, in the South China Sea area, suggest that China may be willing to use military force to effect adjustments in the region.[14]

If this assessment is correct, then it marks a significant change from the track China appeared to be following from the late 1970s through the 1980s. During that period it seemed, in light of its domestic economic reforms and its opening to the world economy, that China had decided to shift away from the kind of tough, territorially aggressive foreign policy that it had pursued in the 1950s (the Korean War), the 1960s (the war with India), and the 1970s (the war with Vietnam). It appeared instead that China was becoming more oriented toward constructing relationships in the region and with the United States that emphasized mutually profitable economic exchange. In sum, using terms suggested by Richard Rosecrance, China gave some evidence in the 1980s of beginning to move down the road of becoming less of a "territorial state" and more of a "trading state."[15]

It should be emphasized that not all of China's recent behavior should necessarily be coded as representing a new interest in national territorial expansion and control. In particular, the case of Taiwan may entail not so much the initiating of new mainland Chinese efforts to retake the island, but simply reaction to efforts by the Taiwanese government to gain new international acceptance. But there remains the troubling matter of the Spratly Islands. In that case, it is China that is seeking to establish a new situation in East Asia, namely, to attain a new level of formal, legal control over the area. Formal control by China of that area would be unimportant economically if, as is likely, Chinese employment of force to take it led to a conflict with other states in the region and possibly with the United States, a conflict which would make it infeasible to exploit the potential oil resources in the area. Yet this is the risk that China appears increasingly willing to run, suggesting that it has shifted its interests in favor of formal territorial ownership, or at least hegemony, even if this new status means the enjoyment of fewer economic benefits.[16]

To the extent that the empirical discussion above is accurate, we need to address three key questions:

1. Why has the Chinese state (or, more precisely, why have top Chinese decisionmakers) shifted that country's orientation from apparently becoming more like a trading state to returning to being more like a traditional territorial state?
2. Why have Chinese leaders apparently come to find intolerable precisely the international framework in which China has been doing so well for the past ten to fifteen years?[17]
3. If Chinese leaders are dissatisfied with the contemporary international and regional status quo, why do they believe they must act assertively *in the near term*? Why do they not wait and, with time and China's projected rate of future growth, become progressively and steadily the hegemon of the region and thereby bring about gradual changes in the regional political status quo so that the latter is more in line with China's interests?[18]

It should be noted again that there might be an important distinction to be drawn between recent Chinese foreign policy in regard to Taiwan and its policy in the South China Sea. To the extent that Chinese leaders believe that it is Taiwan that is seeking to change the regional status quo by its efforts to acquire greater acceptance in the international community, their behavior may be seen more as reactive than assertive. In contrast, China in recent years has seemed to be taking the initiative in the South China Sea case in terms of attempting to create a new level of Chinese control and even sovereignty over the area. And it is precisely China's interest in establishing such control, and its willingness to use force to do so, which may be indicative of a Chinese shift from moving towards becoming more of a trading state to returning to territorialist goals backed by traditional power instruments.

Problems with Current Explanations for the China Puzzle

There are a number of possible answers to the questions posed above. However, differences between Chinese national strategy since the end of the Cold War and those of Germany and Japan, as well as (less pronounced) differences between German and Japanese national strategies, cast doubt on their efficacy.

Germany has responded to the end of the Cold War with a strategy that has made it look more and more like a Rosecrancian trading state. Most important, Germany has markedly reduced its allocation of national resources to military power. For example, German spending on defense decreased from about $46 billion in 1985 (using constant 1993 prices) to $34.8 billion in 1994, and total armed forces have been cut from 478,000 persons in 1985 to 367,000 in 1994.[19] At the same time, Germany has been a principal force (together with France) in European efforts to build stronger regional institutions. These recent efforts include reinvigorating the Western European Union (WEU) military arrangement and, under the auspices of the European Union (EU), working toward Economic and Monetary Union (EMU) and a European Common Foreign and Security Policy (CFSP).

Japan during the Cold War was perhaps more of a trading state than was Germany, and it was vastly less oriented to territorial state goals and instruments than was China. However, and very interestingly, Japan has responded to the end of the Cold War by undertaking a shift along the trading state—territorial state continuum that is similar in direction to that of China, and not Germany, although Japan's shift in favor of greater territorialism is not so great in magnitude as that of China and it certainly has not left Japan at the same point on the continuum as is now occupied by its large neighbor.

On the one hand, Japan has not responded to the end of the Cold War by becoming more assertive or bellicose in Asian regional politics. It has not, for example, sought to attain unilateral control of Asian sea-lanes or ocean resources as has been true of China. At the same time, and in contrast to Germany, Japan has markedly increased its defense spending in recent years. Germany still devotes a larger percentage of its gross domestic product (GDP) to defense (2 percent in 1994) than does Japan (1 percent), but in terms of absolute resource allocations Japan has been able to take advantage of its progressively larger economy to spend more on defense while still staying at the domestically and regionally important 1 percent GDP limit. The result has been that while German, British, and French military expenditures (again, in 1993 constant dollars) exceeded that of Japan in 1985, Japanese expenditures exceeded those of all three countries by 1993–1994.[20] Finally, whereas Germany has worked very hard to assure its neighbors that it remains firmly and indeed increasingly committed to regional cooperation, and is willing to reinforce that commitment through concrete institutional initiatives, Japan has been highly reluctant to accept numerous invitations from Malaysia to help establish a uniquely East Asian regional economic arrangement, and has played a marginal role in the only multilateral security arrangement in the area, the Regional Forum (ARF) of the Association of Southeast Asian Nations (ASEAN).

Keeping in mind these broad-brush characterizations of German and Japanese post-Cold War national strategies, we may identify and evaluate at least four possible arguments about China and its apparent return to territorialism in world affairs:

1. *China has grown in economic power, and thus now has both an interest in changing the East Asian order, and a enhanced base with which to create military power and to use it to bring about such changes in East Asia.*[21]

   Although it is correct that China has greater relative national economic capabilities today than ten or fifteen years ago, this is also true of Germany in Europe and Japan in East Asia. Yet Germany is not seeking to convert its economic strengths into military capabilities; Japan has not started to do so to the same degree as China; and neither Germany nor Japan is seeking to bring about major changes in the status quo of their respective regions. Thus, a major change in relative economic capabilities within a region or the international system as a whole may be a necessary condition for the emergence of a "challenger state" and efforts by it to use force to change the status quo, but such a change is not itself sufficient.[22]

2. *The best path to security for a state is to maximize its national military power and its control over external sources of important resources.*[23]

For this reason China, newly empowered with a growing economy, is acting like a normal, security- and power-maximizing state. This is a useful argument. However, it has a problem in terms of its applicability to the other cases. The German case since the end of the Cold War presents us with an instance of a state that has experienced an increase in overall power but has avoided efforts to increase its political-military power or territorial control. Japan represents a more difficult case: For several decades after World War II it declined to convert its growing economic capabilities into a commensurate level of military power, but in recent years it has enhanced its political-military capabilities quite substantially. At the same time, Japan has not given evidence in recent years that it wishes to overturn any aspects of the Asian regional order, especially in territorial matters.

3. *China is acting more assertively because of fear of a resurgent Russia and the possibility of tensions on its borders with that country.*

Russia during the mid-to-late 1990s has been preoccupied by failed attempts at economic reform at home, the utter collapse of its power position in Europe (symbolized by the expansion of the North Atlantic Treaty Organization to Poland, Hungary, and the Czech Republic), and arguments with the former Soviet republics about the disposition of assets and other matters related to the dissolution of the former USSR.[24] However, China may be concerned that Russia might, as was true of the USSR from the 1960s until well into the 1980s, become an adversary at some point in the future, and therefore is enhancing its capabilities and political status in the world in order to meet that potential challenge. The problem with this argument is that another country that might clearly be fearful of Russia—Germany—has not responded with increases in military power or greater assertiveness in world affairs. Moreover, China has not acted since the end of the Cold War in ways that have brought it into conflict with Russia (and indeed it has sought to improve relations with that country), but instead it has come into more frequent disagreement and conflict with the (more distant) United States.

4. *China has a cartelized political regime, and these regimes are highly likely to become more bellicose militarily as they attain greater economic power and face increasing domestic demands for domestic political reform.*[25]

This is a strong proposition, and it is buttressed by the contrast between China and Germany since 1989. However, rising autocratic states are not unconditionally aggressive. After its success against France in 1870, Germany under Bismarck was an example of a country with a very fast-growing economy and a very conservative foreign policy. In addition, as is moderately suggested by recent changes in Japanese national policy, modern democracies may also shift away (at least slightly) from a trading-state orientation and toward a territorial, military-power-conscious orientation.

Accounting for the Cases:
Possible Paths for Going Forward

Clearly a focus on domestic political variables is needed to account for the apparent return by China to a territorialist as opposed to a trading-state foreign policy, and its greater emphasis on such a national strategy as compared to Japan or Germany. In this regard China's recent behavior might be examined and explained in part by reference to the recent work of such scholars as Jack Snyder and Charles Kupchan. However, to the extent that recent Japanese national strategy can be differentiated from German national strategy in the sense that Japan has increased its military power in recent years while Germany has gone in the opposite direction, then space will be opened up to go beyond a purely domestic argument about the sources of change in strategy of those two countries as well as China. In particular, if the description provided above is correct—that both China and even to some degree Japan (the latter in terms of enhancing its military power) are shifting their orientation away from a trading-state strategy and toward a more traditional territorial approach to its neighbors, while Germany is becoming even more of a trading state—then the question arises as to whether there are fundamentally different regional-level (as opposed to either domestic or global) forces at work today in Asia and in Europe that are contributing to this differentiation in behavior. These forces in East Asia may be pushing not just China to move toward a return to territorial-state behavior, but may even be causing the seemingly hard case of Japan to make some movement in that direction, whereas an absence of such forces may be leading to a different experience for Germany in post-Cold War Europe.[26]

At least two regional-level factors may be bringing about the differentiation in strategy between China and Japan on the one hand, and Germany on the other: greater instability in Asia in relative economic capabilities, and a lower level of trust between nations.

Regional-level turbulence in relative capabilities. Even with the reunification of Germany, changes in overall relative economic capabilities among the main Western European countries have not changed dramatically since 1990; in contrast, there is a great deal of turbulence in relative capabilities in East Asia.[27] Compared to China, and by consequence Japan (if

the latter is basically increasing its capabilities to offset the growing challenges from the former), Germany and its neighbors may be having less
difficulty in calculating the winners and losers, and the more influential
and less influential states, in post-Cold War Europe.

Social capital as a legacy of the Cold War. This line of analysis would involve following up on Miles Kahler's argument that the countries of
Western Europe enjoy greater institutional density and, relatedly, more
favorable endowments of transnational "social capital" than is true of
East Asia. It is especially the difference in regional social capital—or mutual trust—that might help explain why China believes it must act in the
near term to translate its economic growth into a more favorable territo-
rial-diplomatic regional position, which in turn may be provoking Japan
to enhance its own military capabilities. But why did the two regions develop such different levels of social capital? At least one possible argument would be that the difference in social capital reflects the manner in
which the Cold War was conducted in the two regions.[28] That is, the
geopolitical realities of the Cold War in Europe required the Western
states to permit German rearmament, but to offset the risks of German
unilateralism the return of German power took place *early* under the auspices of European and Atlantic institutions.

The Cold War, in a word, required Franco-German reconciliation and
the development of trust between those two countries, and this set the
stage and even served as the motor for a wider institutionalization of
state relationships in Western Europe. In East Asia the Soviet and Chinese threat was met by an American network of bilateral defense treaties.
By consequence, the countries in the region that received American protection did not have a need to reconcile with Japan. Moreover, when
China joined the American-led coalition of Pacific Rim states against the
USSR in the 1970s, its joining was based on an informal entente with the
United States and not a formal regional arrangement involving other regional states. Thus, while the Cold War induced cooperation and reconciliation in Western Europe, and set the stage for the formation of institutions and social capital able to withstand the shocks of 1989–1990, it left
Asia without either a habit of institutionalized cooperation or a reservoir
of mutual trust able to contain or channel growing Chinese power.

Conclusion

The modest improvement in U.S.-Chinese relations during 1997 and
1998, including an exchange of state visits between President Bill Clinton
and President Jiang Zemin, the quieting of Chinese–Taiwanese relations,
the smooth takeover of Hong Kong by the mainland, and China's for-
bearance in the midst of the financial crises of 1997–1998 might yield the

conclusion that fears expressed earlier in the decade about China were misplaced or overdrawn. Yet, at least two of China's core concerns were not yet resolved by the end of the 1990s: Taiwan was still a separate entity that showed signs of a desire for independence, and ownership of the Spratly Islands was still an open matter. These two political problems are likely to engender regional tensions in the years ahead; one or another might even be the basis for a full-fledged political-military crisis involving China and the United States. While economic turbulence in Asia during the last years of the 1990s might raise questions about China's growth trajectory, it remains likely that China will continue to become an economic powerhouse during the next twenty years. Thus, there is a good chance that we will continue to be faced with the combination of growing Chinese capabilities and growing Chinese ambition in regard to Taiwan and the Spratlys.

So we are left with several questions. What will China do with its growing power? What does it want from the international system? What can the United States and its main allies do to smooth the way for China as it grows into its new status in world politics? Should the United States facilitate or impede the growth of China and the enhancement of its power? These will be the troubling questions that we will need to address in the years ahead, in part as a consequence of the peace and victory achieved by America in 1989.

Notes

1. I thank John Mueller for his very helpful comments on an earlier draft of this paper, and Giacomo Chiozza for his excellent research assistance for this project.

2. On this point see Jing-dong Yuan, "Threat Perception and Chinese Security Policy After the Cold War," *Pacific Focus* 13 (Spring 1998): 62.

3. See World Bank, *The World Bank Atlas: 1996* (Washington, 1996): 18–19.

4. See Richard Halloran, "The Rising East," *Foreign Policy*, No. 102 (Spring 1996): 11. Joseph Nye correctly points out that it is important to be cautious in making straight-line projections about China's future economic status, but even with such caution there are strong grounds to believe that China will be a major economic center over the next twenty years: See Nye, "China's Re-emergence and the Future of the Asia-Pacific," *Survival* 39 (Winter 1997–1998): 66–68. For analyses of China's economic challenges regarding both domestic economic restructuring (in particular, in dismantling what is still a very large and inefficient state-owned industrial sector) and external financial linkages, see Neil C. Hughes, "Smashing the Iron Rice Bowl," *Foreign Affairs* 77 (July/August 1998): 67–77; and Nicholas R. Lardy, "China and the Asian Contagion," *Foreign Affairs* 77 (July/August 1998): 78–88.

5. See International Monetary Fund, *Direction of Trade Yearbook: 1996* (Washington, 1996): 3–5; and *Direction of Trade Statistics Quarterly* (Washington, June 1998):

2. On China's dramatic trade success during the past decade, also see "China: A Funny-Looking Tiger," *Economist*, August 17, 1996, p. 18.

6. It should be noted that the bilateral trade figures provided by both states to the International Monetary Fund for 1994, and presented in the latter's 1996 *Direction of Trade Yearbook*, cited above in note 5, differ dramatically as a result of the manner in which each country then treated trade that transited through Hong Kong: According to China, in 1994 it enjoyed a merchandise trade surplus with the United States in the amount of about $7.4 billion; according to the United States that figure was about $32.0 billion.

7. See James Shinn, "Engaging China: Exploiting the Fissures in the Facade," *Current History* (September 1996): 243. According to the 1995 World Bank annual report, the World Bank committed $13.937 billion in loans to China between 1990 and 1995; the next largest recipient was India, to which $11.851 billion was committed during the same period. See World Bank, *Annual Report: 1995* (Washington, 1995): 69, 75.

8. For a very helpful discussion of the concept of state revisionism in world politics, see Randall L. Schweller, *Deadly Imbalances: Tripolarity and Hitler's Strategy of World Conquest* (New York: Columbia University Press, 1998).

9. For helpful discussions of the Spratly Islands/South China Sea dispute, see Gerald Segal, "East Asia and the 'Constrainment' of China," *International Security* 20 (Spring 1996): especially 116–123, and Michael G. Gallagher, "China's Illusory Threat to the South China Sea," *International Security* 19 (Summer 1994): 169–184.

10. For a helpful overview of China's international military sales programs, see Robert S. Ross, "China," in Richard N. Haass, ed., *Economic Sanctions and American Diplomacy* (New York: Council on Foreign Relations, 1998), pp. 21–28. It should be noted that Ross argues that China became more cautious about making arms sales to Middle Eastern countries after 1988.

11. See Robert S. Ross, "Beijing as a Conservative Power," *Foreign Affairs* 76 (March-April 1997): 35–38; Nye, "China's Re-emergence," pp. 68–70; and especially Avery Goldstein, "Great Expectations: Interpreting China's Arrival," *International Security*, 22 (Winter 1997/98): 42–54.

12. See International Institute for Strategic Studies, *The Military Balance: 1995/96* (London, 1995), p. 271.

13. See Alastair Iain Johnston, "China's New 'Old Thinking': The Concept of Limited Deterrence," *International Security* 20 (Winter 1995/96): 5–42.

14. For further discussion of the possibility that China's policies may be highly destabilizing in East Asia (especially if and as they evoke a Japanese response involving a renationalization of its national security policy), see Aaron L. Friedberg, "Ripe for Rivalry: Prospects for Peace in a Multipolar Asia," *International Security* 18 (Winter 1993/94): 5–33; Richard K. Betts, "Wealth, Power, and Instability: East Asia and the United States After the Cold War," *International Security* 18 (Winter 1993/94): 34–77; and Barry Buzan and Gerald Segal, "Rethinking East Asian Security," *Survival* 36 (Summer 1994): 3–21. For a critical assessment of this line of analysis, see David Kang, "The Middle Road: Security and Cooperation," *Asian Perspective* 19 (Fall-Winter 1995): 9–28.

15. See Richard Rosecrance, *The Rise of the Trading State: Commerce and Conquest in the Modern World* (New York: Basic Books, 1986).

16. Robert Ross, a close observer of China who finds that it is generally pursuing a conservative, cautious national strategy, notes that the exception to China's overall caution is its assertive policy regarding the Spratly Islands; see Ross, "Beijing as a Conservative Power," pp. 41–42.

17. That China is becoming disenchanted with the international status quo in spite of gaining from it would appear to be in accord with the power-transition thesis. On its argument that rising powers come to find the existing international order unacceptable, and are willing to use force to change it, see, for example, A.F.K. Organski and Jacek Kugler, *The War Ledger* (Chicago: University of Chicago Press, 1980), especially p. 23; and Robert Gilpin, *War and Change in World Politics* (Cambridge: Cambridge University Press, 1981), pp. 93, 186–210.

18. This question is prompted by Michael Gordon's discussion of Germany and Great Britain at the turn of the century: In terms of projected power trajectories Germany (clearly becoming Europe's economic hegemon) should have been confident and patient, whereas Britain (clearly a relatively declining power) should have been easily provoked and yet was rather reticent to respond to German pressure. See Michael R. Gordon, "Domestic Conflict and the Origins of the First World War: The British and German Cases," *Journal of Modern History* 46 (June 1974): 191–226. It is also informed by Jack Levy's discussion of the argument by A.F.K. Organski and Jacek Kugler that rising challenger-states will display a tendency to use military force to topple the then-hegemon and thereby bring about what for the rising state is a more favorable international order. Levy asks about this posited tendency: "Why should the challenger incur the risks of fighting while it is still inferior? Why doesn't it wait until existing trends in economic and military power, which Organski and Kugler consider to be irreversible, catapult it into the stronger position?" See Jack S. Levy, "Declining Power and the Preventative Motivation for War," *World Politics* 40 (October 1987): 84.

19. IISS, *Military Balance 1995/96*, p. 264.

20. IISS, *Military Balance 1995/96*, p. 264; also see p. 172, at which the IISS reports that this shift between Japan and the three European middle powers occurred in 1993, and that it was reinforced by 1995 projected defense spending by the major powers, and that "With the possible exception of Russia, Japan now spends appreciably more on defence on any other country apart from the US."

21. This is a line of analysis that might follow the work by Gilpin, *War and Change*, and by Organski and Kugler, *War Ledger*.

22. This conclusion is noted by Organski and Kugler, *War Ledger*, p. 51.

23. This view is put forward most effectively by John Mearsheimer, in "The False Promise of International Institutions," *International Security* 19 (Winter 1994/95): 11; also see Fareed Zakaria, "Realism and Domestic Politics: A Review Essay," *International Security* 17 (Summer 1992): 190–196.

24. For overviews of Russia's truncated status in world politics, and its interactions with former Soviet republics, see Michael McFaul, "A Precarious Peace: Domestic Politics in the Making of Russian Foreign Policy," *International Security* 22 (Winter 1997/98): 5–35; and Daniel Drezner, "Allies, Adversaries, and Economic Coercion: Russian Foreign Economic Policy Since 1991," *Security Studies* 6 (Spring 1997): 65–111.

25. The argument linking domestic authoritarianism, and specifically political cartelization, to external state aggression is pursued by Jack Snyder in *Myths of Empire: Domestic Politics and International Ambition* (Ithaca: Cornell University Press, 1991). In addition, see Charles A. Kupchan, *The Vulnerability of Empire* (Ithaca: Cornell University Press, 1994).

26. Such a possible movement by Japan toward traditional national strategy concerns and behavior is especially interesting insofar as recent literature would probably consider that country to be a highly unlikely candidate for such traditional statecraft. For compelling arguments that Japan has moved decisively away from traditional foreign policy goals and means, see Rosecrance, *Rise of the Trading State*; in addition, and for arguments that put special weight on Japan's contemporary culture and internal political structures as constraints on such a return to traditionalism in foreign affairs, see Thomas Berger, "From Sword to Chrysanthemum: Japan's Culture of Anti-Militarism," *International Security* 17 (Spring 1993): 119–150; and Peter J. Katzenstein and Nobuo Okawara, "Japan's National Security: Structures, Norms, and Policies," *International Security* 17 (Spring 1993): 84–118. For analyses which suggest that Japan's foreign policy is more likely to be a function of external constraints and threats than internal domestic political and cultural conditions, see Barry Buzan, "Japan's Defence Problematique," *The Pacific Review* 8 (1995): 25–43; and Michael Green and Benjamin Self, "Japan's Changing China Policy: From Commercial Liberalism to Reluctant Realism, *Survival* 38 (Summer 1996): 35–58.

27. I pursue this argument in "Systemic Sources of Variation in Regional Institutionalization in Western Europe, East Asia, and the Americas," in Helen Milner and Edward Mansfield, eds., *The Political Economy of Regionalism* (New York: Columbia University Press, 1997), pp. 164–187.

28. For this line of analysis, see Joseph M. Grieco, "Realism and Regionalism: American Power and German and Japanese Institutional Strategies During and After the Cold War," in Ethan Kapstein and Michael Mastanduno, eds., *Unipolar Politics: Realism and State Strategies After the Cold War* (New York: Columbia University Press, 1999).

9

Human Capital in
the Twenty-First Century

RONALD L. ROGOWSKI

That a professor emphasizes the importance of human capital will, I suppose, surprise no one. Yet when the organizers of this volume asked the contributors to speculate on "an innovation or discovery of the twentieth century that will have greatest impact in the twenty-first," and when, recalling the occasion that unites these essays, I narrowed that search to innovations or discoveries that resonate particularly with Richard Rosecrance's work, I felt compelled to give pride of place to Gary Becker's invention, or re-invention, of the concept of human capital, and to our growing realization of how central human capital is to economic and political development.

In the spirit of some of Rosecrance's own best work, I will gladly label everything I have to say on this topic "speculative." In a phrase that our late UCLA colleague Richard Ashcraft often used, I hope to "unsettle" questions rather than to "settle" them; to explore some new and strange terrain rather tentatively. I may well have missed important strains of literature, be ignorant of important facts and findings. I will welcome collegial correction and criticism.

The concept of human capital is not difficult to grasp: Humans, like computers, can be "programmed" to do certain tasks. What in computers we call "software" in humans we call "skills." Humans however download more slowly—some students, we will all ruefully acknowledge, must be rebooted several times before installation is even moderately satisfactory—and must curtail productive activities to acquire the skills they need. However, a person who acquires new skills becomes more productive: The same hours of labor yield more output.

In this sense human capital, like physical capital, is a factor of production, an argument in such familiar production functions as the Cobb-Douglass or the constant elasticity of substitution; in some of the "new" growth theory human capital is in fact treated as a factor of production (Barro and Sala-i-Martin 1995, esp. chap. 5). In other, and I think more important, senses, human capital is a factor quite unlike other factors of production. I will focus here on six differences:

- COMPLEMENTARITY. Human capital complements, rather than substitutes for, physical capital. Countries with a lot of labor or land ordinarily employ less physical capital: They rely on more labor- or land-intensive production. Countries abundantly endowed with human capital, as we shall see, employ more physical capital. This connection between the presence of human capital and the use of physical capital is what makes human capital the sine qua non of economic growth.
- PORTABILITY. Land cannot be moved at all, most physical capital only with great difficulty. Of all possible investments, human capital—which one literally carries around in one's head and hands—is the most portable. This fact has both economic and political implications, for example, with respect to migration.
- INCREASING MARGINAL RETURNS. Economics 101 states it as axiomatic that the first plow a farmer buys increases her production more than the second, the second more than the third. Similarly a billion dollars of new physical capital will produce a much bigger increase of productivity in a very poor country (with little physical capital) than in a very rich one (with a lot). The reverse seems to be true of human capital: Later years of education have a higher return than earlier ones, and the same educational input yields more in an educated society than in an unschooled one. Indeed a plausible estimate (as, again, we'll see) is that each year of additional education in a society actually multiplies its productivity at a constant rate (just under 1.5), so that in absolute terms two years of high school adds a lot more than two years of primary school.[1]
- ATTENUATED EFFECT OF OTHER ENDOWMENTS. Human capital permits and encourages human innovations, some of which defy our traditional view of factor endowments. Germany in World War I lacked nitrates, crucial to her land-scarce agriculture; but her scientists quickly synthesized them, literally out of thin air. Any prediction that land-scarce India would ever be

self-sufficient in cereals seemed risible, yet Norman Borlaug's "Green Revolution" yielded exactly this result (Easterbrook 1997).

- AGGLOMERATION. Human capital is most productive when surrounded by other human capital. The isolated genius is the rare exception, Silicon Valley or Route 128 is the rule (see more generally Krugman 1991).
- ENVIRONMENTAL IMPROVEMENT, DAMPING OF POPULATION GROWTH. More generally, human capital substitutes for the factors of land and labor. Agricultural innovations, by making existing acreage more productive, retard and reverse environmental despoliation;[2] and parents' propensity to invest in the education of a few children leads them to produce fewer offspring (Easterbrook 1997, 77–78).

These points, and particularly the claim about increasing marginal returns, will be controversial enough; but I shall compound my sin by venturing even shakier conjectures about the implications for international politics. The first section lays out the essentially economic story I have just outlined. The second considers some first-order social and political effects. The third addresses some major policy issues that will likely arise. And the fourth offers some conclusions.

The Peculiarities of Human Capital

Begin by looking at the relationship between human capital per worker and physical capital per worker at the level of the nation-state (see Figure 9.1) Here we proxy human capital (very imperfectly) as mean years of education in the population aged twenty-five or more years, as reported in the UN *Human Development Report*; and we proxy physical capital by flow rather than stock, that is, new investment in physical capital, per person, as reported by the World Bank.[3,4] The data points are the ninety-seven countries for which such information was available in 1991.

Immediately apparent is the strong positive association between human and physical capital, which turns out to be linear in the logarithm of investment (see Figure 9.2). Roughly, the estimated regression equation tells us that each additional year of education in a country's adult population adds 50 percent to annual investment in physical capital:[5] A country with twelve years' average education in its populace will have 120 times (1.49^{12}) the investment of one whose subjects are totally uneducated. And this formulation probably states correctly the direction of causation: As pathbreaking research on economic growth by Robert Barro and Xavier Sala-i-Martin has consistently shown, level of human capital appears to be one of the best predictors of subsequent physical in-

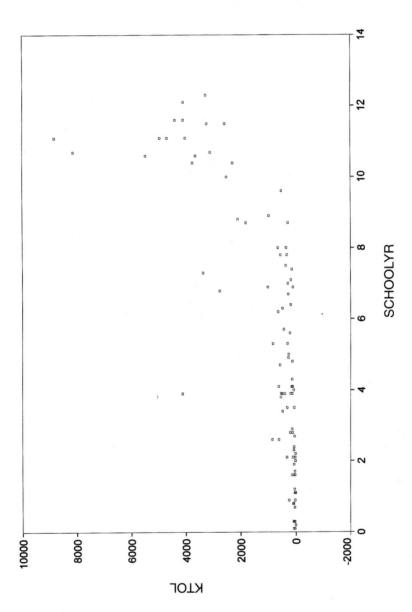

FIGURE 9.1   Investment vs. Human Capital Per Person: 97 Countries, 1991

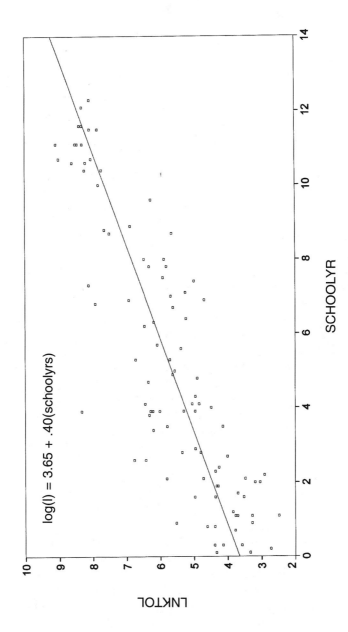

FIGURE 9.2   Log of Investment *vs.* Human Capital Per Person: 97 Countries, 1991

vestment, and hence of economic growth or decline (Barro 1991; Barro and Sala-i-Martin, 1992 and 1995). More anecdotally, the extremely rapid growth of Japan and the Asian tigers had its origins in educational investment; the pathetic decline of many postindependence African states in the corruption and violence that interrupted education.

Now the relation depicted in Figures 9.1 and 9.2 is a rather peculiar one between two nominally independent factors of production. If we plotted instead labor/land and capital/land, we would expect to see a lot more "scatter" and an overall negative relationship: Japan for example has a lot of labor and a lot of capital, Bangladesh a lot of labor and little capital; Australia has little labor (i.e., a low labor/land ratio) and much capital, Argentina little labor and much less capital. On the whole, however, labor-scarce countries will face high wage rates and be likelier to substitute capital for labor; labor-abundant countries will be under no such constraint.

The pattern of Figures 9.1 and 9.2 suggests that human and physical capital are complements rather than substitutes in production: the more you have of one, the more (not the less) you want of the other; and a lot of one is useless without a lot of the other.[6] An educated populace, then, tends to attract physical capital; and the two together guarantee economic growth. Again, however, the effect is exponential. Figure 9.3 illustrates that years of education relate linearly to the *logarithm* of per capita gross domestic product (GDP): each additional year of education raises social product per head by about 48 per cent, so that a nation that averages twelve years of education will have 108 times (1.48^{12}) the per capita product of one with no education at all. Except perhaps among extremely educated populations, human capital is characterized by increasing marginal returns.

One explanation is doubtless the one widely used by adherents of the "new" growth theory, namely the *positive social externalities* of human capital. A worker's skills benefit not only herself but fellow workers, indeed the society at large: Even if I remain an ignorant toad, the kiss of Minerva that transforms you into a prince showers me with diamonds.[7]

This point is closely related to the ones about agglomeration and portability. Workers with particular skills (say, in software design or automobile or musical-instrument manufacturing) find their marginal product (and hence, normally, their wage) to be less when they are dispersed, much higher where they are geographically concentrated. Hence they are strongly drawn to major centers of such activity, and the total portability of their human capital eases their migration.[8] Of all established factors of production, the stock of human capital is likely to be the most "footloose."[9]

To reiterate: Human capital is a peculiar factor of production. Given its growth and productive importance, it is crucial that we understand at least the first-order social and political consequences of these peculiarities.

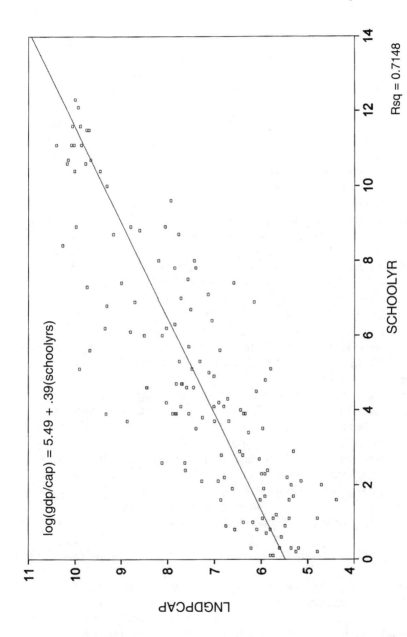

FIGURE 9.3   Log of GDP Per Capita vs. Human Capital Per Person, 1991

First-Order Effects of the Peculiarities

I confine the discussion here to five areas in which human capital's peculiarities have significant implications: inequality of nations and regions; migration and "brain drain"; social underinvestment and political failure; democratization; and wars and warfare.

Inequality

If human capital indeed has increasing marginal productivity, then existing inequalities between nations and regions will tend to persist or grow. Merely by investing the same share of output in new human-capital formation, an already highly educated society can increase production more than one less skilled; and of course the fact that returns to investment are less in the latter society means that actually less will be invested.

In turn, the strong complementarity of human and physical capital that we have already observed means that the skill-poor economies will also attract less investment in new plant and machinery. Absent significant imports of technology from more developed countries, the less developed will suffer in addition from greater environmental degradation; and their low returns to human capital will mean continued high rates of population growth.

The overall result seems clear: Instead of the "convergence" of economies that neoclassical growth theory predicts (Barro and Sala-i-Martin, 1995, esp. chaps. 1 and 2), the natural working of markets will lead to divergence: an increasing gap between developed and less developed economies.[10] Political interventions can forestall such divergence, but they may prove fiendishly difficult to engineer. I discuss these policy issues in a later section.

Divergence can only be augmented by the attenuation of factor-endowment effects noted earlier. Advanced societies, rich in human capital and innovative capacity, can readily find substitutes for most of the land-, labor-, and resource-intensive products of less developed economies.[11] As substitution becomes an ever cheaper alternative, the terms of trade of less developed economies worsen.

"Brain drain" and other migration[12]

Divergence plus agglomeration implies migration. Able people in backward regions will know that skills are highly rewarded in world centers of activity, will acquire skills, and will move: Indian engineers, Nigerian financial wizards, Chinese statisticians, Russian computer experts[13] will flock to places like Los Angeles, Palo Alto, Route 128, London. As the most talented individuals leave, and as their presumptively more talented offspring benefit other regions' gene-pools, the backward areas become yet more backward: Divergence is exacerbated. The complementarity of physical capital and increasingly fluid financial markets—a change that Rosecrance has rightly stressed—imply that new investment will also flow disproportionately to the advanced economies.

Insightful urban historians and sociologists have noted that precisely these highly remunerated possessors of human capital, facing high opportunity costs on their time, generate swelling demand for the labor-intensive services that are not easily automated: cleaning, cooking, childcare, gardening. Because such services are, almost by definition, nontraded, the result is growing migration also of *low-skill* third-world labor to agglomerations of "intelligence-intensive" activity and the rise of what these scholars—foremost among them UCLA's John Friedmann (Friedmann 1986, 1995, more generally Knox and Taylor 1995)—have labeled "world cities." World cities, in this view, are characterized by widening class divisions and intense ethnic conflicts: A cosmopolitan, extremely prosperous elite lives cheek-by-jowl with ethnically specific enclaves of hardscrabble third-world service workers. Perhaps the least controversial observation of this school is that Los Angeles is not unique: London, Paris, Frankfurt, Hong Kong, even Mexico City display quite similar divisions.

Social underinvestment

That human capital has significant positive externalities means (as even most conservative theorists have recognized) that a purely private market will entail significant underinvestment: An individual will acquire skills only up to the point that the marginal return *to her* equals her marginal cost, and this point will be significantly below the one at which marginal social return equals marginal cost. Hence governmental subsidization can improve welfare; but where government is weak or corrupt, market failure will go unremedied. In short the peculiarity of human capital implies a high welfare cost to political failure and great social benefit from good governance.

Democratization

Empirically, the cross-national association between human capital and democracy is very strong, and considerably stronger than that between wealth and democracy (see Fig. 9.4 cf. Londregan and Poole 1996).[14] The likely reason, as I argue elsewhere (Rogowski 1997), is that the portability of human capital gives subjects well endowed with such capital a

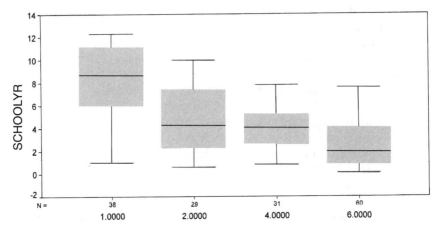

FIGURE 9.4   Mean Years of Education by Gastil Ranking of Democracy: 158
Countries, 1991

more credible threat to emigrate (cf. Bates and Lien 1985). But the economic divergence emphasized above then implies a political divergence:
a First World of democracies, a Third World of nondemocracies.[15] And if,
as some have argued, democracies are likelier to subsidize education, the
political divergence re-intensifies the economic one.

Wars and warfare

If we take as facts the frequent observations that democracies do not fight
each other[16] and that they win most fights with nondemocracies (Lake
1992), we must also envision a pacific First and a bellicose Third World.
Countries rich in human capital will rarely fight each other, countries
poor in it will do so frequently; and the rare (and seemingly irrational)
fights between rich and poor will only devastate the latter. From the
standpoint of the twenty-first century, both the Iran-Iraq conflict and the
Gulf War will have been depressingly accurate auguries.

I re-emphasize that these are but *first-order* effects. They can be countered by other influences, including sensible policy. What that policy
might be, however, is far from clear. It is to this topic that I next turn.

Policy Issues

The good news about human capital seems almost to be outweighed by
the bad. Policy interventions have been proposed, and others may readily
be envisioned, that supposedly would counteract the bad effects while re-
taining most of the good. Again I shall consider only the most obvious.[17]

Third-world education

The seemingly "no-brainer" remedy for almost all of these ill effects is massive subsidization of third-world education—the avenue, as noted earlier, by which supposedly first Japan, later the Asian tigers, and now some regions of India and China have escaped their natural calling as exporters of labor-intensive manufactures and have risen (or are rising) so rapidly into the ranks of the developed countries. Surely the third-world governments themselves, and even enlightened first-world states, should be pouring money into third-world schools.

Yet if a marginal dollar of human-capital investment generates far higher returns in the first world than in the third, it cannot be in the interest of first-world governments to divert money from domestic (high-return) to foreign (low-return) education.[18] Indeed, any such transfer diminishes world welfare and (depending on one's distributional assumptions) may actually make the third-world "beneficiaries" worse off.

But won't third-world rulers find it in their (enlightened) self-interest to educate their subjects? Not necessarily, for three reasons: (1) Given the increasing marginal return to human capital, the most skill-deprived societies will have the least incentive to curtail current consumption and invest in education.[19] (2) The poorest societies are likely to be the most politically unsettled, and rulers' resultant high discount rates—the knowledge that their hold on power will be fleeting—makes the inevitably long-term payoff from education even less attractive. (Indeed, it can rarely hold a candle to the more traditional Swiss bank account.) (3) Even where (1) and (2) hold with less force, rulers must consider the likelihood of "brain drain": that is, the likelihood that much of the human capital they subsidize will simply migrate (together with its possessors) to more highly educated societies and (except in the form of remittances) be lost to their countries of origin.

The implication seems clear: Education, and particularly high-end research apprenticeships, will concentrate even more in the first world. Able third-world students will have to trek to the first to be trained. In doing so, of course, they will acquire the languages that make their subsequent emigration to the metropole all the easier.

Emigration tax

Exactly these considerations have led some astute third-world rulers, and indeed a few world-class economists (most notably Jagdish Bhagwati: see particularly Bhagwati and Partington 1976), to take seriously a policy option that one might have thought perished with the Soviet Union, namely an emigration, or more specifically a "brain drain," tax. In its strongest variants (*not* embraced by Bhagwati), this approach would mean either imposing a lump-sum emigration tax or requiring students to work off at home any educational subsidy received (see description and analysis in Miyagiwa 1991, 757–758). Thus if the Taiwanese state had subsidized my undergraduate and Ph.D. training to the tune of $100,000, I might have to pay back the full amount if I emigrated immediately; $90,000 if I emigrated after one year; $80,000 if I waited two; and so on. In the Bhagwati version a (higher) income tax is imposed on those who work and earn abroad.[20]

Again the instrument is blunt and raises equally blunt objections. Most obviously, any such measure diminishes subjects' incentives to amass human capital in the first place: Knowing that education will earn me less, I acquire less of it. By that long-term route, and in the short run as well, such a tax diminishes world welfare: The third-world engineer can earn more in Boston than in Botswana because she is more productive in Boston; keeping her in Botswana makes her, by definition, less productive; and most tax schemes assure only that the most mediocre engineers will remain in Botswana—the best will still emigrate (Miyagiwa 1991, 750–751). Add that the tax will mean fewer future Botswanan engineers, and the damage is compounded. In the extreme case, such a tax may even make the home government worse off, if, for example, the difference between home and foreign salaries is so extreme that local earnings would be less than foreign remittances.

Multinationals and the "big push"

As students of the "new" growth theory have long argued, the only possible answer is a massive, rapid, and credible growth of the overall productive structure—including, in particular, the knowledge base—of the less-developed economy (see, e.g., Murphy, Shleifer, and Vishny 1989). Such an effort may require broad state intervention (cf. Wade 1990), heavy involvement of multinationals (whose cross-national ties partially substitute for geographical agglomeration), or both. The task is daunting in the best of circumstances; in the poorest third-world countries, typically extremely knowledge-scarce and politically corrupt, it is probably impossible.

Technological exports and assistance

Again the Green Revolution, hatched by American agronomists working in a Mexican research center and backed by Rockefeller Foundation funds and the political clout of first-world fertilizer firms (which rightly foresaw huge new markets for their product), demonstrates the large impact that even modest exports, or gifts, of first-world technology can produce.[21] A plausible scenario has human capital concentrating increasingly in the first world but finding fertile soil for its technological innovations in poorer countries.

Plausible but, I think, not likely. The whole internal history of today's rich countries is one of growing regional imbalance: Appalachia, the Italian *mezzogiorno*, the North of England, increasingly the U.S. Great Plains, all have neither formed their own agglomerations of talent nor prospered by importing the technology that others produce; rather, they have simply "emptied out," becoming deserts whose few oases are sustained only by governmental transfers. The likelier international scenario is a replication of what most third-world countries have already experienced internally, namely massive migration into urban agglomerations or "edge-city" agglomerations. This is a future of mobile factors that is worthy of Rosecrance's analysis.

But again the Green Revolution suggests how enlightened first-world governments and foundations, fearing something like the nineteenth-century Irish famine (and emigration) on a world scale, may simply give away the needed technologies, or indeed may provide larger-scale subsidies.

The dilemma of first-world education

As the stock of human capital increases in rich countries, so (apparently) does its marginal productivity and so (presumably), its positive externalities. To maximize social return, subsidies to education must rise; but subsidies to what kind of education, and in what form? Governments are notoriously bad at anticipating the market and at delivering services efficiently, and stories of utterly misguided educational outlays abound. In the nineteenth century, while German universities were pioneering organic chemistry, optics, and electrical engineering, Oxford and Cambridge sneered at all but classical and theological pursuits (Landes 1969); present-day U.S. schools notoriously emphasize "self-esteem" to the neglect of science and mathematics and seem better at multiplying administrators than at educating pupils.

Subsidies are required, but how can governments best guarantee that they will generate the human capital their economies actually require? Although it will hardly please professors to admit it, traditional direct state supply of education (for example, through the public school or university) provides about the worst possible incentives to "market-conforming" provision of human capital. Far better, though still imperfect, are "voucher"-type partial subsidization of the student and subsidization of student loans. Clearly many first-world governments are moving in this direction.

Conclusion

In a rare scholarly consensus, human capital has emerged in the last decades of the twentieth century as the magic key to economic and political development. At the same time, peculiar characteristics of human capital as a factor of production—increasing marginal productivity, agglomeration effects, strong complementarity with physical capital—suggest a twenty-first century of divergent growth and increasing inequality between and within nations.

So what, if anything, is to be done? Two initially unpopular prescriptions appear to offer the most promising results, namely that first-world states should lower remaining barriers to trade and migration and increase market-conforming subsidies to education, including scholarships and loans to promising third-world students and (under particular circumstances) subsidies directly to third-world education.

To take the first suggestion first, trade in goods, as we know, substitutes mutually for trade in factors; and blocking the import of labor-intensive goods (e.g., sugar) into developed countries is a sure of way of increasing immigration of unskilled labor. Those who purport to be troubled by such immigration should particularly press for freer trade. With barriers to trade dismantled, people will migrate only because their marginal product in the new country is genuinely higher than in the old; and then, by definition, their migration improves world welfare (and that of the country of destination, usually a developed one).

As for the second suggestion, educational subsidies compensate for the growing positive externalities of first-world education and thus help to bring the total supply of human capital closer to the social optimum. But policies that restrict such subsidies to one's own citizens are foolish. Able youth from any part of the world will gain from a first-world education (at least at the graduate level) and, given a higher marginal product due to agglomeration effects, will in all likelihood remain there. There is even a case for first-world subsidies to third world education—*if* the third-world government commits irrevocably not to restrict subsequent emigration and indeed undertakes to ease it, for example by providing universal instruction in English.

Perhaps the strongest arguments against alternative policies come from experience with regional inequalities within states (the North-South divides in Italy and England, the East-West one in Germany, increasingly the efforts of the European Union to assist declining regions throughout its jurisdiction). Efforts at "structural adjustment" or inter-regional subsidies seem only to have worsened the problem; barriers to trade or migration (which Germany actually experienced so long as it remained two states) inflict yet greater damage. Only the dismantling of barriers and the provision of good public services—above all, good education—in all regions has effected solid results.

Better policies may surely emerge. But the beginning of any wisdom is to understand the significance of human capital as a factor of production and the special characteristics of that factor.

Notes

1. I hasten to point out to graduate students that this process has to stop somewhere. More seriously, the curve flattens out after about the eleventh year.

2. In 1950, the world produced 692 million tons of grain on 1.7 billion acres of cropland; in 1992, 1.9 billion tons on 1.73 billion acres: That is, per-acre yield grew by a factor of 2.75. One plausible estimate is that, had the productivity gains of the Green Revolution not occurred, India alone would have had to plow an additional 100 million acres, an area roughly equivalent to that of California. Easterbrook 1997, 78.

3. I commit this heresy for the good reason that much better data, for far more countries, are available about investment than about the stock of capital. Whereas economic theory would lead us to expect that new investment would correlate negatively with existing capital, in practice the converse appears to hold (cf. Barro 1991). For fifty-four of the ninety-seven countries examined here, the Penn World Tables (on-line database, May 1996) offer estimates of capital stock per worker for at least one year in the period 1990–1992 at 1985 international prices. The correlation between those values and the ones for investment per capita used here is r=.93.

4. The numbers used here are actually products of two figures reported by the World Bank, namely gross domestic investment as a share of GDP and (dollar) GOP per capita. (World Bank 1992, Tables 1 and 9). The product approximates (dollar) investment per capita, since (investment/GDP)(GDP/population) = investment/population.

5. Delog both sides by raising to be a power of the natural number e, so that

$$e^{\log(\text{investment/cap})} = e^{3.65 \,+\, .40(\text{schoolyrs})} \rightarrow \text{investment/cap} =$$
$$e^{3.65} * e^{.40(\text{schoolyrs})} = 38.5 * (1.49)^{\text{schoolyears}}.$$

6. I think the economic jargon for this is a Leontieff technology.

7. This explanation of course implies that the private market will fail to provide adequate motivation for training and education: Individuals, guided only by market incentives, will substantially underinvest in human capital formation. That effect and the policy issues it raises are addressed below.

8. Migration, however, is never costless; barriers of culture, language, and politics (state barriers to migration) remain significant even for highly skilled workers.

9. New physical investment probably flows even more easily, but—as noted earlier—the *stock* of physical capital is far less mobile.

10. For endogenous-growth models that do not imply convergence, see Barro and Sala-i-Martin 1995, chap. 4.

11. Examples include synthetic yarns, rubbers, and fertilizers.

12. A convincing model of brain drain based on economies of scale in higher education is developed in Miyagiwa 1991.

13. Just to mention cases personally known to me in Los Angeles. Yes, I *know* that is merely anecdoctal.

14. The resource-rich but human-capital poor states, including particularly those of the Arab Gulf, pull down the association between wealth and democracy.

15. Other variables of course increase the odds of democracy, particularly in states of middling human capital (and, usually, middling wealth), for example, pressure by stability-seeking domestic elites and by other states in the region (particularly instructive is the Spanish experience: Londregan and Poole 1996, 24–25). To the extent that poorer countries become and remain democratic, the dire predictions about warfare in the next section are attenuated.

16. The pioneering statements were Doyle 1983 and 1986. The by now voluminous literature is surveyed in Lake 1992, 28, and Mansfield and Snyder 1995, n. 1.

17. One frequent prescription of the past, namely Soviet-style forced saving to accumulate physical capital, I shall pass over as a clear nonstarter—not only by reason of historical experience, but for a reason laid out above, namely that physical capital is unproductive without accompanying human capital. The skills are crucial, not the iron.

18. Unless, of course, the third-world government commits credibly not to restrict emigration of their ablest, thus in effect adding them to the first-world pool. More on this in the conclusion.

19. A secondary issue is whether low-skill countries gain greater marginal benefit from primary, or from higher, education. Unfortunately the national-level data from which I am working here allow no firm inferences on that point; but the general argument about economies of scale suggests that tiny islands of highly educated people, in seas of ignorance, will be highly unproductive.

20. For the original proposal, see Bhagwati and Dellalfar 1973; its reception and evolution are traced in Bhagwati 1976. As Miyagiwa (1991, 757–758) shows, the crucial effects of the various proposals are quite similar, except that the Bhagwati proposal, if it included highly progressive taxes on immigrants, would be more effective at keeping the most talented at home.

21. In the first year, yields in India rose by 70 per cent; in the second year, by 98 per cent. In 1965, Pakistan harvested 3.4 million tons of wheat, India 11 million; today's figures are 18 million tons for Pakistan, 60 million for India. Averaged over the intervening thirty years, that amounts to an increase of about 5.8 percent each year. Easterbrook 1997, 78.

References

Barro, Robert P. 1991. "Economic Growth in a Cross Section of Countries." *Quarterly Journal of Economics* 106: 407–443.

Barro, Robert J., and Xavier Sala-i-Martin. 1992. "Convergence." *Journal of Political Economy* 100: 223–251.

_____ 1995. *Economic Growth*. New York: McGraw-Hill, Inc.

Bates, Robert H., and Da-Hsiang Donald Lien. 1985. "A Note on Taxation, Development, and Representative Government." *Politics & Society* 14: 53–70.

Bhagwati, Jagdish N. 1976. "The Brain Drain Tax Proposal and the Issues." In Bhagwati and Partington 1976, chap. 1.

Bhagwati, Jagdish N., and William Dellalfar. 1973. "The Brain Drain and Income Taxation." *World Development*, 1: 94–101; reprinted with minor revisions as chap. 2 of Bhagwati and Partington 1976.

Bhagwati, Jagdish N., and Martin Partington, eds. 1976. *Taxing the Brain Drain.* Amsterdam: North Holland Publishing Co.; New York: Elsevier Publishing Co.

Doyle, Michael W. 1983. "Kant, Liberal Legacies, and Foreign Affairs." *Philosophy and Public Affairs* 12: 205–235 and 323–353.

———— 1986. "Liberalism and World Politics." *American Political Science Review* 80: 1151–1169.

Easterbrook, Gregg. 1997. "Forgotten Benefactor of Humanity." *The Atlantic Monthly* 279: 74–82.

Friedmann, John. 1986 [1995]. "The World City Hypothesis." *Development and Change*, 17: 69–84. Reprinted as Appendix to Knox and Taylor 1995.

———— 1995. "Where We Stand: A Decade of World City Research." In Knox and Taylor 1995, chap. 2.

Knox, Paul L., and Peter J. Taylor, eds. 1995. *World Cities in a World-System.* Cambridge: Cambridge University Press.

Krugman, Paul R. 1991. *Geography and Trade.* Cambridge, MA: MIT Press.

Lake, David A. 1992. "Powerful Pacifists: Democratic States and War." *American Political Science Review* 86: 24–37.

Landes, David S. 1969. *The Unbound Prometheus: Technological Change and the Industrial Revolution in Western Europe from 1750 to the Present.* London: Cambridge University Press.

Londregan, John B., and Keith T. Poole. 1996. "Does High Income Promote Democracy?" *World Politics* 49: 1–30.

Mansfield, Edward D., and Jack Snyder. 1995. "Democratization and the Dangers of War." *International Security* 20: 5–38.

McCubbins, Matthew, and Paul Drake, eds. 1997. *The Origins of Liberty.* Princeton, NJ: Princeton University Press.

Miyagiwa, Kaz. 1991. "Scale Economies in Education and the Brain Drain Problem." *International Economic Review*, 32: 743–759.

Murphy, Kevin M., Andrei Shleifer, and Robert Vishny. 1989. "Industrialization and the Big Push." *Journal of Political Economy* 97: 1003–1026.

Rogowski, Ronald. 1997. "Democracy, Capital, Skill, and Country Size." In McCubbins and Drake 1997.

Wade, Robert. 1990. *Governing the Market: Economic Theory and the Role of Government in East Asian Industrialization.* Princeton, NJ: Princeton University Press.

World Bank, 1992. *World Development Report 1992: Development and the Envrionment.* New York: Oxford University Press.

10

The Continuing Conundrum
of Internal Conflict

MICHAEL E. BROWN

There are good reasons for being optimistic about the prospects for peace in many corners of the world. The incidence of interstate war has plummeted in recent times. Since 1945, no great-power wars have taken place, and Western Europe, North America, and South America have experienced only one interstate war, over the Falkland Islands.[1] Moreover, with the end of the Cold War and the growing robustness of international economic ties, the future of international affairs—as many of the contributors to this volume would argue—appears to be comparatively bright.

I would argue that, although North America and Western Europe are unlikely to experience major interstate wars in the foreseeable future, we should be careful about making sweeping generalizations about the prospects for war and peace in the international system as a whole. Internal or intrastate conflicts are still widespread.[2] As of 1995, major armed conflicts—that is, conflicts in which at least 1,000 people have been killed—raged in over thirty-five locations around the world. In thirteen of these conflicts—in Afghanistan, Angola, Azerbaijan, Bosnia, Burundi, Cambodia, Indonesia, Iraq, Liberia, Rwanda, Somalia, Sudan, and Tajikistan—more than 50,000 people had been killed; in at least six—in Afghanistan, Angola, Cambodia, Iraq, Rwanda, and Sudan—over 500,000 people had been killed. My expectation is that this tragic state of affairs will continue: Horrifyingly violent internal conflicts will continue to be widespread.

I would argue, moreover, that internal conflicts should be thought of as important international phenomena. Internal conflicts almost always have regional dimensions—few are hermetically sealed—and they therefore pose threats to regional stability and security. Violent internal conflicts can trigger refugee flows, disrupt regional economic activities, and lead to military incursions in neighboring states. Neighboring states often meddle in the internal conflicts of others to distract and weaken regional rivals. Interstate wars can result. If regional security is an important international concern, then internal conflict should be as well.

Internal conflicts are also important because they undermine regional and international organizations, such as the United Nations (whose stated purpose is the promotion of peace and security); international norms of behavior and international law (with respect to human rights, for example); and international order in general. These costs are difficult to measure, but they are real and they are paid by every actor in the international system. Policymakers in Washington and other international capitals should not be allowed to claim—as they often try to do—that internal problems in far-off lands are of no consequence to distant powers and the international community in general. These problems are consequential.

In this chapter, I will discuss the causes of internal conflicts and then develop some guidelines for international responses to these problems. Although violent internal conflicts will, in all probability, be part of the international landscape for years and decades to come, they are not impervious to international influence. The international community can take constructive steps to prevent, manage, and resolve these deadly disputes.

The Causes of Internal Conflict

Many policymakers and journalists believe that the causes of internal conflicts are simple and straightforward. The driving forces behind these violent conflicts, it is said, are the "ancient hatreds" that many ethnic and religious groups have for each other. In Eastern Europe, the former Soviet Union, and elsewhere, these deep-seated animosities were held in check for years by authoritarian rule. The collapse of authoritarian rule, it is argued, has taken the lid off these ancient rivalries, allowing long suppressed grievances to come to the surface and escalate into armed conflict.

Serious scholars reject this explanation of internal conflict. This simple but widely held view cannot explain why violent conflicts have broken out in some places, but not others, and it cannot explain why some disputes are more violent and harder to resolve than others. It is undeniably true that Serbs, Croats, and Bosnian Muslims have many historical grievances against each other and that these grievances have played a role in the Balkan conflicts that have raged since 1991. But it is also true that other groups—Czechs and Slovaks, Ukrainians and Russians, French-speaking and English-speaking Canadians—have historical grievances of various kinds that have *not* led to violent conflict in the 1990s. This single-factor explanation, in short, cannot account for significant variation in the incidence and intensity of internal and ethnic conflict.

The starting point for analyzing the causes of internal conflict is recognizing that different types of conflicts are caused by different things. The challenge for scholars is to identify these different types of conflicts and the different sets of factors that bring them about.

Types of Internal Conflict

Internal conflicts can be categorized according to whether they are triggered by elite-level or mass-level factors and whether they are triggered by internal or external developments. There are, therefore, four main types of internal conflicts, and they can be depicted in a two-by-two matrix. (See Table 10.1.)

First, conflicts can be triggered by internal, mass-level phenomena, such as rapid economic development and modernization or patterns of political and economic discrimination. To put it more prosaically, they can be caused by "bad domestic problems." The conflict in Punjab, for example, was galvanized by rapid modernization and migration.[3] Another example is the conflict over Nagorno-Karabakh, which was triggered by problematic ethnic geography and patterns of discrimination highlighted by the breakup of the Soviet Union.

The proximate causes of a second set of conflicts are mass-level but external in character: swarms of refugees or fighters crashing across borders, bringing turmoil and violence with them, or radicalized politics sweeping throughout regions. These are conflicts caused by the "contagion," "diffusion," and "spillover" effects to which many policymakers, analysts, and scholars give much credence.[4] One could say that such conflicts are caused by "bad neighborhoods." The expulsion of radical Palestinians from Jordan in 1970 led many militants to resettle in Lebanon, where Muslim-Christian tensions were already mounting. This influx, one could argue, was the spark that ignited the civil war in Lebanon in 1975.

The proximate causes of a third set of conflicts are external but elite-level in character: They are the results of discrete, deliberate decisions by governments to trigger conflicts in nearby states for political, economic, or ideological purposes of their own. The external fomentation of conflict only works, one must note, when the permissive conditions for conflict already exist in the target country; outsiders are generally unable to foment trouble in stable, just societies. Nevertheless, one could say that such conflicts are caused by "bad neighbors." Examples include the Soviet Union's meddling in and subsequent 1979 invasion of Afghanistan, which has yet to emerge from chaos, and Russian meddling in Georgia

TABLE 10.1   The Proximate Causes of Internal Conflict

	Internally-driven	Externally-driven
Elite-triggered	Bad Leaders	Bad Neighbors
Mass-triggered	Bad Domestic Problems	Bad Neighborhood

and Moldova in the 1990s. Another example is Rhodesia's establishment of RENAMO in 1976 to undermine the new government in Mozambique.

The proximate causes of the fourth and final type of internal conflict are internal and elite-level in character. Variations include power struggles involving civilian (Georgia) or military (Nigeria) leaders; ideological contests over how a country's political, economic, social, and religious affairs should be organized (Algeria, Peru); and criminal assaults on the state (Colombia). To put it in simple terms, conflicts such as these are triggered and driven by "bad leaders."

The Importance of Domestic Elites

The scholarly literature on the causes of internal conflict is strong in its examination of structural, political, economic, social, and cultural forces that operate at a mass level—indeed, it clearly favors mass-level explanations of the causes of internal conflict—but it is weak in its understanding of the roles played by elites and leaders in instigating violence. The latter have received comparatively little attention. The result is "no-fault" history that leaves out the pernicious effects of influential individuals—an important set of factors in the overall equation.

Although mass-level factors are clearly important underlying conditions that make some places more predisposed to violence than others and although neighboring states routinely meddle in the internal affairs of others, the decisions and actions of domestic elites often determine whether political disputes veer toward war or peace. Leaving elite decisions and actions out of the equation, as many social scientists do, is analytically misguided. It also has important policy implications: Underappreciating the import of elite decisions and actions hinders conflict-prevention efforts and fails to place blame where blame is due.

The proximate causes of many internal conflicts are the decisions and actions of domestic elites, but these conflicts are not all driven by the same domestic forces. There are three main variations: ideological struggles, which are driven by the ideological convictions of various individuals; criminal assaults on state sovereignty, which are driven primarily by the economic motivations of drug traffickers; and power struggles between and among competing elites, which are driven by personal, political motivations. Admittedly, these compartments are not watertight. It is nonetheless important to make these distinctions, however rough they might be: There are several, distinct motivational forces at work here— several identifiable proximate causes of internal violence. It is important to have an appreciation of the multifaceted nature of the problem, particularly if one is interested in enhancing international efforts to prevent, manage, and resolve internal conflicts.

Ideological Conflicts.   Some internally driven, elite-triggered conflicts are ideological struggles over the organization of political, economic, and social affairs in a country. Some ideological struggles are defined in economic or class terms; others are fundamentalist religious crusades guided by theological frameworks. Ideological struggles over how political, economic, and social affairs should be organized have not gone away with the end of the Cold War, but they have tended to take on new forms. Class-based movements with Marxist agendas have faded from the scene in many parts of the world, including Southeast Asia, the Middle East, Africa, and Latin America, although some rebels in Colombia and Peru have remained largely true to form. Some rebel movements have mutated and taken on the political agendas of indigenous peoples and ethnic minorities. In many places—Afghanistan, Algeria, Egypt, India, Iran, Sudan—conflicts have formed around new secularist-fundamentalist fault lines. These ethnic and fundamentalist movements draw on many of the same sources that impelled class-based movements in the Cold War era—patterns of political, economic, and cultural discrimination, and widespread dissatisfaction with the pace and equitability of economic development—but they are channeled in different directions. In other words, many of the underlying causes of these conflicts are the same, but their proximate causes have changed.

Criminal Assaults on State Sovereignty.   Some internally driven, elite-triggered conflicts are in effect criminal assaults on state sovereignty. In several countries, in Asia and Latin America in particular, drug cartels have accumulated enough power to challenge state control over large tracts of territory. This is certainly true in Afghanistan, Burma, Tajikistan, Brazil, Mexico, and Venezuela, for example. In Colombia, most notably, drug barons and their criminal organizations have directly challenged state sovereignty. This problem shows no sign of abating. A related problem is that, with the end of the Cold War and reductions in financial support from Moscow and Washington, many ethnic groups and political movements turned to drug trafficking to finance their activities. This is true, for example, of various groups in Colombia and Peru. In addition to its other pernicious effects, drug trafficking complicates the nature of the conflicts in question and therefore makes conflict management and resolution more difficult.

Power Struggles.   Finally, some conflicts are in essence power struggles between and among competing elites. Of the three types of internally driven, elite-triggered conflicts outlined here, raw power struggles are clearly the most common. Some are sustained government campaigns to repress ethnic minorities and democratic activists. This would seem to be a fair characterization of the conflicts in Burma, Cambodia, Guatemala, Indonesia, Iraq, and Turkey, for example. Government repression is a prominent feature of other conflicts as well, but power struggles are particularly intense and the "ethnic card" is played very aggressively. Examples abound: Angola, Bosnia, Burundi, Croatia, Kenya, Liberia, Philippines, Russia/Chechnya, Rwanda, Somalia, and Tajikistan.

One type of power struggle is particularly prominent and particularly pernicious: It accounts for the slaughter in the former Yugoslavia and Rwanda, and has played a role in the conflicts in Azerbaijan, Burundi, Cameroon, Chechnya, Georgia, India, Kenya, Nigeria, Romania, Sri Lanka, Sudan, Togo, Zaire, and elsewhere.[5] The starting point is a lack of elite legitimacy, which sooner or later leads to elite vulnerability. Weakening state structures, political transitions, pressures for political reform, and economic problems can all bring about vulnerabilities. Those who are in power are determined to fend off emerging political challengers and anxious to shift blame for whatever economic and political setbacks their countries may be experiencing. In cases where ideological justifications for staying in power have been overtaken by events, they need to devise new formulas for legitimizing their rule. Entrenched politicians and aspiring leaders alike have powerful incentives to play the "ethnic card," embracing ethnic identities and proclaiming themselves the champions of ethnic groups.

This produces a shift in the terms of public discourse from civic nationalism to ethnic nationalism and to increasingly virulent forms of ethnic nationalism. Ethnic minorities are often singled out and blamed for the country's problems: Ethnic scapegoating and ethnic bashing become the order of the day. When power struggles are fierce, politicians portray other ethnic groups in threatening terms and inflate these threats to bolster group solidarity and their own political positions; perceived threats are extremely powerful unifying devices. When leaders have control over the national media, these kinds of campaigns are particularly effective: A relentless drumbeat of ethnic propaganda can distort political discourse quickly and dramatically. Political campaigns such as these undermine stability and push countries towards violence by dividing and radicalizing groups along ethnic fault lines. In the former Yugoslavia,

Serbian leader Slobodan Milosevic and Croatian leader Franjo Tudjman rose to power by polarizing their societies, even though Serbs and Croats had coexisted peacefully for decades.

Why Do Followers Follow?   It is easy to understand why desperate and opportunistic politicians in the midst of power struggles would resort to nationalist and ethnic appeals. For many politicians, tearing their countries apart and causing thousands of people to be killed are small prices to pay for getting or keeping power. The more interesting question is: Why do followers follow?[6] Given that politicians all over the world employ ethnic appeals of one kind or another, why do these appeals resonate in some places but not others? Why do large numbers of people follow the ethnic flag in some places at some times, but not others?

Two factors are particularly important in this regard: the existence of antagonistic group histories and mounting economic problems. If groups have bad histories of each other and especially if they see themselves as victims of other, aggressive communities, ethnic bashing and inflated threats seem plausible. If economic problems such as unemployment and inflation are mounting and resource competitions are intensifying, ethnic scapegoating is more likely to resonate and more people are likely to accept a radical change in a country's political course, including armed confrontation. In short, the emergence of elite competitions might be the proximate causes of conflicts in places like the former Yugoslavia and Rwanda, but hostilities escalate only because of the existence of other underlying problems or permissive conditions—problematic group histories and economic problems.

It appears that all three factors—intensifying elite competitions, problematic group histories, and economic problems—must be present for this kind of conflict to explode. Russians and Ukrainians, for example, have had to contend with collapsing economies and standards of living, and many Ukrainians do not have benign historical images of Russians. However, Ukrainian politicians have by and large refrained from making the kinds of nationalistic appeals that have caused trouble elsewhere. They undoubtedly recognize that provoking a Russian-Ukrainian confrontation would not bode well for Ukraine or their own positions as leaders of an independent state. Some Russian politicians have been far less responsible in this regard, but their nationalistic appeals have not yet taken over the Russian national debate. Whether or not nationalistic and pseudonationalistic politicians remain confined to the margins of the Russian political debate is certainly one of the keys to its future and to the stability of a large part of the world.

A few parts of the world have experienced economic turmoil and power struggles but have been blessed with homogenous populations and few internal ethnic problems. Finland, for example, has experienced a sharp economic decline since the late 1980s but has not experienced interethnic strife, because minorities are few and small and because intergroup relations are relatively harmonious. Similarly, Poland has gone through a complete political and economic transformation since 1989, but it has few minorities and few intergroup problems: Nationalistic appeals have no audience. Poland's hotly contested 1995 presidential election was consequently fought along ideological lines.

Other parts of the world have deeply troubled ethnic histories and leaders who have not hesitated to do whatever was necessary to get and keep power, but they have been spared massive bloodlettings because of their comparatively rosy economic pictures. Much of Southeast Asia experienced considerable turmoil during the Cold War but was quite stable in the 1990s because of the economic boom that swept most of the region. Much of this can be traced to a track record of sustained economic growth, which gives groups, even relatively disadvantaged groups, incentives to avoid conflict and destruction of a system that is bringing more and more economic benefits to more and more people.

One can also point to East-Central Europe, which has experienced more than its share of turmoil in the past and which is not blessed with leaders steeped in the principles of Jeffersonian democracy, but which has nonetheless avoided the carnage that has consumed the former Yugoslavia a few hundred miles to the south. East-Central Europe has been comparatively peaceful, even though every country in the region has been going through a political transition of the most profound sort; elites have been jockeying for position ever since 1989. If one had to point to one reason for East-Central Europe's stability, one would point to its comparatively good economic performance and its comparatively good economic prospects. The fact that the states of this region have a good chance of joining the European Union at some point in the not-too-distant future gives people powerful incentives to ignore nationalistic appeals and not rock the boat. This point is driven home with even greater force when one looks at differences within the region: Nationalistic appeals have been less successful in Hungary, which has an ethnic diaspora but one of the region's strongest economies and one of the region's best chances of joining the European Union quickly, than in Romania, which has struggled economically.

Economic developments have also marked important turning points in the Middle East and Africa. The Middle East experienced considerable domestic turmoil in the 1950s and 1960s, when weak states were unable to meet societal demands, but less instability in some places in the 1970s and 1980s, when high oil prices and high levels of foreign aid from the United States and the Soviet Union gave governments more largesse to spread around. Potential opposition forces were pacified and, in essence, bought off. The fact that oil prices and foreign assistance levels have declined sharply in the 1990s does not bode well for the region's future.

Much of sub-Saharan Africa has experienced similar problems for similar reasons. Many governments in West, Central, and East Africa were able to hold their heads above water in the 1970s and 1980s—even though they were riddled with ethnic problems and run by corrupt, incompetent leaders—because they received substantial amounts of financial support from two external sources: the superpowers and Western Europe; and international financial institutions such as the International Monetary Fund (IMF) and the World Bank. In the late 1980s, however, two things happened: The Cold War ended and international financial institutions changed their ways of thinking about how financial assistance would be handed out. Direct aid from Washington and Moscow dried up, and most aid from Western Europe was redirected to Central and Eastern Europe. In addition, international financial institutions threatened to withhold aid unless governments overhauled their corrupt political systems and ineffective economic systems.

This placed many leaders in Africa between a rock and a hard place: If they overhauled their patronage systems they would lose the support of their domestic constituencies and subsequently lose power; if they told the IMF and the World Bank that they would not implement political and economic reforms, they would not get financial assistance from abroad, their governments and economies would collapse, and they would lose power anyway. Many leaders in West, Central, and East Africa failed to resolve this dilemma and consequently threw their countries into turmoil in the late 1980s and early 1990s. Nigeria, which had substantial oil reserves, suffered similar financial setbacks when oil prices dropped and its government mismanaged the country's oil income. Although parts of Africa—southern Africa, in particular—have stabilized since the end of the Cold War, much of the continent has moved in the other direction.

Economics and Internal Conflict

Although economic developments can affect the prospect for internal conflict, as discussed above, the relationship between economics and internal conflict is complex.

First, countries at different stages of economic development have to contend with different kinds of economic problems. In industrialized countries or regions, public dissatisfaction can intensify even if economies are growing, if they are not growing as fast as they once were or fast enough to keep pace with societal demands. Countries in the process of making transitions from centrally planned to market-based systems usually have to contend with a host of economic problems, ranging from high levels of unemployment to rampant inflation. Countries that are in the process of modernizing have to contend with migration, urbanization, and other social and economic dislocations. In addition, growing public demands and expectations in modernizing countries can overwhelm the capacities of political institutions to respond.[7] In multiethnic countries, these kinds of economic problems invariably have ethnic reverberations. Economic problems, regardless of their source, can aggravate existing ethnic tensions or generate new tensions, especially if they take place in a context where different ethnic groups have unequal economic burdens, different standards of living, and different economic opportunities—which is almost always the case. These tensions are often compounded by domestic elites, who, in campaigns designed to either preserve or enhance their own political positions, blame ethnic minorities for whatever economic difficulties their country may be experiencing.

Second, although economic booms can dampen ethnic tensions and reduce the potential for ethnic violence—as seen in Malaysia, Indonesia, and Thailand in the 1990s, for example—economic growth is not a panacea. Indeed, economic booms can generate ethnic problems of their own. In Thailand, for example, the country's growing economy has attracted illegal immigrants from Burma, where good jobs are scarce. In Indonesia, the Chinese minority, which heads the business community, has benefited disproportionately from the country's economic upswing. This disparity has generated a great deal of resentment in other ethnic quarters. The economic boom in China has benefited some regions more than others: Coastal areas have prospered much more than remote interior areas, many of which are minority regions. Again, this disparity is of course resented in these minority areas. China's economic boom, moreover, was sparked by economic decentralization, which has led to a reduction in the center's control over remote minority areas. This has led to relaxed border controls, which have allowed outside money and arms to stream into minority areas. As a result, some minorities along China's periphery have growing capacities for independent action. The net effect of China's economic boom, therefore, is that many of China's minorities are both more dissatisfied with the central government and more capable of pursuing their own political agendas.

Third, economic developments should not be thought of as immutable facts of life. Leaders make decisions about the kinds of economic systems that will be put into place as well as specific economic policies. Leaders also make decisions about whether or not they will try to mitigate the impact of economic problems on the relevant ethnic communities. In short, this is an area where domestic elites have considerable influence over the course of events.

International Responses to Internal Conflict

To develop guidelines for international action with respect to internal conflicts, one needs to consider two related but distinct questions: First, what *can* international powers and international organizations do to prevent, manage, and resolve internal conflicts? Second, what *should* international powers and international organizations do with respect to these problems? I contend that international powers *can* do a great deal and *should* do more than they have done in the 1990s. I will develop six general arguments about what the international community can and should do with respect to internal conflicts, as well as three clusters of specific arguments about conflict prevention, conflict management, and conflict resolution.

The first of my general arguments is that the problems posed by internal conflict are formidable, but that options for international action do exist. The track record of international efforts to deal with the problems posed by internal conflicts is mixed: Some efforts have succeeded; others have failed. The challenge for scholars is to identify the conditions under which success is most likely. The challenge for policymakers is to act accordingly. Second, internal conflicts are complex, so actions taken to address these problems have to be multifaceted. There is no silver bullet for the internal conflict problem. Third, internal conflicts have deep roots, so long-term efforts will be needed if prevention, management, and resolution efforts are to succeed. There are no quick fixes to these problems. Fourth, internal conflict is widespread and international resources are limited, so difficult choices will have to be made about when and where to act. This means, in effect, addressing some problems and ignoring others—*triage*. Fifth, the international community should favor actions that have high probabilities of success and low costs. This would be a banal thing to say, but for the fact that the international community often does precisely the opposite. The goal should be building a track record of success that lends credibility to international undertakings.

Sixth, internal conflicts fall into two basic categories as far as international actors are concerned: cases where local parties are willing to work for peace and give their consent to international involvement; and cases where they are not. There is a sharp line between cases where local authorities have given their consent to international intervention and cases where they have not. It is imperative for intervenors to know if they are engaged in cooperative or coercive exercises. Operations that have the approval of local authorities have higher probabilities of success and lower costs than their coercive counterparts, and should therefore be given a higher priority. This does not mean that coercive actions should never be undertaken: Coercive actions are indeed warranted when important interests are engaged or when moral outrages, such as genocide, are being committed. In cases such as these, the international community can still do much to prevent or end violence, but the costs of action are higher and the probabilities of success are lower, because international powers are in the coercion business. Coercive actions should therefore be undertaken selectively, with great care, and with great determination.

The Importance of Conflict Prevention

The idea of conflict prevention has a lot of intuitive appeal: Conflict management and conflict resolution clearly have to contend with far more inflammatory situations. Conflict prevention, however, is far from simple.[8] Conflict is, after all, inherent in political, economic, and social life, even if violent conflict is not. Conflict, broadly defined, cannot be extinguished, only controlled. That said, I would suggest three broad guidelines for international actors interested in preventing internal conflicts.

Adopt a Two-Track Strategy for Conflict Prevention. Those interested in conflict prevention should have a two-track strategy. One track should be a series of sustained, long-term efforts focused on the underlying problems that make violence likely. The other track should be a series of more aggressive efforts focused on the proximate causes of internal conflicts—the triggers that turn potentially violent situations into armed confrontations. Both tracks need to be pursued. Long-term efforts to address the permissive conditions of internal conflicts are relatively low-risk undertakings, but they tend to be neglected by policymakers in national capitals and international organizations who are inevitably preoccupied with the crisis *du jour*. At the same time, the catalytic factors responsible for triggering violence—often in places where bloodshed could be avoided—merit careful attention and vigorous action.

Place More Emphasis on Underlying Problems and Long-Term Solutions. Long-term efforts aimed at the underlying problems that make violence likely need to be given more emphasis and made more effective. This is easier said than done. If a simple formula existed for dealing with these problems, the world would be a more tranquil and happier place than it currently is.

To the extent they change at all, the structural, political, economic, and cultural problems that predispose some places to violence change slowly. This means that international efforts to influence events will have to be long-term undertakings. It also means that international efforts to address the root causes of internal conflict will have to be multifaceted in character. Efforts will have to be undertaken in several areas.

Security concerns and arms races contribute to instability and the potential for violence. One way to reduce the uncertainties that often drive arms races is to promote transparency and adopt confidence-building measures. In many cases, the challenge will be convincing governments that they face these kinds of instability problems and that they should agree to outside involvement in domestic security matters.

When people feel that existing political arrangements are unjust and incapable of being changed peacefully, the potential for violence increases dramatically. International actors can help promote peaceful political change by extending technical advice about constitutional and electoral reforms, for example. They can also exert considerable influence by linking financial assistance and the development of closer economic ties to political reforms—that is, by making financial aid and economic relationships conditional. They can also link membership in international economic, military, and political institutions to domestic political reforms. This approach has worked fairly well in East-Central Europe, where states are eager to join the European Union and the North Atlantic Treaty Organization and willing to do whatever is necessary to improve their chances of being offered early admission to Western institutions.

A country's economic situation and economic prospects have tremendous implications for its potential for violence. If international actors are serious about preventing internal conflict and civil war, they have to do more than treat the military dimensions and military manifestations of the problem; they have to address the economic sources of conflict in troubled societies. International actors can help promote economic reforms the same way they can help promote political reforms: by extending technical assistance; by linking financial assistance and economic relationships to the implementation of reforms; and by linking membership in international organizations and institutions to reforms. States, international financial institutions, and other international organizations should work together to develop "mini-Marshall Plans" for countries in need of special economic attention. Nongovernmental organizations should devote more of their resources to these "silent emergencies," as opposed to *post hoc* responses to crises that have already exploded into violence and chaos.

Finally, international actors need to address the cultural and perceptual factors that lead some countries towards violence. This means working to overturn patterns of cultural discrimination by safeguarding rights with respect to language, religion, and education. This also means working to revamp the distorted histories groups often have of each other. Governments could be asked to enter into international dialogues about group histories and to publish foreign criticisms of school curricula and textbooks.[9] Scholars and teachers should be brought into these dialogues.

Pernicious group histories play important roles in galvanizing internal conflicts, and they need to be given much greater attention in conflict-prevention circles.

Neutralize the Proximate Causes of Internal Conflicts. Those interested in conflict prevention should also pay more attention to the proximate causes of internal conflicts. As discussed above, internal conflicts can be triggered by any one of four clusters of proximate causes: internal, mass-level factors; external, mass-level factors; external, elite-level factors; and internal, elite-level factors. That said, many internal conflicts are triggered by domestic elites, and many of the conflicts that fall into this category are raw power struggles. It follows that international actors interested in conflict prevention should focus on this problem area.

Conflicts triggered by internal, mass-level factors—bad domestic problems—are often driven by ethnic strife. The key to negating pressures for ethnic violence is overturning perceived patterns of political, economic, and cultural discrimination. When tension is building, violence is looming, and distrust is mounting, international actors can help defuse potentially explosive situations by internationalizing the dialogue and injecting impartial observers and mediators into the equation. Fact-finding missions can be launched to help identify the origins of specific problems, human rights monitors can help ensure that injustices do not go unnoticed, and election monitors can help guard the integrity of political processes. The United Nations can be very helpful in this regard. Ethnic bashing and scapegoating in the media can be countered by international organizations and the international media, thereby helping to promote less emotionally charged debates.

Conflicts triggered by external, mass-level forces—bad neighborhoods—are sparked by waves of refugees or troops crashing across international borders, bringing turmoil and violence with them. Waves of refugees and motley gangs of renegade troops are hard to deter or control because they lack effective leadership. The international community can try to prevent refugee problems from becoming regional problems by setting up refugee camps and safe areas in the country where violence first started. To be effective, however, international actors will have to move quickly and convince refugees that safe areas are genuinely safe. This will not be easy to do, given the international community's track record in Bosnia and Iraq. Preventive military deployments are another option.

Internal conflicts triggered by external, elite-level forces—bad neighbors—would seem to be easier to prevent. Specific actions can be proscribed, potentially troublesome governments can be identified, and a wide range of coercive actions can be threatened or taken with respect to renegade states. States are powerful actors, however, and they can therefore be difficult to dissuade, especially if leaders believe important national interests are at stake. Deterring bad neighbors from causing trouble in nearby states is particularly difficult when the neighbors in question are large and powerful. Russia, for example, clearly played a key role in triggering conflicts in Georgia and Moldova, but it was hard to influence because of its size, its position on the UN Security Council, and its firm conviction that Georgia and Moldova were part of its sphere of influence.

Finally, conflicts triggered by power struggles between opportunistic and desperate politicians are common, and should therefore receive special international attention. Since economic problems make escalation and violence more likely, emergency economic relief packages should be part of the equation when tensions rise and danger looms. Cynical campaigns to mobilize ethnic support, polarize ethnic differences, and blame other ethnic groups for whatever troubles a country may be experiencing are often responsible for inciting violence and leading countries into all-out civil wars. It follows that international actors interested in preventing these conflicts from becoming violent and escalating out of control should endeavor to neutralize hate-mongers and their propaganda. At a minimum, this means launching international information campaigns and antipropaganda efforts to ensure that reasoned voices can be heard and alternative sources of information are available in political debates. In more extreme cases, when leaders call for the extermination of their adversaries or entire ethnic groups, as in Rwanda in 1994, more forceful measures will be called for. Taking coercive action is a big step, but some situations—such as calls to commit genocide or slaughter—should lead to forceful international action.

Many internal conflicts are triggered by self-obsessed leaders who will do anything to get and keep power. They often incite ethnic violence of the most horrific kind for their own political ends. If the international community is serious about preventing internal conflicts, it needs to think more carefully about the kinds of political behavior that should be proscribed and the kinds of actions it will be willing to take to steer or even seize control of domestic political debates. These are extremely difficult problems, both intellectually and politically, but they have to be confronted if international actors are to prevent the deadliest internal conflicts.

The Challenge of Conflict Management

Once violence breaks out and fighting begins, escalation becomes much more difficult to control. Security concerns and arms races intensify, and attacks on civilians can spiral out of control. Compromise and settlement become more difficult. Conflict management is more challenging than conflict prevention, and should therefore be undertaken more selectively and with great care. The costs and risks can be high. The following three guidelines should be kept in mind.

Act Early to Keep Violence from Escalating.   International actors worried about emerging internal conflicts should act sooner rather than later. Internal conflicts often begin with limited clashes that escalate only gradually. Put another way, a window of opportunity for crisis management exists even after violence breaks out. The longer international actors wait, the more intense conflicts become, and the more difficult conflict management becomes. International actors have a wide range of policy instruments at their disposal, including cooperative instruments such as mediation and the deployment of traditional peacekeeping forces, and coercive instruments such as arms embargoes, economic sanctions, and the use of military force.

Unfortunately, international motivations to take action are weakest in the early stages of internal conflicts, when levels of violence are low and windows of opportunity are open. Motivations to take action increase as levels of violence increase, but rising levels of violence also make conflict management efforts more difficult. In other words, international motivations to act are weakest when options are strongest, and motivations to act are strongest when options are weakest.

Keep Internal Conflicts from Becoming Regional Conflicts.   International actors interested in conflict management should strive to keep internal conflicts from becoming regional conflicts. Internal conflicts usually become more difficult to control and resolve when neighboring states become involved. Additional sets of interests are injected into the equation, and additional resources are made available to combatants. Fighting often intensifies, and negotiations almost always become much more complicated.

Achieving this goal means addressing two problems. First, it means working to minimize the impact of internal conflicts on neighboring states, including refugee problems, economic problems, military problems, and instability problems. These kinds of problems often lead neighboring states to launch defensive or protective interventions. Second, international actors should work to discourage neighboring states from engaging in opportunistic acts of aggression, such as supporting rebel forces in order to influence the regional balance of power or launching opportunistic invasions.

There are reasons for being optimistic about the international community's ability to take effective action in this area. The problems that internal conflicts pose for neighboring states are easy to identify, even if they are not all easily solvable. The actions that neighboring states should be discouraged from taking are also easy to identify. Plus, the UN Charter provides a legal foundation for taking action to maintain international peace and security. In addition, international actors are dealing with established governments in neighboring states, and governments can be engaged and influenced in ways that amorphous political movements and rebel groups cannot. If necessary, the full array of international policy instruments can be brought to bear on troublesome or potentially troublesome neighboring states, including threats to use economic sanctions and military force.

Distinguish Between Cooperative and Coercive Actions.   It is essential for international actors contemplating intervention to distinguish between two fundamentally different kinds of problems: cases where the local parties are ready to stop fighting and are receptive to international involvement, and cases where they are not. The track record of international efforts to bring fighting to an end is good in the former, bad in the latter, and truly awful when the line between cooperations and coercive undertakings is blurred.

During the Cold War, peacekeeping operations were usually deployed to monitor cease-fires, and they were deployed with the consent of the relevant local parties. These operations consequently enjoyed a high rate of success. It was understood that there was a sharp line between these kinds of undertakings and the coercive operations launched under Chapter VII of the UN Charter.

This line began to get blurred in 1992, when UN secretary-general Boutros-Ghali suggested that future peacekeeping operations might not depend on the consent of all local parties.[10] The UN-authorized missions to Somalia and the former Yugoslavia that followed were deeply troubled exercises, mainly because the line between cooperation and coercion was blurred. UN humanitarian operations in these two countries were presented as impartial efforts to relieve human suffering, but they were seen quite differently by local leaders, who correctly understood that humanitarian relief had implications for the local balance of power. International efforts to put pressure on local leaders and open the way for humanitarian supplies failed, first, because international actors insisted on pretending that they were not engaged in coercion and, second, because they did not have sufficient forces on the ground to engage in effective coercion. In fact, the deployment of lightly armed units to escort humanitarian relief convoys was counter-productive: UN peacekeepers became prepositioned hostages, and hostage-taking completely undercut international efforts to bring the fighting to a quick end.

UN officials, to their credit, have learned from these mistakes, and by 1995 it was again an article of faith in UN circles that there was a sharp line between cooperative and coercive undertakings.[11] Some scholars and analysts continue to argue, however, that there is a gray area between cooperation and coercion, and that a "third option" or "middle option" exists.[12]

My view is that the new thinking at the United Nations is correct: Cooperative and coercive operations are fundamentally different kinds of undertakings, and it is essential for international actors to keep these two kinds of activities separate.[13] The UN-authorized missions to Somalia and Bosnia ran into trouble because whatever consent had once been given began to evaporate when mission objectives expanded and international actors began to engage in more and more coercion.

This is not to say that international actors should eschew coercion, only that they need to distinguish between cooperative and coercive undertakings and be prepared to play hardball when they are engaged in the latter. Coercion *can* work, and the international community has many coercive policy instruments at its disposal. Individuals can be held accountable for their actions through the establishment of international criminal tribunals. Arms embargoes can be imposed on one party or another. Economic sanctions can be powerful sources of leverage, especially when one is dealing with central governments, neighboring states, and other easily identifiable and targetable actors. Military force can be threatened or used and, contrary to current thinking in the U.S. Department of Defense, it can be used in limited ways in support of limited objectives: Safe areas can be established and protected; heavy-weapon exclusion zones can be established and enforced; and air power can be directed at specific targets such as arms depots, communications and transportation links, military bases, and forces in the field.[14]

Successful coercion depends on several things. First, international actors must recognize and admit that they are engaging in coercion: They should not delude themselves or try to delude their publics into thinking that threatening to use military force, for example, will be seen as a form of cooperative engagement. Coercion is not aimed at "conflict": It is aimed at governments, groups, and individuals who will see threats and coercive acts as forms of aggression. Second, international actors need to be clear about both their long-term political objectives and their short-term operational objectives. This requirement of clarity is one of the reasons why coercion worked in Haiti and failed in Bosnia. UN mandates, which should be secured whenever possible, should be clear on these counts as well. Third, coercive actions need to be pursued with great political determination and with sufficient resources. When military forces are involved, this might mean deploying large numbers of heavily armed troops guided by clear and liberal rules of engagement. Lightly armed peacekeepers should not be sent out to wage war or into situations where they might reasonably be expected to engage in open combat. It is reckless and irresponsible to place peacekeepers in such jeopardy.

Although coercion can work, the international community should emphasize cooperative conflict management actions over their coercive counterparts. Cooperative actions—such as sending mediators to help negotiate cease-fires and sending peacekeepers to help monitor cease-fires—are relatively low-cost, low-risk undertakings. They should be the mainstays of international efforts in this area. Coercion is more expensive and riskier, and should be employed only when important interests are at stake or when crimes against humanity, such as genocide or the deliberate slaughter of civilians, are being committed. The international community should engage in these kinds of high-cost, high-risk undertakings only when the stakes are high and only when it is determined to see a serious campaign through to the bitter end.

The Potential for Conflict Resolution

The end of the Cold War has led to the resolution of a number of conflicts—in El Salvador, Mozambique, Nicaragua—driven in large part by the geostrategic competition between Washington and Moscow. The international community, under the aegis of the United Nations, has played an active and important role in helping to bring these conflicts to an end. It has also helped to bring to an end the conflicts in Haiti, Namibia, and South Africa, which were not driven by Cold War dynamics, and it has helped to dampen tensions in Cambodia, Iraq, Tajikistan, and Western Sahara.

Conflict resolution is an enormously tricky proposition: It is hard for people to lay down their arms, rebuild ravaged political and economic systems, reconstruct civil societies, and reconcile when large amounts of blood have been spilled and vengeance has come to dominate political discourse. There are, however, reasons for being hopeful about the prospects for conflict resolution in some parts of the world, and about the ability of the international community, through the United Nations, to facilitate these conflict resolution processes—as longer international actors observe the following guidelines.

Help Those Who Want to Be Helped. The international community's resources are not unlimited, and difficult decisions will inevitably have to be made about where and when to try to lend a helping hand. The guiding principle should be: First help those who want to be helped.

When people are determined to keep fighting, the international community can do little to bring hostilities to an end unless it is willing and able to impose peace. Imposing peace means employing coercive instruments with a heavy hand, and in most cases it probably means unleashing a massive, crushing military blow followed by the long-term deployment of military forces and the imposition of an international trusteeship under the supervision of the United Nations. These operations are bound to be exceedingly expensive and open ended. It is therefore highly unlikely that the international community will be inclined to go down this path. It did not do so in either Somalia or Rwanda, where humanitarian crises were intense and local military forces were comparatively weak.

Given that the international community has limited resources to devote to peace processes and a limited tolerance for pain, it makes sense for international efforts to be concentrated in places where combatants are tired of fighting, ready for peace, and looking for help. There is a lot the international community can do to help resolve conflicts and make peace under these conditions, when it has the full consent and cooperation of the local parties. It can provide humanitarian assistance to refugees and others in need. It can launch fact-finding and mediation missions to help resolve outstanding political differences. Traditional peacekeeping forces can help keep former adversaries apart while cooperative disarmament efforts get under way. Multifunctional peacekeeping operations can help with political and economic reconstruction. The track record of international efforts in postconflict settings such as these is good: Again, international actors can do a lot to help people who genuinely want to make peace.

The key is making sure that one is dealing with people who genuinely want peace. Most people want peace, of course, but on their own terms. When they agree to peace settlements and elections, leaders of factions often assume that electoral triumph is in the offing. Problems can arise when elections turn out in unexpectedly unsatisfying ways: Peace settlements that were attractive when high office appeared to be part of the package are much less attractive when it is not. When leaders don't get the electoral results they were hoping for, they may conclude that resuming the fight in the bush or the jungle is preferable to being a political non-entity. This is what happened in Angola after the September 1992 elections, which Jonas Savimbi lost. The challenge for international actors is to make sure that local parties are acting in good faith and that local leaders fully understand the potential ramifications of the peace process.

Launch Multifaceted Undertakings.   Since the forces that drive internal conflicts are complex, conflict resolution efforts have to be multifaceted undertakings. The United Nations has launched a number of multifunctional peacekeeping operations since the end of the Cold War. The UN missions in Cambodia, El Salvador, Haiti, Mozambique, Namibia, and

Nicaragua are the most prominent examples. As noted above, these wide-ranging, multifaceted operations have a fairly good track record, and offer some useful lessons for the future.

Ideally, international efforts to help resolve internal conflicts will address four sets of problems. The first order of business must be to bring military hostilities to an end and address attendant military and disarmament problems. Cease-fires have to be negotiated, implemented, and monitored. International mediators and peacekeeping forces can be tremendously helpful in this regard. Military adversaries then have to be persuaded to hand in their arms; buy-back schemes have been successful in El Salvador, Haiti, and Mozambique. Over time, rebel military forces and militia have to be demobilized, and national military forces, including appropriate representation from all relevant ethnic and political groups, have to be reconstituted. The key to continued progress is addressing the security concerns that former adversaries will inevitably have as disarmament and demobilization processes unfold. International actors can help to reassure local parties by monitoring these processes carefully and promoting transparency.

Second, international actors can help with political reconstruction. In the short term, this means helping to establish transitional governments, as well as fair and effective police forces and courts. In El Salvador, Nicaragua, South Africa, and elsewhere, the United Nations has helped to organize and supervise elections. The United Nations can also provide technical expertise with respect to constitutional reforms: the creation of a federal system, the establishment of minority rights safeguards, and the like.

Third, international actors can help—indeed, they must help—with the long and difficult problem of economic reconstruction and the promotion of economic development. Many countries torn apart by internal conflict were in poor economic shape to begin with; years of war have only made matters worse. As noted above, "mini-Marshall plans" involving the combined efforts of governments, international financial institutions, international development organizations, regional organizations, and multinational corporations will generally be needed.

Finally, international actors will have to help with the complex problem of rebuilding civil societies. This can involve activities ranging from the repatriation of refugees to the creation or re-creation of a free and fair press to the founding of schools. Getting groups to come to terms with the distorted and pernicious aspects of their histories and inculcating the values of compromise and tolerance in political and social discourse are among the most important problems war-torn countries face. In short, education is one the keys to long-term political stability. This is surely an area where the international community can make a difference.

Make Long-Term Commitments. One of the most depressing aspects
of internal conflict is its recurring nature. In place after place, from Angola to Zaire, conflicts sputter to a halt, only to start up with renewed
fury years or decades later. Internal conflict seems to go into a state of
suspended animation from time to time, but it never seems to go away.

Conflict resolution is not easy, and it cannot be brought about in
months or even a year or two. Conflict resolution is a long-term process,
and if international actors are to contribute in useful ways to this process,
they have to be willing, able, and prepared to make long-term efforts.
Consider the magnitude of the problems most countries face in the after-
math of civil war: State structures have to be rebuilt; legal institutions
and police forces have to be reconstituted; political institutions and electoral processes have to be re-established; industrial and agricultural activities have to be relaunched; communication and transportation systems have to be reconstructed; schools have to be reopened; and so on.

The goal should be creating a lasting peace that would allow international actors to walk away at some point: Peace would be self-sustaining.
This is not an impossible dream, but it most certainly is not a short-term
proposition. Politicians in Western capitals who need immediate gratifi-
cation and crave regular diplomatic triumphs need not apply. This is a
job for serious international actors capable of making long-term commitments to deep-seated problems.

Enduring Dilemmas

What should the international community do about internal conflicts?
The central dilemma confronting the international community is that
peace, order, and stability are not the only values policymakers should
seek to maximize. Political, economic, and social justice are equally important, and these two sets of values are not always in perfect harmony.
Although policymakers should try to prevent conflicts as a general rule,
they should not necessarily work to keep oppressed peoples from rising
up against totalitarian leaders who will not accept peaceful political
change. Although policymakers should try to keep armed conflicts from
escalating as a general rule, they should not work to keep arms from people who have been attacked by others or who are being slaughtered in
large numbers. And, although policymakers should try to resolve conflicts quickly, this mission becomes complicated when aggressors have
the upper hand, which they often do. Under these conditions, bringing a
war to a quick conclusion might not be compatible with bringing it to a
just conclusion.

The challenge, of course, is to promote both sets of values—peace,
order, and stability on the one hand; political, economic, and social jus-

tice on the other—at the same time. The best way to meet this challenge is for the international community to devote more effort to political and economic development and the broadening and deepening of civil societies. Internal conflict is not just a military problem: It is fundamentally a political, economic, and social problem. Addressing the military manifestations of internal conflict means dealing with the political, economic, and social roots of organized violence.

This need leads to yet another policy dilemma. Although the international community's best bets for peace and justice are long-term conflict prevention efforts, the moral concerns and national interests of international actors are engaged most acutely when people are being killed or displaced in large numbers—that is, when an intense war is under way. In other words, the international community's motivations to act are strongest when the options for taking effective action are weakest.

This brings us to a final policy dilemma. When policymakers contemplate intervention in internal conflicts, the costs of international action are easy to measure and they have to be paid immediately: They include the financial costs of economic sanctions and military deployments; the risks to troops placed in harm's way; and the domestic political risks that policymakers might have to run. The costs of inaction are much harder to measure and are usually realized only in the long term: They include damage to core political values, international norms of behavior, international law and order, and regional and international stability. It is important to remember that almost all internal conflicts have regional dimensions, implications for regional security, and implications for international order. Internal conflicts are rarely self-contained pockets of turmoil. The costs of inaction are therefore real, as is the moral diminishment that attends inaction in the face of slaughter. Unfortunately but inevitably, the costs of action receive more attention than the costs of inaction in policymaking debates. Politicians invariably focus on the calculable, short-term costs that they will have to bear as political figures. Statesmen worry more about the long-term costs to national and international security that accumulate only with the passing of time—but true statesmen are few and far between.

Notes

1. See Kalevi J. Holsti, *The State, War, and the State of War* (Cambridge: Cambridge University Press, 1996), pp. 21–25. For more discussion, see John Mueller, *Retreat From Doomsday: The Obsolescence of Major War* (New York: Basic Books, 1989).

2. My discussion of internal conflict draws on my contributions to Michael E. Brown, ed., *The International Dimensions of Internal Conflict* (Cambridge, Mass.: MIT Press, 1996); and Michael E. Brown and Sumit Ganguly, eds., *Government Policies*

and *Ethnic Relations in Asia and the Pacific* (Cambridge, Mass.: MIT Press, 1997). By "internal conflicts," I mean violent or potentially violent political disputes where the main disputants are domestic actors; where the main objects of contention are domestic political, economic, and social arrangements; and where armed violence takes place (or threatens to take place) primarily within the borders of a single state. Examples include violent power struggles involving civilian or military leaders, armed ethnic conflicts and secessionist campaigns, challenges by criminal organizations to state sovereignty, armed ideological struggles, and revolutions.

3. See Sumit Ganguly, "Conflict and Crisis in South and Southwest Asia," in Brown, The International Dimensions of Internal Conflict, pp. 141–172.

4. See, for example, John A. Vasquez, "Factors Related to the Contagion and Diffusion of International Violence," in Manus I. Midlarsky, ed., *The Internationalization of Communal Strife* (London: Routledge, 1992), pp. 149–172; Ted Robert Gurr, *Minorities at Risk: A Global View of Ethnopolitical Conflicts* (Washington: U.S. Institute of Peace Press, 1993), pp. 132–135. For an excellent overview of this literature, see Stuart Hill and Donald Rothchild, "The Contagion of Political Conflict in Africa and the World," *Journal of Conflict Resolution*, Vol. 30, No. 4 (December 1986), pp. 716–735.

5. See Human Rights Watch, *Slaughter Among Neighbors: The Political Origins of Communal Violence* (New Haven, Conn.: Yale University Press, 1995).

6. See Donald L. Horowitz, *Ethnic Groups in Conflict* (Berkeley: University of California Press, 1985), p. 140.

7. See Samuel P. Huntington, *Political Order in Changing Societies* (New Haven, Conn.: Yale University Press, 1968); Ted Robert Gurr, *Why Men Rebel* (Princeton: Princeton University Press, 1970). For an overview, see Saul Newman, "Does Modernization Breed Ethnic Conflict?" *World Politics*, Vol. 43, No. 3 (April 1991), pp. 451–478; Jack A. Goldstone, "Theories of Revolution: The Third Generation," *World Politics*, Vol. 32, No. 3 (April 1980), pp. 425–453.

8. See Stephen John Stedman, "Alchemy for a New World Order: Overselling 'Conflict Prevention,'" *Foreign Affairs*, Vol. 74, No. 3 (May-June 1995), pp. 14–20. For other views, see Michael S. Lund, "Underrating Preventive Diplomacy," *Foreign Affairs*, Vol. 74, No. 4 (July-August 1995), pp. 160–163; John Stremlau, "Antidote to Anarchy," *Washington Quarterly*, Vol. 18, No. 1 (Winter 1995), pp. 29–44.

9. See Stephen Van Evera, "Hypotheses on Nationalism and War," *International Security*, Vol. 18, No. 4 (Spring 1994), pp. 5–39.

10. See Boutros Boutros-Ghali, *An Agenda for Peace: Preventive Diplomacy, Peacemaking, and Peacekeeping* (New York: United Nations, June 1992), p. 11.

11. See Boutros Boutros-Ghali, *Supplement to an Agenda for Peace: Position Paper of the Secretary-General on the Occasion of the Fiftieth Anniversary of the United Nations*, S/1995/1, January 1995, paragraphs 33–35; Shashi Tharoor, "United Nations Peacekeeping in Europe," *Survival*, Vol. 37, No. 2 (Summer 1995), pp. 121–134; Shashi Tharoor, "Should UN Peacekeeping Go 'Back to Basics'?" *Survival*, Vol. 37, No. 4 (Winter 1995/1996), pp. 52–64. See also Charles Dobbie, "A Concept for Post-Cold War Peacekeeping," *Survival*, Vol. 36, No. 3 (Autumn 1994), pp. 121–148.

12. See Adam Roberts, "The Crisis in UN Peacekeeping," *Survival*, Vol. 36, No. 3 (Autumn 1994), pp. 93–120; Donald C. F. Daniel and Bradd C. Hayes, "Securing

Observance of UN Mandates Through the Employment of Military Forces," manuscript, March 1995; Donald C.F. Daniel and Milton E. Miles, "Is There a Middle Option in Peace Support Operations? Implications for Crisis Containment and Disarmament," Paper Prepared for the UN Institute for Disarmament Research, November 1995; Adam Roberts, "From San Francisco to Sarajevo: The UN and the Use of Force," *Survival*, Vol. 37, No. 4 (Winter 1995/1996), pp. 7–28.

13. It is certainly true that peacekeeping operations often engage in coercion at a tactical level (against renegade elements or in the context of monitoring a cease-fire), in the course of policing activities (to stop looting), and in self-defense. However, this kind of coercion takes place with the consent of local leaders and usually within the framework of a cease-fire agreement. There is a big difference between this kind of "tactical" coercion and "strategic" coercion designed to secure an agreement from local leaders, change their political goals, or change the correlation of local military forces. Tactical coercion is normal and acceptable. Attempting to engage in strategic coercion with lightly armed peacekeepers deployed under misleading or obsolete pretenses is deeply problematic, as we have seen in the Horn of Africa and the Balkans.

14. I concur with Ivo Daalder, who argues that the Pentagon's all-or-nothing approach to the use of force limits U.S. military intervention to cases where vital interests are engaged. This puts the cart before the horse. National interests should define policy objectives, and policy objectives should determine how force is used. If interests and objectives are limited, one should be able to use force in a limited way. If one is unable to use force in a limited way for doctrinal reasons, then bureaucratic dogma is damaging national interests. See Daalder, "United States and Military Intervention in Internal Conflict," in Brown, *The International Dimensions of Internal Conflict*, pp. 461–488.

11

Trading Up and Trading Down: The Impact of Technological Change on the International System

CHERIE J. STEELE

One of the distinguishing aspects of both the work and the teaching of Richard Rosecrance has been his focus on change over time. While conventional international relations theory has identified continuities across countries and throughout history, or highlighted structures that persist across systems, Rosecrance has focused on historical, contemporary, and potential changes in both state behavior and the international system. The dramatic changes apparent in politics, economics, and society bought about by the end of the bipolar Cold War conflict have convinced other scholars to move in Rosecrance's direction: to focus on change, even if only to explain the greatly unexpected rapid triumph of capitalism and the demise of communism. Scholars today are focusing on the changing nature of threat, as well as the appearance of new opportunities for peace and prosperity. Still, Richard Rosecrance urged the study of the dynamics of the international system long before the end of the Cold War convinced more conventional scholars to undertake that study.

This chapter focuses on the roots of change in the international system. It seeks not so much to identify the cause of changes in a specific distribution of power in a system, such as that brought about by the demise of the Soviet Union and the end of the Cold War, as to discover the basis of more general changes in the elements of system structure. These dynamic features include changes in the role of international institutions as major actors in the system, changes in the territorial versus trading strategies adopted by individual states, and the origins of the dramatic changes in norms and ideas we are seeing at the end of this millennium. By identifying the roots of these changes, one can ground speculation about the new millennium more firmly in a study of changes in the present—and changes in the past. This paper will first lay out the theoretical underpinnings for an argument about systems change, then review changes in the recent past (since World War II), and finally lay out some expectations for the future.

Realism and Liberalism

The fall of the Soviet Union in 1989 signaled an end to the dominance of realism in the field of international relations. This parsimonious and powerful theory suddenly appeared problematic even to its most fervent proponents: Neorealists had predicted stability for the bipolar system[1] and therefore instability for a unipolar system (in which lesser powers would challenge the dominant state until balance was restored). Yet the Soviet Empire broke apart without a major war or conquest from a challenging power, and, thus far at least, no alliance of lesser states has emerged to challenge the dominance of the remaining superpower. Hence, some of the assumptions underlying those realist predictions have had to be reconsidered. These assumptions include notions that states are the major actors in the system, that the system is anarchic, that the system therefore forces all actors to be functionally undifferentiated, and that each state therefore necessarily seeks to improve its relative position. A state's relative position is determined by how powerful it is— and power, to the neorealists, is fungible, with military power paramount. The anarchic structure of the system forces states to guarantee their own security: Military protection of borders is the most fundamental function of the state. The structure therefore ensures states will all behave similarly (a consequence of being functionally undifferentiated), pursuing strategies that will maximize their relative power and position.

Neorealism, of course, had its critics long before the fall of the Soviet Union. Many of these critics were lumped together in the "liberal" theory camp, despite diverse critiques. Although most liberals did not specifically predict the fall of the Soviet Union, many focused on changes in the international system, arguing that these changes were real and lasting, and that the realists failed to foresee any true change in the system. Liberal critiques ranged from specific challenges to Waltz's assumptions concerning functional differentiation[2] to arguments that increasingly powerful nonstate actors were challenging the dominance of states,[3] to arguments that military power was no longer predominant,[4] to arguments that states pursued absolute gains in many cases.[5]

What these liberal theories shared was an assumption that power is *not* necessarily fungible, and that, at different times, different issue areas are dominant.[6] Liberal theorists placed an emphasis on economic strategies, which the realists tended to treat as secondary concerns for states. By turning to a focus on trade and economic matters, liberal theorists argued that there can be more change in the system than the realists foresaw, that cooperative strategies can be followed, possibly even at the expense of a state's relative position, and that institutions and norms are established to further guarantee cooperation. Liberal theorists shared the view that strategy is what determines structure—that, as Richard Rosecrance argued, a trading strategy and increased interdependence can create a system in which states are essentially playing a mutually beneficial "assurance" game.[7] For realists, given their focus on relative (military) power, states persist in playing the more competitive "prisoners' dilemma" game, and the system remains static. For liberals, new actors (institutions, multinational corporations, and others), functional differentiation, new norms, and shifts in the dominant actors in the system all can occur from the pursuit of new strategies.

These two schools of thought—neorealism, with its treatment of power as fungible and its argument that structure determines behavior, and liberalism, with its treatment of power as not fungible and its argument that strategy can determine structure—have continued to conflict. Realists argue that their theory remains a powerful predictor of state behavior, as it was during the superpower era. Liberals argue that realists continue to deny the fundamental changes in the system even during that era. Differences between the two schools today are perhaps most strikingly obvious in their predictions for the next millennium: Realists continue to argue that military threats will re-emerge, generally through ethnic conflict and more specifically through the "Clash of Civilizations."[8] Liberals argue that a peaceful, cooperative world will continue to evolve, as less powerful states imitate the trading strategies of the powerful: Either the world will be peaceful and boring as we see "the end of history,"[9] or else it will be lucrative and ever more interdependent with the rise of the "virtual state."[10] What is missing is a sense of what systemwide variables might lead a system in a new direction—or keep it stable and unchanging. Without a theory of change—of what types of changes occur and whether they can be lasting—not only will specific changes in the distribution of power (like the fall of a superpower) be impossible to predict, but theoretical disagreements about what elements in the international system are essential will continue. An understanding of system dynamics is needed to know whether actors pursue absolute or relative gains, whether they seek military or economic power (or whether power really is fungible), whether self-help is the organizing principle of the system, which actors matter, whether norms matter, and whether institutions are merely epiphenomenal.

The Dynamics of the System

Technology is the motor that drives systems change. As described in a general framework of system dynamics (drawn from Steele 1995[11]), all individual states at all points in history are interested in both security and prosperity. The trade-offs they are willing to make between the two goals are a function of three factors. The first factor is the domestic situation: the leaders, the culture, and the type of governmental system within the state. The second is the history of the individual state's interaction with other states and the current strategies of those states, including the level of conflictual strategies versus trading strategies. The third is the level of incentives in the international system itself for states to adopt certain types of strategies. Underlying changes in any of these three factors is technological change. Technological changes, both in the security and in the commercial realm, can lead to changes in incentives in the international system. At certain times, the system may therefore be more conducive to cooperation and trade; at other times, it may be more conducive to territorial conflict and war.

Innovations in technology can create disproportionate returns for investments in one strategy as opposed to another. If returns for warmaking strategies increase, the system *as a whole* will become more belligerent. If returns for strategies of commerce increase, the system as a whole will become more peaceful. That is, as technology changes, states find they can better reach their security and prosperity goals by pursuing either more cooperative or more conflictual strategies. The workings of this principle lead to a system of more territorial states at some points in history (which tend to be geographically large states, or even empires), or more trading states (which tend to be smaller geographically). If returns to both cooperative and conflictual strategies stay constant, no real change in system's incentives will occur, and little change in the mix of states will be expected. If the returns to both increase in parallel, or decrease in parallel, there will be no real change in the mix of trading and territorial states in the system (although states may find it easier or harder to reach their goals as technology changes). It is only when the returns to one type of strategy increase or decrease relative to the other type of strategy that the system as a whole becomes more cooperative or more conflictual.

This focus on technological change is broader than just a focus on offensive or defensive weapons. Other authors have described periods in which either offense or defense is clearly dominant and the effect this dominance has on war[12] or even offered the offense/defense argument as an explanation for certain shifts from eras of war to eras of peace (such as the devolution of the fairly peaceful period during the Concert of Europe into the World War I period). But this argument explains only very specific and limited periods or specific wars, both because it is often hard to tell which type of weapon is dominant, and because the dominance of one type of weapons technology often leads to the pursuit of a technology that can counter it, so that the dominance of one type of technology is short-lived.[13] In addition, those who focus on weapons tend to neglect other types of technology that affect trade as well as military strategies, such as improvements in communications or transportation, which lower transaction costs and bring better returns to trading strategies. Finally, technology does not just affect the success of war or trade but can also change the purpose of strategies and the goals states pursue. For example, the value of territory itself changes as it becomes more costly or cheaper to defend, and as territory becomes more useful or less useful as a source of goods to trade, or a help or a hindrance in moving or exchanging goods. Thus the utility of military expansion may go up or down as territory becomes more highly valued—independent of the types of weapons that may be dominant.

As Richard Rosecrance has pointed out, the prospects for peace and stability become enhanced as more states adopt trading strategies and diminish as they adopt territorial strategies.[14] In order to make predictions for prospects of peace and war, or for territorial expansion and trade in the new millennium, we have to focus on trends in technological change and innovation.

The theory presented here is a path-dependent one, in which innovations serve as breakpoints in a model of punctuated equilibrium. Major changes in the structure of the system are rare and depend, in part, on where innovations occur and how they diffuse, on who the existing major actors are, and on what rules and institutions are in place. When periods of intense innovation lead to reversals in the returns states expect from their investments in one type of power versus another, systems change does occur. Institutions and norms will be established that enhance the benefits states glean from following particular strategies. That is, if military power is predominant, institutions will be formed which lower the costs of conflict, such as institutions in which it is easy to coordinate alliances, write treaties, and make diplomatic contacts. If economic power is predominant, on the other hand, institutions will be developed to lower the costs of trade and financial interactions, such as institutions to disseminate information, ease negotiations and contracts, and foster coordination. Through institutions and norms, great-power states structure the system so that they can maximize gains from the strategies they follow. This system then provides incentives for other states to adopt similar strategies: conflictual ones in a world in which military power and territory predominate; cooperative ones in a world in which economic power and trade predominate.

The Recent Past

The international system before World War II was already a strong military-political one. Territorial competition drove states into two destructive World Wars, and culminated in the detonation of the atomic bombs at Hiroshima and Nagasaki. The United States and the Soviet Union emerged as two superpowers in a strongly bipolar world. Power depended on territory and on military capabilities (particularly nuclear weapons) to protect each state's own survival and interests. The colonial system was dead, replaced by a system of allies and satellites. States strove for self-sufficiency except in the nuclear realm, in which some states did strive to attain their own nuclear capabilities, whereas others were content to find protection under the nuclear umbrella of the superpowers.

The two great areas of innovation in the postwar period were first, in the military sphere, in the form of nuclear weapons and their delivery systems, and second, in the commercial/economic sphere, in the form of advances in information and communications, including the use of satellites and computers, which had an impact on both economic and military power.

Innovations in military power over the last fifty years have raised the cost of the use of force everywhere. This change was brought about in part (but not exclusively) by the development of nuclear weapons. The realists argue that the postwar bipolar system was extremely stable because of the disparity between the superpowers and the rest of the system that nuclear capability created. But the effects of nuclear weapons are felt throughout the system. All states face an unprecedented degree of threat because of the great costs associated with using them. Part of these costs come from the technology itself: possible "nuclear winters," the well-publicized risks of any radiation in the atmosphere, and the impact of nuclear accidents like Chernobyl have convinced all actors that grave costs would be incurred by both the aggressor and target states in any nuclear confrontation. Additional costs come from the deterrence doctrines of the nuclear powers and the system of alliances in the system. A decision to use any force must include the consideration of the costs associated with using nuclear weapons, because any conflict theoretically can escalate into a nuclear one.

Nuclear weapons have not been the only military innovation in the last fifty years, of course. Improvements in conventional weapons include dramatic improvements in firepower and accuracy, in the range and the reach of that firepower, and in the speed with which attacks can be delivered, all of which are also attributes of nuclear weapons themselves. Fighter planes and bombers are faster, better cloaked, better able to identify targets, and better able defend themselves against attack. Missile technology has continued to develop, including intercontinental-ballistic missiles (extremely long-range), SAMs (cheap, mobile surface-to-air missiles), antiballistic missiles (seen as destabilizing), cruise missiles (which can be launched by ship, submarine, or air), and the neutron bomb, which kills people (through enhanced radiation) but leaves real estate intact.[15] Because the time period in which weapons can reach their target is now so short, and because the geographical reach of these weapons is now so great, territory today is less important as a defense against attack. It no longer serves as a buffer against enemies.

Improvements in chemical and biological weapons have led to greater fears of mass devastation, just as nuclear weapons have. In addition, high technology weapons have been developed since World War II. Such weapons include sensors, antipersonnel weapons, and precision-guided "smart" munitions. Again, these have improved accuracy and lethality. High-tech conventional weapons have become more costly to develop and deploy, but, like nuclear weapons, they are also more lethal, can extend that lethality over greater distances, and can wreak havoc in very brief periods of time, leaving little time for diplomatic resolution to crises. Finally, although high-tech weapons are costly to develop and deploy, their development depends more on knowledge and level of technical sophistication than on natural resources—making territory, which provides natural resources, less valuable. Thus the potential for widespread devastation from military strategies has increased, the costs for advanced weapons have skyrocketed, and territory has become less useful as a means of protection against attacks or as the basis of resources needed for the development of military power. The returns for investing in military power, taking into account the increase in expense, the increase in risk, the increase in the cost of devastation, and the diminishing benefits of taking new territory, have fallen.

During this same post-World War II period, dramatic innovations have occurred in communications, transportation, and computer technology. These innovations have profoundly influenced both military and economic strategies. Focusing first on this technology's impact on military strategies, instantaneous communication improves command and control of military forces, and has enabled the development of precision-guided weapons; satellites allow for early warnings for mobilization of forces or missile launches[16] and, of course, would be the basis for a Strategic Defense Initiative (SDI, or "Star Wars") system. Thus the impact on military strategy is mixed: Weapons are more accurate (for those who can afford high-tech weaponry), but military strategies designed to take territory are more difficult—surprise attacks are no longer possible.

Such technology has also helped make territory itself less vital as a means for security and prosperity. As already described, territory is less vital as a buffer if weaponry has a long reach, and the natural resources that come with territory are less important for information-based technologies. But information technology has also made it more difficult to control populations once territory is taken. Borders are now more permeable, as access to computers, faxes, and broadcasts means that individuals or groups can spread information (and/or propaganda) independent of government control and oversight. Central governments no longer have a monopoly over the control of information and can no longer lie with impunity. Of course, this permeability is not absolute: Many leaders try to use this same technology to spy on their own citizens, and they also try to control citizens' access to information—as China has succeeded in doing, to a great extent. But such efforts to control access to information are very expensive. On balance, information technology at times makes weaponry more accurate and rapid (possibly making war more devasting once war is declared), but it has decreased the importance of taking and holding territory (and so there is less reason to go to war).

On the commercial side, information technologies have dramatically lowered transaction costs for trade. Coordination between manufacturers, the delivery of goods, and access to markets have all improved. As trade has increased, interdependence between states has increased, leading to greater state specialization based on comparative advantage. Communications and computer industries show increasing returns, in which specialization is more profitable than competition because of the lockout phenomenon. These industries require few raw materials for production, and entail high research and development costs. Investments in infant industries such as electronics are risky: It is difficult to predict which of several viable models will become the standard for the industry. The prevalence of knowledge-based industries in which people "learn by doing" means that firms increase returns over time as the workforce gains expertise, and spin-off industries further increase profits.

Specialization and interdependence in the economic realm inevitably affects the security realm. Countries that have developed these kinds of industries, such as Japan and the European Community (EC), have chosen not to seek self-sufficiency in their military strategies. Instead, they rely to a great extent on the U.S. nuclear umbrella. They also rely on increasingly interdependent economic ties to provide "cheap deterrence": that is, they rely on the fact that it is more costly to bomb trading partners than independent competitors. Cooperation has come not only out of trading relationships (the pursuit of absolute gains) but also as a means of lowering risk and development costs in high-tech industries. The returns to trade have been so great that the relative returns from investments in military and economic power have shifted to the point where returns for productive investments and strategies are greater than for military strategies.[17] The incentives of the system have encouraged investments in the economic sector and the pursuit of economic strategies in order to pursue both security and prosperity.

As the incentives in the system shifted over the last fifty years toward trading strategies, the major powers in the system established norms and institutions. These norms and institutions fell into two categories: first, those aimed at making war less likely (and hence, any possible escalation to the use of weapons of mass destruction), and second, those aimed at facilitating trading strategies and creating further incentives for states to follow such strategies. The costs associated with actually using nuclear weapons were so devastating, the security costs were so great in a world in which nuclear weapons could be used, and the trade-offs for prosperity so unacceptable, that the great powers were able to agree to these norms, which lessened the likelihood of war, lowered security threats, and freed resources to invest in productive strategies. These included norms against nuclear proliferation and nuclear testing and use[18] in order to lower the risk of nuclear exchanges. Arms control agreements covered both nuclear weapons and other weapons of mass destruction.[19] Other agreements encouraged the move toward stabilization, verification of arms control, and stable nuclear strategies.[20] Anticolonial norms and norms against territorial expansion were established to further lower the risk of a possibly devastating war: Breaking the norm would entail a cost so high as to make the benefits of territorial challenges not worth the costs. Institutions like the United Nations[21] have provided a forum for diplomacy and cooperation, as well as establishing a mechanism to set formal rules and to enforce sanctions.

Norms and institutions were also established to foster trading strategies and further lower transaction costs. Formal institutions were established and have become primary players themselves in managing the world economy. They have included broad arrangements such as The Bretton Woods agreement and the establishment of the International Monetary Fund (IMF) starting in 1944, successive rounds in the General Agreement on Tariffs and Trade (GATT), and eventually the World Trade Organization (WTO) in 1994, as well as regional arrangements such as the European Union.[22] The impact of these organizations continues to grow: Today, even less developed states that dislike IMF policies find themselves bargaining with the IMF and following their stabilization requirements in order to have access to international loans. Even China is now ready to join the WTO. As interdependent ties are formalized and commitments are made, further cooperation is fostered. Rules are clear, compliance is verified, and sanctions are administered. As transaction costs for trade decrease, returns increase, and states have greater incentives to follow trading strategies.

Those Left Out of the System

To argue that certain institutions (like the United Nations or the IMF) have emerged as major players in the system, or to argue that new rules and norms have been established to allow for the reward and punishment of certain state behavior, or to argue that the dominance of one type of power (military or economic) limits certain possible strategies and expands others, is not to say that statesmen and stateswomen no longer have any real choice of policy. This paper does suggest that some new opportunities are created, and that the costs and the payoffs that accompany different choices may change. In other words, the incentives in the system for states to follow certain choices but not others can shift dramatically. But not all states can take advantage of these incentives.

Historically, Great Powers have been most able to respond to incentives (and to shifts in incentives) in the system. Indeed, Great Powers are often even instrumental in establishing the institutions and norms that create some of those incentives. Not all Great Powers will always make predictable choices, even when the incentives are clear (leaders may have many conflicting interests), but at least they are able to take advantage of the incentives when they choose. Other states, however, have severely constrained choices. This constraint could be for one of several reasons. First, they could be so beset by threats to their security (either from domestic unrest or from external enemies) that they have no choice but to follow military strategies, even in a world in which economic power is dominant. Second, they can be either too poor or too lacking in resources (natural resources, an educated work force, and so forth) to take advantage of trading strategies. Third, they may be excluded from certain international institutions, or generally treated as pariah states, either for geographical or political reasons, and so be unable to take advantage of many of those incentives. Thus an overly optimistic view of the future, based on a recognition of the increasing incentives to follow trading strategies rather than territorial ones, will leave scholars and policymakers alike unable to predict or prepare for continuing conflict around the world.

One recent example is the newly erupting nuclear arms race between India and Pakistan. Both countries seem to be making irrational choices, given the incentives for trading strategies in the international system, accepted norms against proliferation and testing,[23] and the need both have for economic investment by the Great Powers (who support the norms against proliferation). Not only are they failing to make choices that take advantage of incentives toward trading strategies and away from military strategies, but they actually seem to be flaunting existing norms (such as the Non-Proliferation Treaty [NPT]) and are in fact suffering economic sanctions (in the form of the loss of aid and investment) because of their behavior.

The Bharatiya Janata Party (the largest group in the coalition ruling India at the time of the blasts) was so proud of their achievement following their May 1998 nuclear tests that they handed out sweetmeats to celebrate the blasts, discussed building a monument at Pokharan (the test site) to be "a shrine of strength" to be visited by pilgrims, and talked of sending samples of sand from the test site all over the country so that "the whole nation could partake of the glow."[24] While local villagers expressed concern about radioactivity, public opinion around Delhi supported the blasts as enabling India to achieve great-power status.[25] The leading spokesman for India's nuclear policy, K. Subrahmanyam, the retired director of the Institute for Defence Studies and Analyses, has not only argued that nuclear weapons are the currency of international power, but has suggested that India may even be able to "parlay its nuclear program into a seat on the UN Security Council."[26] Pakistan decided to respond to India's testing with its own six tests.

The NPT is seen by these nations (and other nuclear "wanna-bes") as an unfair attempt by the existing nuclear powers to ratify the status quo and keep nuclear power for themselves.[27] The actual international response has been to condemn both India and Pakistan. Indeed, both suffered economically, as the rupee in India fell to a historic low, prices skyrocketed, and the stock-market index fell, and in Pakistan the United States is backing off from its previous commitments for both military and economic aid. Both India and Pakistan appear unrepentant.

Thus, throughout the same post-Cold War period in which the existing nuclear powers have been building down their nuclear arsenals and have been turning more toward trading strategies, less developed nations or those which are only marginally members of international institutions have continued to pursue military power and territorial strategies. India and Pakistan have shown some restraint in actually using nuclear weapons (as opposed to trying to capitalize on them politically, as noted above), but the same may not be true for other states which have embarked on nuclear programs, including North Korea and Iraq. India and Pakistan are limited in their ability to take advantage of international incentives to follow trading strategies, and so may have turned to nuclear testing for prestige. North Korea and Iraq, as marginalized or even pariah states, may be so isolated from the international community that they feel they have little to lose in flaunting existing norms. Certainly Iraq, at least, appears to be less constrained in its use of force generally.

Still, the majority of states in the international system have turned away from territorial strategies and toward trading strategies, increasingly over the course of the Cold War and very dramatically since the end of the Cold War. At the end of World War II, two outcomes were possible for the system as a whole: a continuation of a stable bipolar military-territorial world, which, perhaps, allowed the use of nuclear weapons to determine the structure of the system (although threatening to end every system), or a world in which actors became more interdependent and wealth again became the currency of power. Innovations leading to lower returns on the production and use of military power (especially given the destructive capacity of nuclear weapons) and higher returns on the investment and use of economic power (especially as improvements in transportation and communications have led to a decline in transaction costs) provided incentives for norms that lowered the risk of war (by further raising the costs of going to war). As the ratio for returns on military and economic investment reversed, incentives rose for interdependent behavior and the specialization of states' roles as producers, providers of capital, markets, labor bases, and the providers of military force. As the rules of the system changed, incentives shifted away from an emphasis on self-sufficiency.

Opportunities arose for new actors to become important players in the system, including new nonstate actors (e.g., multinationals and supranational organizations) and newly independent states (as the costs of fighting nationalist movements outweighed the benefits of defending or expanding territory). Diffusion of these innovations is not equal, and states unable to maintain security or increase prosperity in the new system may still try to do so using military power in regional conflicts, but the changing relative prices for military and economic power in the system as a whole have changed and, along with them, the structure itself has changed. New rules and principles, as well as new actors, suggest a new international system is indeed emerging. These systems changes are much more far-reaching than just the change in the distribution of power in the system evident in the fall of the Soviet Union—and these systemic changes, in actors, in institutions and norms, in differentiation and specialization among actors, began much earlier than 1989.

Into the Next Millennium

I clearly share the view of many liberal theorists that incentives in the system do increasingly favor economic strategies. We are on a trajectory of more trade and cooperation. However, those who are most likely to take advantage of such incentives are the more developed states. To the extent that rogue states survive (those politically isolated from the system), or to the extent to which states do not have the resources to benefit from the incentives of the system, security problems will flare. Less developed states and pariah states are less likely to be able to benefit from trade or feel constrained by norms. Indeed, in predicting the future, we cannot even be sure future technology will not push the system as a whole back in a more competitive and violent direction. Even if such innovations do not occur, however, the new millennium is not likely to be the completely peaceful trading world envisioned by many optimists. Not all states are convinced capitalism and trade alone promise them a golden future.

Still, it is true that for the majority of states, incentives have changed, and they see greater benefits from trading strategies than from military ones. Territory, a constant sum good, had been the best guarantee of security in the era before the Nuclear and Communications Revolutions. As the Realists described, military power and the maximization of relative position made sense in this earlier era. But once it is clear that innovation can alter the costs and benefits of different elements of power and that different types of power are useful in accomplishing different goals at different times, it becomes clear that the importance of maximizing relative power can change as well. And in fact the importance of maximizing relative power has changed since World War II: Incentives have shifted, encouraging states to pursue economic and trading strategies, which offer the best rates of return. This change does not mean that position is completely unimportant today: Internal capabilities still determine much of each state's strategy, and different types of nations with different relative capabilities will still behave differently. These differences have remained even as relative power concerns and polarity have become less important, as norms have been established to raise the costs of using military power, and as roles for states (as well as other actors) have become more specialized. Not all actors have been able to switch their investment decisions completely—and not all have recognized the possible returns from doing so. Still, the most successful states have at least begun to switch their investment decisions and their strategies (rather than risk suffering the same fate as the USSR), and have worked to change norms and institutions in order to further lower the costs of economic strategies.

If states are to maximize their absolute power, their capabilities and resources (their comparative advantage) will determine the specialized roles they adopt. Resources, for example, will determine which states succeed in competing in leading economic sectors, or in developing new technology. States with large amounts of capital can continue to invest in research and development, perhaps leading to new innovations and further systems changes. Less developed countries may provide labor, raw materials, and markets for goods developed in capital-rich states. Previously, great powers avoided interdependence not only out of fear of changes in relative power from asymmetrical joint gains, but also out of fear of the sensitivity form of interdependence: fear that shocks in one state would lead to economic and political dislocations in other states. Now the former problem has lessened and many large states actually consider sensitivity to economic changes in other states to be an advantage. They see interdependence as lowering the risk of defection and increasing time horizons for state strategies, both of which make it more likely that states will choose cooperative strategies. In other words, long-term interdependence sets up a durable relationship that should also lessen the problem of cheating across other issue areas[28] and raise the prospects that regimes will succeed. Once interdependence exists, even where military power is applied and levels of threat rise (either because actors fail to recognize the inefficiency of military power, because they have no other options, or even because a new innovation promises greater returns), interdependence should continue to serve as a deterrent for at least a reasonable period: At least it ensures that if a state turns on its partner, it will be a more costly decision, since its own economy will suffer.

In the future, the system will continue to provide the same incentives it has since World War II, at least as long as returns on investments in economic strategies outweigh returns on military strategies. That is, incentives will increase for states to cooperate and to specialize. The system will become more heterogeneous in terms of the kinds of actors who are major players. Cooperative institutions have developed during the period after World War II in the economic arena. These institutions, along with trading regimes such as the European Union (EU) and the North American Free Trade Agreement (NAFTA), lower transaction costs, and similar institutions will continue to emerge both to further lower these costs and to take advantage of economies of scale. These regimes will not be territorially based, however, since territory is no longer the currency of power.[29] Territory is no longer the guarantee of security it once was, given the development of air power, missile technology, and satellite information gathering: Distance no longer protects states. In addition, the development of high-technology industries, which require knowledge but fewer raw materials, suggests that territory is less important than it once was even for economic strategies. In fact, in the future, states are likely to become smaller, based on ethnic or religious interests. Nations can be expected to protect their culture and nationalist groups to assert their political and economic rights. The international system will continue to de-emphasize self-sufficiency: If relative position is less important (as constant-sum goods are no longer the sole basis of power), the fear of assymetric gains from interdependence lessens. Accordingly, cooperative ventures will continue to be sought across issue areas—in the security arena as well as the economic one. Multilateral organizations and collective security are more likely in a world in which economic power is predominant.

Defense is still required, but military aggression, at least by major powers, is less likely (in part because of lower returns, in part because norms have made military power even less efficient or useful), and major states are less concerned about asymmetric gains. Once institutions can lower the likelihood of cheating (and therefore uncertainty), actors are less vulnerable and, in an age in which military power gives fewer returns anyway, cooperation is possible even in the pursuit of security.

Norms, such as the norm of sovereignty, will continue to evolve. They raise the costs of pursuing undesirable strategies by establishing sanctions for such behavior. Sovereignty itself, for example, has become "unbundled": its meaning has changed. Some of its component parts are no longer viable; others continue to be desired. The elements of sovereignty that continue as norms include the idea that all states will continue to be treated as the primary actors in the system, although they are no longer the only major actors in an age of multinationals and international organizations. The annexation of territory is now more strongly discouraged than in any earlier period. Others aspects of sovereignty, however, are breaking down. Transnational problems, including environmental ones, make it more difficult for developed states to keep out of the domestic affairs of others (especially in Eastern Europe, with all its current pollution problems, or the developing world, with its emerging pollution problems and depletion of resources such as the rain forests). The permeability of societies from satellite and other communication technology makes it even more difficult to keep outside influences from crossing borders. Through fax machines, telecommunications, and computer networks, subnational and transnational groups link across borders: Governments can no longer control the flow of information in and out of a country. These trends help explain exactly why some old territorial units are breaking up (such as the former USSR, unable to adequately pursue prosperity and no longer in need of such a large territory), while others are forming confederations and actually appear to be ceding their sovereignty (as in the EC). These trends are likely to continue.

Unevenly distributed technical innovations and uneven baselines of resources still suggest growth among nations will continue to be uneven. The core-periphery disparities will be exacerbated. As states differentiate according to comparative advantage, concerns will differ. Highly developed, efficient states may seek to better the quality of life for their populace, including limiting the effects of development on the environment, which may come into conflict with those states still looking ahead to development—and who may be concerned that if they do not continue to develop, they will not be able to fully benefit from new technologies (because of the lock-out phenomenon of high-tech industries) or, indeed, to be truly interdependent with highly developed states and to derive the deterrence benefits as well as the opportunities to pursue prosperity.

Thus, even if there is less concern within each state about preventing gains to other states (because relative power today is less important between large states and small states cannot really compete with large), a less affluent state[30] may still pursue primarily military strategies as it tries to compete in an interdependent world to guarantee security and pursue prosperity. Thus, if a state has few economic resources with which to trade, even in an era of decreasing returns on investments in military power, less developed countries may still choose military strategies. This likelihood will remain as long as they believe that military force can, in the short run, either bring greater prestige or even succeed in capturing new economic resources: The costs and risks of pursuing military strategies will be worth it as long as no other real options appear to be available.

Core-periphery problems will also be exacerbated because of the continuing shift from traditional manufacturing to the production of information-based technologies in the developed world.[31] Once the completely dependent relationships of the colonial era ended after World War I, industrialized states did aid in the development of the former colonial states. They gave this aid in part because of security interests, as the world was carved up into two spheres of influence during the Cold War and a loss of an ally, even in the remotest, least developed part of the globe, was seen as a gain for the other side. Another reason they gave was that manufacturing industries in the industrialized states needed the raw materials, cheap labor, and potential markets of less developed countries (LDCs).

Once nationalism in former colonies increased and anticolonial norms were established, the cost of holding colonies became prohibitively high: Former imperial powers could no longer extract resources by force. The strategy of aiding the development of former colonies promised the greatest returns, especially if these areas became viable markets for manufactured goods rather than merely areas rich in raw materials. The appeal of investment opportunities in LDCs has declined, however, and will continue to appear less attractive than it has been in the past. In part, this decline reflects the fading of security interests in these areas since the end of the Cold War. This trend downward will continue, however, as high-tech industries in the developed world create a much smaller demand for raw materials. The desire for the cheap unskilled labor in LDCs has decreased because these high-tech industries require a highly trained and educated workforce.[32]

It is also difficult for newly developing states to ever compete in high-tech industries. As described earlier, many high-tech industries display the "lock-out" phenomenon, which comes about from increasing returns: Returns increase because workers "learn by doing," because these industries rely much less on depletable raw materials, and because experience increases the ability to develop spin-off products. These increasing returns, plus the risk involved in entering the high-tech field without partners (due to the problems of unpredictable standardization and the high research and development costs these technologies require), preclude the ability to compete by states and firms that enter the market late: Nonindustrialized states with untrained workers and little capital certainly cannot enter the race. Instead, joint ventures between industries within developed nations or between developed nations themselves become more likely, as these industries and states seek to spread out the risks and costs of research and development. Furthermore, because of the lack of need for raw materials and the extreme specialization of high-tech industries, horizontal trade is more common than in an era dominated by manufactured goods. Developed countries will continue to increase trade with one another, leaving nonindustrialized states completely out in the cold.

Furthermore, though norms of territorial integrity are systemwide (a situation originally instituted as a means of mitigating the threat of nuclear war), their effect will continue to be somewhat weaker in areas where nonnuclear countries face other nonnuclear countries, especially since, in the post-Cold War world, such states may not even be allied with countries with nuclear forces. Less developed states, therefore, may occasionally flout the new norms in the system, ready to bear the costs of other states' responses if they believe they can put themselves on a more competitive footing. These strategies will spread if they appear to be successful, either because force succeeds in increasing a state's resources at an acceptable (if not optimal) cost, or because the threat of force leads to economic concessions by developed states (as in the case of the recent agreement to provide light water reactors to North Korea in order to discourage their nuclear program). Still, this tendency should be tempered somewhat by the knowledge that such norms benefit underdeveloped states as well, protecting them from a conventional military force and invasion and allowing them to devote resources to pursuing prosperity. Many small states have endorsed the norms of territorial integrity and are likely to continue to seek nonmilitary means of bettering their economic position and to follow the incentives of the current system where possible (evidenced by the current wave of privatization of industry that is spreading through the LDCs).

War, of course, is still possible, and is most likely to be waged by those denied the benefits of an interdependent strategy. As territory declines in importance as a guarantee of security (as it is no longer necessarily worth the cost of maintaining the territorial holdings of the large states that consolidated during the eighteenth and nineteenth centuries), ethnic groups within states are also likely to engage in conflict in order to seek political and economic rights (and some of these groups continue to look for support from members of their groups in other states, possibly pursuing irredentist strategies). Other domestic political causes of war are also likely to continue: Petty tyrants or irrational leaders may seek aggrandizement or may hope war will turn the focus of their people away from domestic problems; specific interest group pressure or anger at another state's interference in supporting antigovernment groups may also lead to conflict.

The possibility always exists as well for the development of new offensive weapons as investments in research and development continue in states either seeking to control internal unrest or maintaining military capabilities to deal with potential outside threats or in response to demands from domestic interest groups. LDCs may have problems believing that trading strategies can benefit all players if players do not start out with more equivalent resources. If this concern leads to economic strategies that are protectionist, such strategies too may lead to conflict if larger states are not willing to tolerate paying asymmetrical costs and thus retaliate by closing their own markets. In this case, returns on economic strategies would fall. Pressure for such policies in LDCs (as a result of seeing even the economic world in mercantilist constant-sum terms) may be particularly great now that the Cold War has ended and less foreign aid is coming from the superpowers than was the case when they were trying to divide the world into spheres of influence for security reasons.

Here again, Japan may be at the forefront of a new trend, giving foreign aid for economic rather than security reasons and disregarding strategic interests as the primary determinant for choosing trading partners. All states worry less about the danger of joint gains in a world in which there is little incentive to transform economic gains into military resources and little incentive for (costly) military resources to be used by states pursuing their interests in security and prosperity. Still, as long as war is possible, states must plan defense and maintain certain levels of military resources even as they pursue some economic strategies with security externalities.

States that have been very independent and have a great deal invested in their military resources may also take longer to see the world in variable-sum terms or to see the advantages (as opposed to the risks) of interdependence. Thus the United States, for example, has difficulty even in seeing the trading world as a variable-sum world, concerned as they are with Japan's "getting ahead."[33] Protectionists argue that the United States should close markets in retaliation rather than pursue the interdependent strategies that might encourage Japan to open its markets further. This policy is an especially dangerous one to adopt just when other states are increasing their interdependence with each other and their levels of specialization in an attempt to lower the risks and costs of investment in high-tech industries. If a state, even a wealthy one, tries to compete on its own, it may get left behind in a world of increasing returns, which would hurt its absolute power. Joint ventures and interdependence can help minimize the risk of committing high levels of resources to industries with multiple equilibria and uncertain outcomes. Still, systems change can only constrain state choice, not determine it.

Thus, while realist explanations for state behavior in the territorially dominated post-World War II world remain powerful, by the 1970s and 1980s liberal focus on change offered international relations theory the ability to retain its descriptive accuracy and possibly some predictive power. By focusing on change, models for the evolution of the international system become possible. New technology offers the international system the promise of a more cooperative future. However, the next millennium may not be as peaceful or as widely prosperous as some liberals have hoped. Not only is the gap between rich and poor nations likely to widen, possibly creating instability, but there is no guarantee that further developments in technology will necessarily continue to promise greater returns on cooperative economic strategies than on military strategies. Should that ratio shift, further changes in the structure of the system are unlikely to continue to offer hopes of cooperation.

Notes

1. Kenneth N. Waltz, *Theory of International Politics.* (Reading, Mass.: Addison-Wesley, 1979).

2. John Gerald Ruggie, "Continuity and Transformation in the World Polity: Toward a Neorealist Synthesis." in Robert O. Keohane, ed., *Neorealism and Its Critics.* (New York: Columbia University Press, 1986), pp. 131–157.

3. Robert O. Keohane and Joseph S. Nye, *Power and Interdependence: World Politics in Transition,* (Boston: Little, Brown, 1977).

4. John Mueller, *Retreat from Doomsday: The Obsolescence of Major War,* (New York: Basic Books, 1989).

5. See Arthur A. Stein, *Why Nations Cooperate: Circumstance and Choice in International Relations* (Ithaca: Cornell University Press, 1990), p. 149.

6. Keohane and Nye, *Power and Interdependence.*

7. Richard Rosecrance, *The Rise of the Trading State: Commerce and Conquest in the New World* (New York: Basic Books, 1986), p.237.

8. Samuel P. Huntington, "The Clash of Civilizations?" *Foreign Affairs* 72 (Summer 1993): 22–49.

9. Francis Fukuyama, "The End of History?" *The National Interest* 16 (Summer 1989): 1–18.

10. Richard Rosecrance, *The Rise of the Virtual State*. (New York: Basic Books, 1999).

11. Cherie J. Steele, "Altered States: Innovation, Power, and the Evolution of the International System," (Ph.D. diss., UCLA, 1995).

12. See, for example, Stephen Van Evera, "The Cult of the Offensive and the Origins of the First World War," *International Security* 9 (Summer 1984): 58–106, and Stephen Van Evera, "Offense, Defense and the Causes of War," *International Security* 22 (Spring 1998): 3–33.

13. The creation of mobile artillery in the latter part of the fifteenth century, leading to offense dominance as town walls quickly succumbed to mobile cannon fire, was followed by the development of the defensive trace itallienne by the 1520s, which included a series of defensive ramparts and bulwarks able to withstand sustained assaults. The use of air bombing and U-boats in World War I was followed by the development of radar and antiaircraft guns; the development of long-range missiles following World War II was followed by efforts to create effective ABM (anti-ballistic missile) systems and technology, continuing today in the on-again, off-again Star Wars program.

14. Rosecrance, *The Rise of the Trading State*.

15. These last were seen as so clearly offensive (in both senses of the word) that the United States abandoned a 1981 plan to stockpile the weapon.

16. For example, monitoring equipment (in itself an example of how information technology can help to establish and support norms and institutions) enables the analysis of real-time data from 321 geophysical stations in order to detect nuclear testing and to identify violations of the Comprehensive Test Ban Treaty (CTBT). Recent analysis by the International Data Center (IDC) suggested that the yields from both the Indian and Pakistani tests of May 1998 were substantially lower than announced by the respective countries, although evidence confirmed that tests did occur. Although the monitoring system may still not be perfected, the data as presented suggests that Indian claims that they set off an H-bomb in May 1998 may be greatly exaggerated and that the Pakistani claims for the yield of five explosions on May 28 and 30 were also grossly overestimated. India claimed the H-bomb alone had a yield of 45 kilotons; the IDC estimated the yield for all five Indian tests to be between 9 and 16 kilotons. The Pakistani tests were estimated to yield a blast of 16 kt., rather than the 60 kt. claimed by Pakistan. See Brian Barker, Michael Clark, et al., "Policy Forum: Seismology: Monitoring Nuclear Tests," *Science* 281, no. 5385 (1998): 1967–1968, as well as Raj Chengappa, "Is India's H-Bomb a Dud?" *India Today* 28, no. 41 (1998): 22–28).

17. For further information on the impact of information technology, see Cherie J. Steele and Arthur A. Stein, "Communications Revolutions and International Relations," in Juliann Emmons Allison and Glenn A. Oclassen, Jr., ed., *Conflict, Cooperation and Information*, Series on Global Politics. (Albany: State University of New York Press, forthcoming).

18. Including, among others, the NPT (Non-Proliferation Treaty) in 1968, the Limited Test-Ban Treaty of 1963, and the Comprehensive Test Ban Treaty of 1995.

19. Including SALT I and II (the Strategic Arms Limitation Talks of 1972 and 1979), the Chemical Weapons Convention of 1992, the Biological Weapons Convention of 1972, and the U.S./USSR Strategic Arms Reduction Treaty (START) signed in 1990.

20. These agreements included The Open Skies pact (proposed in 1955, signed in 1992), the establishment of the independent monitoring agency, the IAEA (International Atomic Energy Agency), and the ABM (anti-ballistic missile) Treaty of 1972.

21. Established in 1945.

22. Established in the Maastricht Treaty (or Treaty on European Union) of 1992.

23. Scott Sagan has traced the shift in these norms; he reported that testing was "deemed prestigious and legitimate in the 1960s, but is today considered illegitimate and irresponsible," and that international prestige has shifted from those states joining the nuclear club in the 1960s to those joining the NPT in the 1990s (Scott D. Sagan, "Why Do States Build Nuclear Weapons?" *International Security* 21 (Winter 1996/1997): p. 76.

24. Amitav Ghosh, "Countdown: Why Can't Every Country Have the Bomb?" *The New Yorker*, Oct. 26 and Nov. 2, 1998, 186–197.

25. Ibid., p. 188.

26. Ibid., p. 189.

27. Jaswant Singh, "Against Nuclear Apartheid," *Foreign Affairs* 77 (September/October 1998): 41–52.

28. See Robert Axelrod, *The Evolution of Cooperation* (New York: Basic Books, 1984).

29. Even comparing organizations in which states are still the major actors, territory and military power have become less important in determining power within the organization. The UN, for example, was structured so that all peacekeeping operations, as well as the Military Staff Committee, are under the auspices of the Security Council, which also has veto power over all other UN votes. The Security Council, of course, comprises the five great powers. Newer organizations are set up quite differently: The European Union, for example, gives all members equal stature in decisionmaking, with an independent European Court of Justice as the final arbiter of disputes between member states. The World Trade Organization also gives all members equal power, with an independent court to mediate disputes.

30. That is, a state without the ability to develop enough capital accumulation to enter into high-tech industries early enough in the process to compete.

31. Right now, growth rates in third world countries equal or surpass those in the developed world—in part because of slower growth rates in the west as developed countries attempt to decrease deficits and maintain low rates of inflation. But, again, timing matters—if the third world cannot accumulate enough capital quickly enough to compete when high-tech industries are in their infancy, they may be never be able to catch up because of increasing returns.

32. NICs (Newly Industrialized Countries) are benefiting today because wage rates remain low but an educated workforce exists—hence, India has become a

base for farming out the writing of software, and Japan has farmed out (lower value-added) technology to South Korea. Mexico has opened its markets to IBM in exchange for educational support. Brazil, however, which has worked so hard to educate its work force, offering incentives to improve links between the private sectors and universities, trying to create computer hardware, software, and semiconductor industries, and focusing on education, found that, in some cases (such as computer hardware), they entered the market too late to compete. They have now backed away from protectionist strategies and are trying to increase foreign direct investment—but the German and Spanish multinational corporations that have bought out or replaced local investors do not have the same interest as the Brazilian government in education.

33. At least before the recent Asian economic crisis.

12

The Justifying State: Why Anarchy Doesn't Mean No Excuses

ARTHUR A. STEIN[1]

In August 1990 Iraq attacked and conquered its neighbor Kuwait. The Iraqi government provided a justification: "Kuwait is part of Iraqi territory that was severed at some point in the past." This had been done "by the British occupation authorities," and thus, the annexation of Kuwait eliminated "a trace of Western colonialism."[2]

*   *   *

By 1941, U.S. president Franklin Roosevelt was committed to entering the ongoing war in Europe but believed he needed a justification. In August, he met British prime minister Winston Churchill to hammer out joint war objectives. Churchill noted FDR's plans: "The President ... said he would wage war, but not declare it, and that he would become more and more provocative. If the Germans did not like it, they could attack American forces. ... Everything was to be done to force an 'incident.' ... The President ... made it clear that he would look for an 'incident' which would justify him in opening hostilities."[3] As Roosevelt had told much of his staff even earlier, he believed that the United States would eventually join the war, but he wanted his hand forced.[4]

*   *   *

On November 18, 1967, at 9:30 on a Saturday evening, the British Treasury announced a devaluation of the British pound. The event culminated weeks of meetings and discussions with other nations' central bankers and finance ministers, as well as officials of the International Monetary Fund. British officials had justified their decision and took the steps they thought proper and required. They notified the IMF and awaited its approval of their new exchange rate before officially announcing the devaluation. As British Prime Minister Harold Wilson noted in his memoirs, "Devaluation was forced upon us, the whole world recognized that there was no alternative—central banks and governments accepted the decision as necessary."[5]

*   *   *

In each of these cases, a state either justified or looked for justification for its actions, and in each case it is not immediately clear why. When Iraq attacked Kuwait, an entrenched dictatorship that had previously attacked one of its neighbors (Iran) turned on another. Why justify its action? To what end? And to whom? Equally puzzling is the case of FDR, committed to one side in an ongoing war, already supporting that side in every way he could short of cobelligerency, aware of his country's interests, yet looking for a pretext to justify full-fledged military involvement. For whom was the justification needed? After the British had staved off devaluation for years, why had Prime Minister Harold Wilson wanted the world to recognize his country's actions as necessary? Why did he need anything more than his own government's assessment of what Britain required? Why the need for others to recognize that logic?

These are just a few examples of the *justifying state*, a sovereign state justifying its international behavior. Why do states explain themselves, and to whom do they justify their behavior? What values do they emphasize? And what are the implications of such behavior for our understanding of international politics?

The Expectation That States Should Not Justify Themselves

Anarchy means not having to explain yourself. Or it should. Sovereignty means not having to say you're sorry. Or it should.

The conventional understanding of international politics generates an expectation that there should be no justification of foreign policy. In the traditional vision of international politics, that of interacting independent states in an anarchic realm, states are autonomous, sovereign, and self-reliant. They fend for themselves; no one else assures their survival, meets their needs, or enforces their rights. International politics is about power, not rights and obligations. States assess their power relative to others' power. Might alone makes right.

In such a setting, states neither apologize for their behavior nor explain it. Power and interest explain the behavior of states. Self-interest is the sole justification. Unlike interpersonal relations and domestic society, international relations should have no role for justification. Sovereign states should not explain themselves, justify their behavior, or make excuses.

For what would be the point of justifying state behavior in a world guided solely by self-interest? The only justification states could provide for their behavior would be self-interest, and others would already presume that motive.[6] No other rationale would be credible. In short, explaining oneself and one's actions should not be an element of international politics.

Yet history is replete with examples of states justifying their behavior to one another, especially in the modern world. All types of states provide rationales, and they do so in a variety of issue domains. The United States and the Soviet Union justified virtually all their military interventions during the Cold War, usually by explaining that a local client or faction had invited them in. Major economic steps, such as changing exchange rates or altering the rules for cross-border flows, are usually accompanied by justifications. Small states justify their actions, and so do great powers. They justify military as well as economic measures. Allies explain themselves to one another, and so do rivals and antagonists.

I argue that the existence of justification reveals important insights about the nature of international politics. That states justify their actions does not imply the existence of a cooperative world and the absence of conflict. Rather, it explains much about how nations manage the processes of international conflict and cooperation—both at home and abroad. This paper argues that, at the very least, justification in international politics demonstrates that states recognize the centrality of domestic politics for foreign policy. It also highlights the incompleteness of realist theory. Most broadly, justification points to the existence of an international society with common global values.

Justification for Domestic Mobilization

Justifications are directed at audiences, and one such focus is internal. *Mobilizational justification* matters when governments need to mobilize their people. In fact, governments often provide reasons to make their actions acceptable or understandable to ordinary citizens. Bothering to explain implies recognition that people will either tolerate state actions or deem them unacceptable as a function of the reasons provided for them.

States justify their foreign policies to their own citizens when those policies require popular support—when society and economy must be mobilized but when the people would not automatically back their government without acceptable grounds. Governments that must mobilize citizen armies rather than mercenaries, for example, depend on internal support. Representative governments especially rely on popular backing for their foreign policies. "What a President says and thinks is not worth five cents unless he has the people and Congress behind him," President Lyndon Johnson told Israeli Foreign Minister Abba Eban in the days before the Six-Day War of June 1967. "Without the Congress I'm just a six-foot-four Texan. With the Congress I'm President of United States."[7]

Classic liberals criticized monarchies and advocated representative governments precisely because they could not envision democracies ever waging needless war, since their citizens would not agree to risk their lives or empty their pockets without cause.[8] However willing they might be to give even their lives for beliefs they hold dear, they might not be animated to sacrifice in order to maintain the balance of power. People can be mobilized to defend their homelands, to fight for country and a way of life. But mobilization on behalf of expansive aggression or intervention in foreign lands is not self-evidently defensive and requires special justification. At one meeting during the Gulf crisis in 1990, Senator William Cohen (Republican, Maine) cited Mark Twain's observation that people would fight to defend their homes but might have a different view towards their boardinghouse. And, he argued, the American people saw Kuwait and Saudi Arabia as "the equivalent of the boardinghouse."[9]

U.S. entry into war requires justification, and American presidents have typically found the best case for war to be when others attacked U.S. citizens, property, or the nation itself. In 1812, President Madison sent Congress a message that, although not requesting a declaration of war, made the case that Britain was already waging an undeclared war against the United States: "We behold . . . on the side of Great Britain a state of war against the United States, and on the side of the United States a state of peace toward Great Britain."[10]

President James Polk went even further by attempting to instigate an incident that would have the United States responding to provocation rather than initiating the hostilities that he wanted to occur. Polk came to power in 1845 as a dedicated expansionist whose vision for the country included acquiring Texas, Oregon, and California. When diplomatic attempts failed to get Mexico either to accept the U.S. claim that the Rio Grande marked the border of Texas or to sell New Mexico and California to the United States, Polk ordered troops into the disputed area. He instructed them to march to the Rio Grande, but not to initiate hostilities.

They were, however, to treat any Mexican incursion into the disputed territory as an act of war.

In Washington, President Polk and his Cabinet anxiously awaited news from the Southwest, hoping that Mexico would commit an act of "aggression." Tired of waiting, the Cabinet prepared a war message anyway, one justifying war on the grounds that Mexico refused to negotiate and had failed to fulfill promises to U.S. claimants. Still, Secretary of the Navy George Bancroft thought it would be preferable had a hostile act occurred on the border. And in fact, the arrival of U.S. forces at the Rio Grande had already brought Mexican reinforcements, generated a sequence of actions and reactions, and a skirmish. General Zachary Taylor notified Washington, "Hostilities may now be considered as commenced."[11] His note, which took two weeks to arrive, finally got to Polk right after the cabinet decided on Saturday to send a war message to Congress by Tuesday. Polk, given the stronger justification he wanted, wrote his message to Congress in strong terms: "Mexico has passed the boundary of the United States, has invaded our territory and shed American blood upon American soil. . . . War exists, and notwithstanding all our efforts to avoid it, exists by the act of Mexico."[12] He did not even ask Congress for a declaration of war, but simply for recognition that Mexico's actions meant that a state of war already existed between the two governments.

President Polk had searched for a peaceful resolution consistent with U.S. territorial demands of Mexico, but he was prepared to go to war. Even then, he preferred to await an incident that would make the United States the responder rather than the initiator. When Mexico obliged by reacting to U.S. provocations, Polk had his incident, and Congress responded predictably, approving the war message overwhelmingly and swiftly.

Almost a century later, FDR faced different circumstances that delayed U.S. entry into World War II. In the 1930s, FDR wanted to oppose Nazi Germany's expansion in Europe but confronted a Congress dominated by isolationists intent on keeping the United States out of any European war and prepared to keep the president from even assisting those trying to deter German aggression. He struggled against the constraints that Congress and public opinion imposed, and he constantly qualified his commitments to European leaders with references to the constraints under which he labored. Even as he moved the nation toward rearmament and the support of one side in the European conflict, he believed that the nation's actual entry into war would require the justification that it had been attacked first. Ironically, Hitler understood this and decided not to oblige FDR, ordering his navy not to fire on U.S. ships in the Atlantic. Only the Japanese attack on Pearl Harbor and Germany's subsequent declaration of war on the United States made possible full-fledged U.S. entry into the European war.[13]

The United States has often intervened overseas for a variety of economic, strategic, and ideological reasons, but short of an attack on U.S. soil or U.S. troops, the justification that has resonated most strongly at home has been an attack on U.S. citizens. A common justification for overseas intervention that has great domestic salience, therefore, is the need to save American lives. Ronald Reagan, for example, explained the U.S. intervention in Grenada and the toppling of its regime as necessary to save the lives of American medical students on the island.

Sometimes, however, the government has had to search for a justification that the American people would find sufficiently credible to generate the domestic support needed. George Bush tested a series of rationales for sending troops to the Persian Gulf in the wake of the Iraqi absorption of Kuwait. The president emphasized oil, the protection of Saudi Arabia, Iraq's being on the verge of deploying nuclear weapons, Saddam Hussein's taking Americans and other foreigners in Iraq hostage, the brutality of Iraq's occupation of Kuwait, and the importance of demonstrating that naked aggression would not go unpunished.[14] The president "kept shifting his emphasis among various justifications for the U. S. military deployment in the Gulf, as if he were market-testing ads for a new deodorant."[15]

That representative governments might lie or mislead their populations in order to secure support for an otherwise insupportable policy has led some to emphasize the role of an elected legislature and a free press as checks on executive power. Supreme Court Justice Hugo Black held that "Paramount among the responsibilities of a free press is the duty to prevent any part of the government from deceiving the people and sending them off to distant lands to die of foreign fevers and foreign shot and shell."[16]

Governments whose audience is solely domestic can base their justification on narrow, parochial values. They can mobilize on such grounds as nationalism, racism, ethnic solidarity, or religion—on the basis of values that are not universal and, especially, not shared with the nation being opposed.[17] It is a form of justification that can exist in worlds in which domestic societies matter but in which no international society (or only a limited one) exists.[18]

Justification intended for domestic consumption affirms, contrary to the conventional realist wisdom, the centrality of domestic politics for international politics. That view is built on the presumption that states are capable of acting in an interstate arena devoid of domestic constraints. It posits security against outside attack as the key reason for the existence of the state (*raison d'état*), holds that states act in self-interest, and presumes their ability to mobilize support and resources. Yet a state's need to justify behavior implies the existence of domestic constraints on foreign policy. The need to justify means that states cannot just do whatever they want and then argue simply that they acted in the interests of the country. This limitation is especially strong now. The growth in the number of states with representative governments and of literate and knowledgeable citizenries, together with the role of modern communications, translates into a growing need for states to justify their foreign policies in order to obtain domestic support.

Justification As Pretext

Justification does not always address an internal audience. Even when the most totalitarian of regimes have had no domestic reason to do so, they have justified their foreign policies to external ears. Unlike rationales intended for domestic consumption, however, justification to foreigners is not inconsonant with the conventional realist view of a conflict-ridden interstate system populated with autonomous self-interested states. States wage war for a variety of reasons, from self-defense to self-aggrandizement. Nevertheless, states still rationalize their decisions to each other, sometimes creating elaborate ruses before the fact in order to go to war in the first place. They need pretexts to fight even when they believe war is in their interest. Justification is then simply a facet of their cynical, self-serving behavior.

Inhibiting Justification: Signaling Limited Aims

Explaining the need for justification in a way consistent with standard (realist) views of international politics requires arguing that states explain themselves to others in order to get away with aggression. That is indeed one reason states explain themselves: Justification in these cases is intended to make aggressive actions appear reasonable and limited in the hope of preventing the emergence of a countervailing coalition intended to contain the aggressor's future expansion or force it to give up its gains.

Hitler, for example, provided reasons for each predatory step Germany took in the 1930s; he wanted each move to appear reasonable, limited, and certain to be his last. Such measures had the intended effect of delaying the consolidation of a balancing coalition. Astonishingly, Nazi Germany was trying to justify its aggression as late as September 1939 by claiming that its attack on Poland was a response to border violations.

During the Cold War, the superpowers justified their interventions, when they could, by arguing that they had been invited in. The Soviet Union, for example, used this excuse to explain its intervention in Hungary in 1956 and Czechoslovakia in 1968.

Iraq's explanation of its conquest of Kuwait exemplifies the use of limited-aims justification to divide other states and minimize the adverse consequences that aggression might otherwise generate. Iraq knew it could conquer Kuwait and take control of its oil fields easily only if others, especially the United States, refrained from entering the fray. But the Iraqis also knew that U.S. involvement was almost certain if its aggression looked like a first move toward taking control of much of the world's oil supplies—if the invasion suggested, for example, that Saudi Arabia was next on a hit list. Iraq accurately saw its ability to get away with its aggression as depending on its successfully signaling that it had limited ambitions and so dissuading others from a military reaction. So Iraq justified its behavior by arguing that Kuwait had always been considered part of Iraqi territory and was, in fact, its nineteenth province.[19] Making the attack on Kuwait appear the forcible resolution of a long-standing territorial dispute was intended to ease others' fears about subsequent Iraqi behavior. The rationalization did not have to placate all concerned nations, only enough of them to prevent the emergence of a viable countercoalition. This kind of divide-and-conquer strategy is predicated upon the ability of aggressors to generate sufficient uncertainty about their future intentions to prevent the formation of a countercoalition.

Nations justify their behavior by appealing to others in terms that are understandable, if not always acceptable, to their audience. The more values shared among justifier and relevant third parties, the more important the need to justify a norm-breaking action. Thucydides relates that Sparta, having chosen war with Athens, spent "the period before the outbreak of war . . . in sending embassies to Athens with various complaints, so that there should be a good pretext for making war if the Athenians paid no attention to them."[20]

This eminently realist explanation for the justifying state reveals some important aspects of international politics. Revisionist actions by states do not automatically generate countervailing coalitions, which often arise because of their members' expectations about the revisionist's future behavior (its intentions) rather than its past actions. Not only do states not automatically balance adverse shifts in the balance of power, they do not always create balancing coalitions in response to actual aggression. Balancing requires not just revisionist behavior that brings change to the balance of power, but depends critically on threat perception and the expectation of future aggression.[21]

Pretexts are therefore useful even in a realist world, because states not only assess one another's power and look at one another's actions, but evaluate intentions and draw inferences about other states' types and their prospective behavior. Pretexts then play the role of signaling limited aims and ambitions. They minimize the import of aggression. They make states' actions appear to be responses to their environment rather than autonomously driven and chosen.

In this way, justification adds an interesting wrinkle to arguments in psychology about attribution and the actor/observer disjuncture. Experiments show that people see themselves as having less choice than others. They attribute others' actions to their attributes, choices, preferences, and predispositions, but their own actions to the pressures of external forces. Pretexts are a social device by which actors, aware of others' likely attributions, signal that they are in fact reacting to others rather than making independent choices.

Justification as pretext implies that the meaning of actions are not self-evident, but contingent and open to interpretation. States evaluate discrete actions as part of a pattern and remain as concerned about future consequences as immediate ones. Justification plays a role in contextualizing one state's behavior for others. Justifications may be accurate or they may be ruses, and they may or may not succeed, but there is no question that they play a role in international politics.

Defanging Justification: Justifying to Others' Citizens

Justifications as signals of limited ambition can be directed at the citizens of other countries as well as their governing elites. Justification can be useful in affecting the responses of other countries that are constrained by their domestic societies.

A state can signal limited aims in order to make it difficult for other states to mobilize in response when state-society relations in those other states require rationalization for such mobilizations. Even if Saddam Hussein, as an autocrat, did not require a domestic political cover to attack Kuwait, convincingly justifying his actions might have made it more difficult for other countries to mount an opposition. Calling the invasion a response to a long-standing territorial dispute might have made it harder for the democratic great powers to mobilize their populations to expel him from Kuwait. The citizen-audience for justification in such cases is not one's own population but those of relevant others.

Justifying to other countries' citizens need not be solely to prevent unwanted reaction but may also be intended to elicit sympathy. Even when states have good reasons for their actions, they may concoct justifications that get them greater, and more certain, popular sympathy from other countries. The 1967 Israeli attack on Egypt came in response to Egyptian actions that included the closure of an international waterway, an adequate *casus belli* in international law. But since U.S. President Lyndon Johnson had personally impressed upon Israeli Foreign Minister Abba Eban that Israel should "not be the one to bear the responsibility for any outbreak of war,"[22] Israeli Prime Minister Levi Eshkol had delayed the attack, "using time as currency to secure ultimate political support."[23] When Israel did attack on June 5, the first two cables to Washington said that fighting had been initiated by Egyptian forces that had struck Israel. When that story was quickly challenged, the Israelis amended the rationalization and claimed that Egypt had been on the verge of attacking. Israeli officials, who later acknowledged that they had not expected an Egyptian attack at all, feared that even an acceptable *casus belli* under international law would not be enough to secure support. And indeed, President Johnson's first question when informed of the fighting was, "How did it start? Who fired first?"[24]

Justification aimed at others' citizens implies the existence of values that transcend state boundaries. Explanations of foreign policies intended to affect the way in which they are viewed and the nature of the responses to them must be done in terms of common values. Such appeals must be framed in encompassing terms, not exclusionary and narrow ones. Because the justification is nothing less than a claim that one's actions are just and appropriate, securing the understanding and sympathy of other nations' citizens requires that the justification be cast in terms they accept and according to values they share.[25]

The existence of justification and its implications about engaged citizenries and common international values does not assure cooperation and can be consistent with realism. It may indeed be that states must appeal to their own populations and can try appealing to others on the basis of mutual values. Nevertheless, as some of the above discussion implies, states can justify their behavior quite cynically in order to undertake the kind of autonomous and conflictual behavior that realism implies. Realism still describes state interests and choices, but ones whose implementation may require justification. In other ways, world politics remains unchanged.

In important ways, however, an understanding of the uses and roles of justification does in fact change our understanding of international politics. In certain circumstances, justification implies the importance of domestic politics, the existence of shared values, and the contingency of balancing responses to aggression.

Justification and International Society

There is an additional, critical reason for the justifying state, one that must be conjoined with those adduced above: the rise of an international society that tolerates justifiable defections. The growth and changing nature of justification in the past half century both illuminate the development of a community of countries in which the reasons for state actions are as important as actual behavior in determining how other states respond. This emergence of an international society is an important phenomenon, one that makes international politics more like domestic society.

One clear implication of explaining oneself to others is that there must be generalized norm-based expectations for behavior. Justifications and rationalizations represent attempts to explain deviations from others' expectations—from assumed norms. It suggests that the justifying actor recognizes others' expectations and preferences as regards its behavior and realizes that violating them may have adverse consequences that rationalization can mitigate.

States justify in order to get other nations to acquiesce in, if not to support, their actions. Providing a rationale involves explaining behavior in such language and invoking values that others understand and even accept. Obtaining others' understanding can mean avoiding opprobrium or worse; gaining acceptance can even mean securing support. When Great Britain devalued the pound in 1967, the British government worried that important European nations would simply devalue their currencies in turn and negate the consequences of the British devaluation. The British had experienced such reactions before and wanted to make certain that others found the devaluation justified by circumstance rather than an attempt to gain an advantage, because the latter would more likely be countered.

States also justify their behavior in order to avoid punishment for deviating from expected patterns of behavior. Here, international politics resembles civil society. Whether a particular killing is deemed murder or justifiable homicide depends on circumstance and the nature of the justification provided. Societies establish judicial procedures for ascertaining, on a case-by-case basis, whether deviations from code are justified or punishable. When the circumstances are deemed exigent, a nominal offense may be accepted as excusable or even appropriate.[26] Civil societies recognize that some individual departures from customary and expected behavior do not violate norms. They do not fear that leaving the deed unpunished will invite further miscreant behavior by either the same person or others. There is no sense that the failure to punish will create a new calculus that will embolden anyone to flout the rules in dissimilar situations. The social fabric does not unravel as long as behaviors can be distinguished from one another and only justified defections from social norms are left unpunished. Even as simple and straightforward a rule as "thou shalt not kill" can be violated under certain circumstances. Societies consist not only of rules, but of rules for violating rules and procedures for adjudicating individual violations on their merits.[27]

Something similar is at work in international relations. States acting in violation of others' expectations justify their actions in the hope of avoiding punishment. There exists, as discussed below, something akin to an international society with norms of appropriate state conduct.[28]

Prisoners' Dilemma and Justified Defection

By presenting the argument in terms of values understandable to the target audience, the justifier intends to generate a response that is less conflictual and hostile than would occur absent the justification. Imagine a system of self-interested actors interacting in a repeated prisoners' dilemma. At each point in each bilateral relationship, each player has a dominant strategy of defecting. But every actor in every dyadic interaction is better off at every point if both cooperate. In such a system, cooperation can be maintained by everyone's commitment to a grim-trigger strategy: Every actor will defect against any actor who has defected against anyone. One defection unravels such a cooperative world, and cooperation is sustained by the threat that such defection will bring a punishing counterdefection by the victimized state. There is also linkage in such worlds, for others punish the opportunistic defector, approximating what happens in domestic societies. The victims of crime do not themselves punish criminals; not even their immediate families do so.[29] Rather, members of the civic society who typically know neither criminal nor victim punish.

The grim-trigger strategy is a problematic way to sustain cooperation. A single defection unravels everything. Yet the incentives for defection vary, and without some mechanism for distinguishing between cases of situationally induced defection and those caused by wanton greed, cooperation will dissolve at the first defection. The actual payoffs in real world repeated prisoners' dilemmas change—leaving actors to confront situations that magnify their fear and greed and so create exceedingly great pressures for defection. It is important to recognize that defection in the prisoners' dilemma can be explained either by the fear of being taken advantage of (and receiving the worst payoff when the other defects in the face of cooperation) or by the desire for the gains to be made through defecting when others cooperate. Defection can rest on either greed or fear, and there is no way to separate those sentiments and identify the motivation simply by observing defection in the prisoners' dilemma.

Yet social cooperation requires distinguishing between a wanton rule-breaking and a situationally exigent and temporary departure from accepted norms. The former involves actors who do not see themselves as bound by the rules and who cheat opportunistically if they find it worthwhile—if, that is, they deem the odds of punishment sufficiently slight or the severity of retribution sufficiently inconsequential that they expect a net benefit. Situationally exigent defections, on the other hand, involve actors who accept the rules, are prepared to enforce them for others, and recognize them as binding upon themselves. Exceptional circumstances, however, make their continued adherence suddenly costly. An ability to apprise others of the changed situation and gain their acquiescence for departure is desirable, because by taking into account exigent circumstances, it sustains the system of rules that all want maintained in the longer term.

Sustaining international cooperation, therefore, requires some mechanism for distinguishing between justified and unjustified defection. Indeed, the absence of such a mechanism can prevent the consummation of international agreements when farsighted states, recognizing the potential need for defection at some future time, eschew international agreements in the present.[30] If the international world approximated civil society, states would be assured that their agreement to cooperate would not bring punishment should circumstances require their temporary departures from expected behavior. Thus, a world that tolerates justifiable defection makes possible higher levels of cooperation by ensuring that not every defection unravels systemic cooperation.

Exculpatory Justification: International Society and Sanctioned Departures

Indeed, the realm of international relations has increasingly come to resemble civil society. States reach cooperative agreements that stipulate what exigent circumstances would make defection acceptable, and they establish procedures for adjudicating culpability.

This evolution has been particularly dramatic in the international economic arena during the twentieth century, as illustrated by the marked contrast between the pre- and post–World War II eras. During the Great Depression, nations defected from the economic order by raising tariffs and devaluing their currencies. A vicious circle of defections set off the downward spiral of the world economy, as the system of international exchange and finance collapsed in the wake of beggar-thy-neighbor policies. The U.S. depression spread throughout the world. Both criticisms of U.S. policy and analytic arguments about the necessity of hegemons not adopting others' policies in such dire circumstances implicitly recognize the failure of tit-for-tat in sustaining cooperation in such cases and commend an alternative in which a great economic power tolerates others' cheating for its own and everyone else's good.

The construction of the post–World War II world included plans to revive international trade and capital flows. International agreements struck to govern both recognized that dire circumstances might arise. Individual states would confront balance of payments and trade crises and want desperately to alleviate them. No state could be expected to live by the rules in all circumstances. Moreover, the system would collapse if punishment followed every deviation. Hence, these agreements specified conditions that would constitute exceptions to typically expected compliance. They also established procedures by which states could obtain approval for their defections.

The General Agreement on Tariffs and Trade (GATT), for example, delineates the conditions under which states can defect from trade agreements and impose trade restrictions without retaliation. GATT rules prohibit states from imposing unilateral quotas, but provide an exception when imports threaten "market disruption."[31] It also outlines procedures by which disputes involving defections can be adjudicated. States have a forum in which to complain about others' practices and seek permission, as it were, for imposing countervailing measures.

Similarly, in the immediate postwar period, the International Monetary Fund (IMF) established rules for acceptable changes in exchange rates and for the imposition of exchange controls. Its Articles of Agreement includes specific language allowing exchange rates to be changed if the IMF agreed that a country's balance of payments was in "fundamental disequilibrium."[32] Countries experiencing balance-of-payments crises could impose controls as well as devalue their currencies. Indeed, states could get prior private international agreement allowing them to depart from the normally expected and enforced rules.

Modern international agreements are facilitated and sustained by escape clauses that stipulate justifiable and excusable defections from them. States concerned about future contingencies can therefore sign agreements in the knowledge that situations requiring their defection will be recognized and tolerated without retribution. In this way, fears of the future do not derail agreements in states' current interests. Moreover, the occurrence of exigent circumstances leads not to an unraveling of the agreement but to the accepted and excused defections of a few.[33]

Justification and Apologies

The phenomenon of the justifying state is only one indication of the rise of an international society in which states do not just explain their behavior, but even apologize for it. In a striking historical development, governments have apologized to one another and to one another's people. Some fifty years after World War II, for example, Japanese Prime Minister Tomiichi Murayama personally apologized to Korea for his nation's occupation of the region in the first half of the twentieth century.[34] But this initial apology was seen as personal, not official, and as insufficiently contrite. Hence, South Korean President Kim Dae-jung's later state visit to Japan was preceded by extensive intergovernmental negotiations in order to generate a public apology that would facilitate intersocietal reconciliation; it had to be sufficiently remorseful to satisfy Koreans and not too excessive for Japanese sentiment.[35]

Retrospective apologies for past behavior exemplify an altered international environment in which domestic populations play important roles in constraining and shaping state policy. Apologies reflect the continuing centrality of peoples' feelings toward other countries and the importance of easing their anger and hurt in order to move contemporaneous relationships forward. This is a striking development in the evolution of international politics.

Justification: Types and Implications

States, despite sovereignty, justify their behavior. The examples provided above illustrate the types of justification, which vary by purpose, audience, and values emphasized. In turn, the different forms of justification differ in their implications for our understanding of international politics. Tables 12.1 and 12.2 lay out the essential points.

Audience: Justification and Domestic Politics

The need for some governments to mobilize their citizens underlies two reasons that governments provide rationales for their actions. The audience for a justifying state may be its own society, the society of other countries, or other governments. When the audience is a society, the point of justification is mobilization, either to facilitate or to impede the mobilization of social forces. When aimed at a state's own society, the intent is to secure the domestic support needed for the state's foreign policy. When aimed at another country's people, justification is meant either to mobilize foreign support or to prevent a foreign government from mounting an opposition. Justification may make it more difficult, for example, for other states to punish miscreant behavior. At the extreme, a state can hope to generate sufficient internal pressure on foreign governments to obtain the support of those those governments that would otherwise have opposed it.

That states justify their actions underlines the importance of domestic politics for international relations. Were governments certain of domestic support for their policies, justification would be irrelevant. States engaged in revising the status quo can most easily mobilize internal support if they cast their actions as reactions to the provocations of others. Yet states engaged in the balancing responses described by realist analyses of international politics also find the need to offer reasons for mobilizing—citizens do not sacrifice for the balance of power alone. State-society relations are essential elements of the strategic interaction of countries.

TABLE 12.1   Justification: Types, Audiences, Values, and Purposes

Type	*Audience*	*Values appealed to*	*Purpose*
Mobilizational	Own society	Typically exclusive (can be inclusive)	Obtain domestic support
Inhibiting	Other governments	Typically exclusive (can be inclusive)	Preclude opposition by signaling limited aims
Defanging	Other societies	Inclusive	Prevent other countries from mobilizing opposition
Exculpatory	Mostly other governments, but also their societies	Inclusive	Obtain others' acquiescence and approval for norm-breaking behavior or defections

Values

Justification entails an appeal to values and to circumstances. It is an attempt to get others to understand the logic of a state's actions, to see them as appropriate and necessary given some set of basic values, the situation, and the choices available. The presumption is that others can recognize and accept the bases of the state's behavior.

When the support of the target audience is at stake, the values appealed to are inclusive, ones shared by justifier and audience. When such appeals are made internationally, there must be some common values held across national boundaries. Probably the most fundamental value is the right to self-defense against unprovoked attack.

Justification also relies on exclusive values, ones not shared. Domestic appeals to mobilize one's own society against foreigners typically do rely not on universal values but on such parochial ones as religion, ethnicity, race, and nationality. Not surprisingly, therefore, the most virulent forms of racism and nationalism are evident during wartime and comparable extremes of domestic mobilization.[36]

Reliance on exclusive values for international as opposed to internal justification is intended to demonstrate the self-limiting nature of one's expansive interests. States signal to one another, for example, that they want to expand only in order to absorb coreligionists or members of their people's own race and ethnicity. Here, the emphasis on self-limiting rather than universal values is essential to prevent the development of a balancing countercoalition. In contrast to expansion in the service of sup-

TABLE 12.2   Justification: Types and Implications

Type	Implications for our understanding of international politics
Mobilizational	Domestic support not presumable, must be acceptable to populace
Inhibiting	Opposition to revisionist behavior not automatic; balancing not automatic
Defanging	Balancing not automatic, depends on others' ability to mobilize support internally; common values exist that can be appealed to across countries
Exculpatory	International society exists; cooperation does not unravel from every defection; retaliation and punishment a function of explanation and circumstance and not just a response to any action

posedly universal values, which scares all others in the system who do not share those values, expansion in the service of parochial values is inherently limited and does not threaten everyone else.

International Society

Sustained international cooperation depends not only on the existence of mutually beneficial exchanges and agreements, but on the expectation that states will not be adversely affected in the future by the commitments they make today. Like individuals and firms, states cannot draft contracts that include every foreseeable contingency. But they can delineate the foreseeable circumstances of the need to punish hostile transgressions and the need to excuse exigent circumstantial departures. States want to be free to violate their commitments in order to punish miscreants, but they also want to be free to violate their commitments out of necessity without retribution. Both elements are essential to the creation and maintenance of an international order. Without such agreement on acceptable and unacceptable defection (or some mechanism for ascertaining them), many agreements would not be viable. Without such agreement, all accords would be destroyed by the first appearance of difficulty.

The creation of terms of acceptable defection and of institutions for corporate sanctioning (in both its senses, punishment and acquiescence) generates an important international equivalent to domestic society. Domestic social compacts are not just about authoritative enforcement in one entity, they are also about mutually acceptable rules for behavior that excuse cheating and entail mechanisms to determine when and what punishment is appropriate. This development constitutes an important element in the emergence of an international society.

Conclusion

Justification in international politics tells us that the international state system is not composed of autonomous independent entities simply pursuing their interests without needing to obtain domestic support or to explain and justify their actions to foreigners. Justification is an important element in ascertaining the existence of an international society with intersubjectively recognized and accepted guidelines for behavior, in which departures will be punished unless justified. It implies a world in which sustainable cooperation exists. Such cooperation can weather the vicissitudes of circumstance. It also implies the existence of shared values (even if used merely instrumentally) and their effacement (whether justified, excused, or not) in order to pursue contrarian activity.

Justification is of growing importance in a world of more nations with representative governments whose citizens' preferences can allow or scuttle the pursuit of foreign policies. Foreign policy is increasingly a product of domestic politics, and so justification targeted at both one's own and other societies becomes part and parcel of foreign policy.

Justification has also been fundamental to the emergence and maintenance of global interdependence. The very international agreements and institutions that have both made interdependence possible and have dealt with its fallout[37] depend critically on provisions that provide escapes from commitments in exigent circumstances. The possibility of justifiable defection has made possible the gradual construction of global order with rule-governed relations.

Justification confirms the occurrence of important changes in the nature of international politics. The views of citizens matter in the formulation of many countries' foreign policies, and so governments justify their behavior to their own citizens and those of other countries'. Intersocietal justification presumes the existence of common values to which states appeal. Finally, the growth of international agreements depends upon socially sanctioned departures from expectations. In short, the international system increasingly resembles a society in which normative behavioral expectations exist and in which states justify their actions to avoid sanction for their exigent defections.

Notes

1. My thanks to Elizabeth Matthews and Joel Scanlon for research assistance, and to Amy Davis and Cherie Steele for comments and suggestions.

2. The Iraqi justification elicited scholarly responses analyzing the history of Iraqi claims and their legal and historical merits. For an example of this kind of analysis, see Lawrence Freedman and Karsh Efraim, *The Gulf Conflict 1990–1991: Diplomacy and War in the New World Order* (Princeton: Princeton University Press, 1993), pp. 42–44.

3. David Reynolds, *The Creation of the Anglo-American Alliance 1937–41: A Study in Comparative Co-Operation* (Chapel Hill: University of North Carolina Press, 1982), pp. 214–215.

4. For a compilation of the evidence for Roosevelt's desire to be forced into war, see Reynolds, *The Creation of the Anglo-American Alliance*, p. 347, n. 38.

5. Harold Wilson, *A Personal Record: The Labour Government 1964–1970* (Boston: Little, Brown and Company, 1971): see p. 6 for the quote, for the preceding events see pp. 439–459.

6. Justification is also problematic for rational-choice explanations of social and domestic life. If behavior were solely guided by self-interested calculation, then justification would be unnecessary, since the only justification, self-interest, would already be recognized as such by others.

7. Donald Neff, *Warriors for Jerusalem: The Six Days That Changed the Middle East* (New York: Simon and Schuster, 1984), p. 145.

8. This "political liberalism" is discussed in Arthur A. Stein, "Governments, Economic Interdependence, and International Cooperation" in *Behavior, Society, and International Conflict*, vol. 3, pp. 241–324, edited by Philip E. Tetlock, Jo L. Husbands, Robert Jervis, Paul C. Stern, and Charles Tilly (New York: Oxford University Press, for the National Research Council of the National Academy of Sciences, 1993).

9. Bob Woodward, *The Commanders* (New York: Simon and Schuster, 1991), p.339.

10. Bradford Perkins, *Prologue to War: England and the United States, 1805–1812* (Berkeley and Los Angeles: University of California Press, 1961), p. 404.

11. Thomas G. Paterson, J. Garry Clifford, and Kenneth J. Hagan, *American Foreign Policy: A History* (Lexington, Mass.: D. C. Heath and Company, 1977), p. 82.

12. Bradford Perkins, *The Cambridge History of American Foreign Relations*, vol. 1: *The Creation of a Republican Empire, 1776–1865* (New York: Cambridge University Press, 1993), p. 190.

13. For my assessment of U.S. grand strategy during this period, see Arthur A. Stein, "Domestic Constraints, Extended Deterrence, and the Incoherence of Grand Strategy: The U.S., 1938–1950," in *The Domestic Bases of Grand Strategy*, eds. Richard Rosecrance and Arthur A. Stein (Ithaca: Cornell University Press, 1993), pp. 96–123.

14. Some stories of Iraqi brutality turned out to be fabricated products of a Kuwaiti public relations campaign intended to assure public support for military action to oust Iraq from Kuwait.

15. Michael Duffy and Dan Goodgame, *Marching in Place: The Status Quo Presidency of George Bush* (New York: Simon and Schuster, 1992), p. 154.

16. *New York Times v. U.S.*, *U.S. Report*, vol. 403 (1971), p. 717.

17. For the role of these factors in international politics, see my *Blood and Power: Culture and International Politics*, in progress.

18. Alternatively, such particularistic justifications can be consistent with international societies that are really regional subsystems. In ancient Greece, the Peloponnesian League, the Delian League, and what is sometimes called the Hellenic League included somewhat overlapping memberships and were all justified on the grounds of making common cause against the Persians. The initial justification for one league did not, therefore, pose a threat to the others. Donald Kagan, *The Outbreak of the Peloponnesian War* (Ithaca: Cornell University Press, 1969).

19. Iraq also listed a set of old grievances against Kuwait and generated new ones. First, it argued, Kuwait was helping keep world oil prices low and thus hurting Iraq. This explanation did not, however, act to separate Kuwait from Saudi Arabia, since the Iraqis could make a similar claim against the Saudis. Second, Iraq argued that Kuwait was siphoning off Iraqi oil by pumping from a pool lying under their common border. Third, Iraq claimed two islands in the Persian Gulf held by Kuwait. Finally, Iraq resurrected its claim that Britain had inappropriately created Kuwait as an independent nation from historically Iraqi territory. On the Gulf crisis, see Freedman and Efraim, *The Gulf Conflict 1990–1991*.

20. Thucydides, *The Peloponnesian War*, translated by Rex Warner (Baltimore, Maryland: Penguin Books, 1954), p. 82.

21. The prospect that not all aggression is comparably threatening implies that not all aggression should generate the same response. See Kristen Williams, "Nationalist Conflicts: Threats to International Peace?" (Ph.D. dissertation, UCLA, 1998). Moreover, the threats (perceived and real) themselves vary. See Stein, *Blood and Power*.

22. Lyndon Baines Johnson, *The Vantage Point: Perspectives of the Presidency 1963–1969* (New York: Holt, Rinehart and Winston, 1971), p. 293. After making the point directly, the President handed Eban an aide-mémoire making the same argument. See Abba Eban, *Personal Witness: Israel Through My Eyes* (New York: G. P. Putnam's Sons, 1992), p. 390.

23. Martin Gilbert, *Israel: A History* (New York: William Morrow and Company, 1998), p. 375.

24. Neff, *Warriors for Jerusalem*, pp. 210–211.

25. Propaganda efforts intended to obtain outside intervention in war or civil war, for example, have this character.

26. This paper does not distinguish between justifications and excuses. In moral theory, justified actions are warranted, and therefore can be performed by others, should not be interfered with, and should be assisted. Excuses may relieve an actor of blame, but do not make the action appropriate and warranted in the above sense. The argument developed in this paper is that excused defections are indeed deemed warranted, could be performed by others, and are assisted in the sense that they are excused. But unlike justifications, excuses recognize a norm that is being broken for exigent circumstances. For the classic paper, see John L. Austin, "A Plea for Excuses," *Proceedings of the Aristotelian Society* 57 (1956): 1–30. The ethical distinction is often difficult to make in the law; see Kent Greenawalt, "The Perplexing Borders of Justification and Excuse," *Columbia Law Review* 84 (1984): 1897–1927.

27. Robert B. Edgerton, *Rules, Exceptions, and Social Order* (Berkeley and Los Angeles: University of California Press, 1985).

28. Hedley Bull developed the concept of international society, which has been called the defining difference of "the English school." See Hedley Bull, *The Anarchical Society: A Study of Order in World Politics* (New York: Columbia University Press, 1977), and Barry Buzan, "From international system to international society: structural realism and regime theory meet the English school," *International Organization* 47 (Summer 1993): 327–352.

29. Though families have punished in some societies.

30. For this problem, monitoring and transparency are inadequate to generate cooperation.

31. An undefined condition usually interpreted to mean unusual surges in imports that threaten the survival of an entire industry.

32. Another undefined condition meaning that a country has experienced a permanent shift in the international demand for its products.

33. Terms that allow exit and renegotiation can also facilitate agreement in an uncertain environment. But excused cheating is preferable in that the occurrence of exigent circumstances is less likely to unravel agreements.

34. In a similar vein, the Soviet government apologized in 1989 for a host of earlier actions; this apology was offered, however, by a new regime distancing itself from past regimes.

35. Nicholas D. Kristof, "Korean Leader, in Japan, Urges Healing of Old Wounds." *New York Times,* October 8, 1998; and Nicholas D. Kristof, "Japanese Leader Apologizes for Occupation of Korea." *New York Times,* October 9, 1998.

36. This pattern has been repeatedly evident in U.S. history. For one example, see John Dower, *War Without Mercy: Race and Power in the Pacific War* (New York: Parthenon Books, 1986).

37. Stein, "Governments, Economic Interdependence, and International Cooperation."

13

The Cold War and Its Ending in "Long-Duration" International History

PAUL W. SCHROEDER

This essay is a kind of flight forward (*fuite en avant*). Contributors were asked to discuss the most significant development in international relations in the twentieth century and its likely implications for the twenty-first. My choice, an obvious one, was the end of the Cold War. Yet as a scholar whose serious study of international history begins with the seventeenth century but does not extend much beyond 1945 I am ill equipped to analyze the Cold War and its outcome. I could claim, as historians often do, that only a long-range comparative historical perspective enables us to understand so recent a development, and then try to provide that perspective by comparing the end of the Cold War to supposedly analogous historical events or developments over several centuries (for example, the termination of other enduring rivalries). This essay may look like such an exercise in historical comparison, but it is not.

First of all, any such attempt faces grave epistemological and methodological problems in regard to its validity, intersubjective verifiability, and usefulness. A second more immediate concern is that it often generates a response from political scientists, international relations theorists, and policy experts that can be called polite dismissal. They listen more or less attentively to the historical discussion, remark, "That's interesting," and then go back to analyzing the event by their own methods in line with their own concerns about its immediate origins, course, and present and future implications.

Therefore this essay is a bolder and more hazardous attempt to escape the dilemma. Rather than try to draw analogies and lessons from the history of four centuries of European and world international politics to apply to the Cold War and its end, I propose instead to place the Cold War and its end into that long history, as an integral part of it, and to claim that doing so can contribute to how we understand it.

Such a project requires showing (or rather, for reasons of space, asserting) two things. The first is that there is a history of the evolution of European and world international politics from the early seventeenth century that demonstrates certain distinct stages of development—in other words, that this history has gone somewhere, is in some sense directional, and is not simply a kaleidoscopic jumble of contingent events and merely cyclical change—"just one damned thing after another," as the famed historian Sir Richard Pares once termed it. The second assertion is that the Cold War and its termination fit into that general pattern, represent a particular stage in that long history. If these two points could be established, it would mean that even though the Cold War began, ran its course, and came to an end because of particular historically unique late-twentieth-century events and developments and one can adequately account for it in both historical and social science terms on the basis of these factors alone, nevertheless another kind of explanation and understanding of it is also possible and useful, a kind achieved by situating the Cold War and its end within the long history of international politics and conceiving that history in a different way than most scholars have used.

The concept of a history of long duration (*"histoire de longue durée"*) comes, as many will recognize, from the so-called Annales school of historiography, which dominated historical writing in France and strongly influenced it elsewhere from the 1930s until recently. One of the principal Annales theses involved the notion of a history of long duration, of slow, almost glacially paced changes, underlying the more visible middle-range developments of history (*"conjunctures"*) and the kaleidoscopic surface changes of day-to-day and year-to-year events (event history, *"histoire événementielle"*). Annalistes typically found this fundamental history of long duration in the supposed deep structures of society—geography, climate, demography, socioeconomic structures, and certain aspects of collective mentalities—meanwhile consigning the history of politics, especially international politics, to the superficial, inferior category of event history.

Today Annales historiography no longer reigns supreme even in France, though like every other powerful school of historical interpretation it has left behind an important permanent legacy and influence. Two things, besides the normal shifts of fashion and interest among historians, helped end its reign. The first was the realization even among its ardent proponents that the concept of three different levels and paces of historical change—long-, middle-, and short-term, structural, conjunctural, and event—fit the ancient, medieval, and early modern worlds vastly better than the modern and postmodern ones. Science, technology, mass politics and society, and modern economics have rendered the old unchanging structures of society either obsolete and unimportant, or almost as subject to rapid change and deliberate manipulation as other aspects of society. To paraphrase the verdict of one leading exponent of Annales views, a history of long duration is no longer a history of this present world. The other realization was that certain vital arenas of human endeavor—among them, politics—were not well served or understood by Annales methods and presuppositions, and needed different ones.

In this essay, paradoxically, I as a non-Annaliste political historian will argue that this concept of a history of long duration, now considered inapplicable to the modern world, still applies to it, and applies, moreover, precisely to the sort of history, that of international politics, which Annales historians generally despised. I will offer (to repeat, by assertion more than argument and evidence) a broad scheme for a history of long duration discernible beneath the mid-range conjunctural level of international history and the kaleidoscopic event level of everyday international politics. The structure or pattern of long-range history proposed here is, I claim, different from the cyclical ones usually detected and described in histories of international politics (for example, the rise and fall of great powers, shifts in the balance of power, alternations between periods of stability and instability, cycles of war and peace). I will then attempt to show how the Cold War and its termination fit into this pattern, hoping thereby to shed light on the elements both of continuity and change, the familiar and the unprecedented, in them.

Since this statement of purpose is bound to arouse skepticism and seem to promise another grand scheme of history like those offered by philosophers and speculative world historians (Hegel, Toynbee, Spengler, and many more), some disclaimers and qualifications are called for. First, the argument, for reasons of time and space, will be extremely sketchy—hardly even a connected skeleton, more a collection of bones. The meager historical evidence cited is intended for illustration and explanation rather than proof. (Hence also the virtual absence of scholarly footnotes.) Second, though it may appear dogmatic or determinist, the scheme should be understood as provisional and open to change at many points. Obviously many details (dates of periodization, specific so-called turning points, particular alleged causes, facts and interpretations, and so on) are highly debatable. Third and most important, to claim that a certain pattern can be discerned in international history over the last four centuries is not to claim that this must be the only or the dominant pattern or perspective.

A history of long duration by definition underlies conjunctures and events; it does not cancel them out or render them unimportant. The putative pattern, moreover, should be seen as emergent rather than clear and dominant, as compatible with some other patterns while incompatible with others, clearer at some places than others. Finally, since an extended historical exposition, impossible here, would be needed to support this thesis and make it plausible, I expect no one to accept it simply on my word. I ask instead for a provisional suspension of disbelief, in order to consider the question: Assuming that this scheme has a certain validity, what can it tell or suggest about the Cold War and its ending?

That understood, here in bare outline are the successive periods or stages of this putative international *histoire de longue durée* beginning early in the seventeenth century and going up to the beginning of the Cold War:

The Periods and Their Content and Character	Their Dates
1. Emergence of a new order, conflict over its nature and rules, convergence on a concrete definition of peace	1643–1715, 1811–1820
2. More or less stable operation of the new system	1715–1739, 1820–1848
3. Initial crisis, breakdown, and partial transformation of the new system, followed by apparent restabilization	1740–1763, 1848–1871
4. Normal operation of the revised system, marked by rising complications, tensions, and incipient breakdown	1763–1787, 1871–1908
5. Final crisis and breakdown of the old order and pupal stage of the new	1609–1643, 1787–1811, 1908–1945

What follows is an attempt to indicate briefly the salient characteristics of each period or stage and to show that the scheme works historically (that is, broadly makes sense of the evidence and makes a difference in our overall conceptualization of international history). If it fails this prima facie test, it is useless for any other purpose. This is the reason for asking readers to follow what may seem some remote and irrelevant historical argument, in the hope that it will lead to ideas applicable to today's world.

Emergence of the New Order

This stage is the most difficult to explain and to defend historically; it therefore requires somewhat more exposition. It will help if three defining characteristics or elements of it are kept in mind. (1) A real, definitive break with the past occurs in the 1643–1715 and 1811–1820 periods. Not only later historians but also contemporaries sense this, and they believe that the old order is no longer sustainable or tolerable and that something new and different must replace it and is doing so. (2) At the same time, there is no agreement but instead widespread, deep uncertainty about the exact nature and rules of the new order. No one, including those most convinced that the old order must be supplanted, knows at first precisely what the new one will be, or how and whether it will work. This uncertainty helps generate and prolong a more or less protracted period of struggle over the new rules of the game—who will run it, how the costs and benefits will be distributed, how much of the old will be saved, restored, or transmuted in the new, and so on. (3) Out of this struggle, a new consensus or convergence on the rules of the game eventually emerges—enough agreement among enough key players to render the new system legitimate and more stable and enforceable than the old for a considerable period of time.

If we keep these defining characteristics in mind, it is easier to understand two peculiarities in the dates of this scheme of periodization. One is that two famous turning points in international history, 1648, the date of the Treaties of Westphalia and the birth of the so-called Westphalian system, and 1814–1815, the date of the Vienna Congress and birthday of the Vienna system, become simply parts of longer periods. The other is that the first of these periods takes seven decades, so that the new order is supposedly emerging and crystallizing all the way from the end of the Thirty Years War through the wars of Louis XIV to 1715, while the same process takes less than a decade in 1811–1820. These aspects not only seem odd, but suggest, contrary to much historical scholarship and international relations theory, that the Treaties of Westphalia did not found a new international system, but only marked the beginnings of a process by which one finally emerged with the Treaties of Utrecht, Rastatt, and Baden in 1713–1715, ending the War of the Spanish Succession.

Obviously this is not the place to quarrel over periodization in history, a theme of interest only to professional historians. What counts for our purposes, besides indicating how these apparent anomalies do fit the main historical facts, is to show how they reflect a fundamental characteristic of international history. The interpretive pattern presented here involves a basic assumption or premise: that change in the international system involves above all changes in the reigning assumptions, dominant understandings and conceptions, and collective mentalities of political leaders. In other words, it insists that international politics represents human conduct, not just behavior. Systems do not change simply or mainly because power relationships change and leaders respond in more or less routine and predictable patterns of behavior to these changes, but because states, governments, leaders, and peoples react purposively, with conscious ideas and aims, to changes in power and to other concrete problems and circumstances. They act, moreover, within a generally shared understanding of the prevailing system, meaning thereby what some call political culture—the expectations, norms, and rules governing the common practice of international politics, and their understanding of the prevailing incentives or payoff structure. This understanding limits and to some extent governs what they attempt to do and their strategies and hopes for success. Systems change, then, when the reigning ideas about the system change fundamentally and durably.

It follows, then, that in this scheme the emergence of a new, more stable and durable international order (in other words, peace) involves and depends on a change in collective understandings, assumptions, and outlooks among leaders and governments. Peace further involves and requires a convergence or consensus among the major players on a new, concrete, practical definition of peace—something only possible through a process involving a long time and much struggle. It starts with an initial widespread recognition that the old system has hopelessly broken down and must be replaced with something new, and ends, if it comes to fruition, with a substantial working agreement on a new order with different rules, norms, and incentives. Peace treaties and settlements can play a role in creating this consensus, but do not always or even usually do so. The 1815 treaties, true, were exceptionally successful in turning an emerging consensus on a new order into a comprehensive, concrete peace settlement in a remarkably short time. Yet it nevertheless took a difficult, perilous process starting about 1811 and not completed until about 1820 to reach a common definition of peace, and even then there remained old dissents and new emerging rifts. Most peace settlements in European history, including some of the most important (1763, 1919, 1945), did not arise from any such consensus or serve to create one.

Nor did the Westphalian treaties of 1648. Though they represent a vital turning point in international history, this is because they finally ended an old era, the long sixteenth-century Habsburg-Valois/Bourbon contest for universal monarchy and undisputed leadership of a unified Christendom—a contest essentially ended or abandoned even before 1648—without founding a new system or consensus. The treaties did not even bring general European peace. War between France and Spain lasted until 1659, war in Northern Europe until 1660. Nor did they settle all the vital issues, or try to. The treaties deliberately omitted many vital aspects of an enduring settlement or left them vague and subject to dispute.[1]

More important is the widespread notion that the Treaties of Westphalia initiated a new brand of European international politics that was secular rather than religious in character, was played by absolutist princely states rather than feudal units with overlapping rights and jurisdictions, was based on state sovereignty and juridical equality, and operated on principles of *raison d'état* and balance of power. Although Westphalia undoubtedly represented an important stage in the process that led to this change, these generalizations clash with so many realities of seventeenth- and even eighteenth-century politics that they should be used only with extreme care and qualification.

In fact, the Treaties of Westphalia, which did replace the fragile religious peace of 1555–1608 in Germany (the Holy Roman Empire) by a new, more solid one, thereby *founded* the pattern of politics based on religion and confession in Germany, which lasted into the mid-nineteenth century. The granting of *ius foederis* (the right of making foreign alliances) to the estates of the empire was not, as often supposed, decisive in establishing princely sovereignty and reducing the empire to a hollow shell. It actually restored an earlier fifteenth- and sixteenth-century practice, and while it is true that many German princes tried to acquire full sovereignty over their territories and some succeeded, most units remained semifeudal, characterized by divided sovereignty and limited, overlapping jurisdictions. The Holy Roman Empire continued to exist and to operate on the basis of hierarchy, not autonomy, and the emperor at Vienna after 1648 regained much of his lost influence and authority over the estates. France's relations with its many allies were overwhelmingly those of patron and client rather than juridical equality. Seventeenth-century rulers great and small continued to play both sacral and secular roles, seeking both real power and territory and traditional feudal rights, status, and glory (for example, Louis XIV, Emperor Leopold I, John Sobieski of Poland). The balance of power principle did not become clear or dominant until at least the early eighteenth century.

Although much more could be said on this theme, the point is that for our purposes it makes better sense to see the whole conflict-ridden period of 1643–1715 as one of the kind of general uncertainty and shakedown required before any general consensus on a definition of peace and on the nature and rules of politics under a new system could arise. Even the narrow and fragile consensus reached after the long, exhausting War of the Spanish Succession (1702–1713) emerged only late in the game. Once again a common generalization, that Britain and its European allies were fighting for decades against Louis XIV's hegemony and for a balance of power, and that they finally imposed peace on that basis on France in 1713–1715, gravely oversimplifies and distorts both the process and the final outcome.

To take just two of the problems: Although balance of power was a good slogan to use against Louis XIV's supposed attempt at "universal monarchy," it is easy to show that under the rubric of "balance of power" every power allied against France, as one would expect, fought for its individual aims, usually dynastic, religious, and territorial. Moreover, many princes were Louis's allies rather than opponents, and all of his opponents, including the most important, the Dutch stadholder William of Orange, who became Britain's King William III and led the various coalitions, made deals with Louis at various times that promoted his expansionist ambitions. As for Louis, though he certainly loved war, sought glory, and aspired to hegemony in Europe (that is, a recognized superior position, not unchallenged domination) for much of his reign, by 1697 he had tacitly given this ambition up and by 1708 was desperate for peace at almost any price, while as late as 1710 the British and Austrians, if not the Dutch, still wanted all-out victory and empire ("no peace without Spain"). In the end, peace came when a new government in Britain worked out moderate terms with the enemy, France, and helped impose these terms on its own allies, especially the Habsburg Empire.

What counts is that through this long messy process a change in collective outlook and a new understanding of international politics finally did develop and that it prevailed after 1715. A new system, based on a balance of power as Britain and France understood the term and enforced it, became accepted as the basis for peace in western and southern Europe, even though attempts to extend this system to northeastern Europe once again failed and peace would not come there until 1721. In operational terms, the system depended on shared Anglo-French hegemony more than on balance of power. These two dominant powers set the rules of peace in the treaties and enforced them or supervised their revision thereafter.

In this respect and others the Utrecht settlement, the first real peace system modern Europe enjoyed, thus shows a pale but recognizable resemblance to the Vienna settlement a century later. They both recognized some of the same basic international principles (such as the sovereignty, independence, and juridical equality of all units, and a distribution of power sufficient to prevent empire or "universal monarchy" in Europe), and used similar devices for enforcement and management of the system (a hegemonic partnership, dominant alliances, treaty revisions imposed by the great powers, and conferences and congresses to settle outstanding questions)—means more characteristic of concert and collective security than balance of power.

Stable Operation of the System

This stage requires less explanation. In both 1715–1739 and 1820–1848 periods the stability of the system or lack of it depended on how broad and deep the original consensus was on the definition and requirements of peace, how committed the victors were to maintaining and enforcing it, and how successful they were in repressing, channeling, or controlling ideological and power-political ambitions and rivalries so as to preserve the essential consensus. On all these counts the Vienna system, as one might expect, proved superior to that of Utrecht. There was more peace and less conflict over a longer period, a broader and deeper original consensus, a more precise and comprehensive treaty settlement, less need or pressure for later revisions of the treaties, greater willingness and ability of the managing powers to make the needed adjustments, more general cooperation and less defection and resistance, more success with international conferences and congresses, and more ideological conformity among the major powers and/or willingness to overlook and transcend their ideological differences in the interests of managing crises and solving problems.

The differences are stark enough to raise the question of whether the post-Utrecht period was comparable to the Vienna era at all. Yet the earlier era shows enough solid evidence of progress in peacemaking and peacekeeping, particularly when contrasted with the decades that preceded it, and includes enough examples of developments and ideas that would prove fruitful later, to justify including it.[2]

Crisis, Breakdown, Transformation, Restabilization, but an End to Consensus

Most historians would probably accept this summary as reasonably accurate for the international history of the 1740–1763 and 1848–1871 periods. Each began with a crisis in the old system. In 1740 it came suddenly and dramatically with a Prussian attack on Austria followed by a joint Franco-Bavarian assault, launching a general war and threatening to bring the Habsburg monarchy down. In 1848 it came as a series of domestic revolutions and counterrevolutions leading to serious international crises and some armed conflict in Italy, Germany, and the Balkans. In both cases the initial crisis led to a further breakdown of the system. In 1740–1763 the breakdown involved two long, exhausting general wars. In 1853–1871 it involved five wars, none general and all less bloody and protracted than their eighteenth-century counterparts, but even more important in transforming European power relations and the rules of the game. In both instances the wars seemed at last to restabilize the system and allow international politics to resume its normal course. The only point some historians might object to is the phrase, "an end to consensus." There was in fact widespread agreement after both 1763 and 1871, they might claim, as to the winners and losers, the new balance of power, and the new prevailing rules of the game.

This claim is true—and shows the difference between agreement on the outcome and the prevailing on the one hand, rules and consensus on a concrete, practical definition of peace on the other. After 1763 and 1871, what some governments saw as a concrete, practical definition of peace, a new status quo to be defended, represented for others latent war, a condition of insecurity, injustice, and threat to be changed or overturned. Still others seized on the split between defenders and opponents of the new status quo as an opportunity to exploit.[3] Moreover, in both cases the wars had proved that power was the final arbiter, meaning that the only serious way to change the system was not European Concert decision or great-power cooperation but unilateral actions of the kind that risked or produced war. In other words, agreement on the nature of the game and its recent results, current standings, and operating rules not only failed to include a consensus on a definition of peace, but actually precluded a consensus on legitimate means of peaceful change and sanctioned violence.

Changes in collective attitudes underlay the crisis of the old system and the successful challenge to it in both periods. One such change is obvious and needs little discussion. It was the growth of widespread dissatisfaction with the old system and its rules and restraints among many leaders and governments, derived from frustrated ambitions, demands and pressures for change coming from those they governed, and their belief that the system was worn out and unjust. The second source for the crisis and challenge is less obvious: optimism.

A striking characteristic of the periods 1740–1763 and 1848–1871 was that leaders in both were much more willing to gamble than their predecessors, deliberately risking or provoking war with bold initiatives in the sanguine expectation of short-term gains and long-term success. Sometimes the gambles paid off at least in the short term—witness the spectacular gains made by Frederick II of Prussia in 1740–45 or Cavour and Bismarck in the 1850s and 1860s. More often risky strategies failed even in the short-term—witness the failures of French and Bavarian policy in the early 1740s, or Austria's in the Seven Years' War, or those of Prussia and Sardinia-Piedmont in 1848–1850, Russia and Britain in the Crimean War, and Napoleon III throughout the 1860s. Yet this widespread willingness to gamble for immediate gains is less remarkable than the optimistic belief (usually an unarticulated assumption) that these gambles, if successful in the short term, would prove durable and beneficial in the long run. The risk-takers in both periods assumed optimistically that the international system, as a whole would survive the shocks and changes they administered to it and continue to function in their favor. After they, so to speak, had broken the law and changed the rules, their gains would be accepted as legal and they themselves recognized as legitimate, respectable fellow statesmen, while a new consensus on the governing rules and norms of international practice would more or less automatically emerge. In ordinary parlance, their attitude was, "Don't worry—they'll get over it; things will settle down."

After 1763, this obviously failed to happen. What developed instead was a quick revival of wars and crises, despite the general war-weariness, and a marked decline in international norms, demonstrated most clearly by the First Partition of Poland in 1772. As for the period after 1871, a restabilization seemed to happen under Bismarck's leadership, but the apparent stability was always fragile and deceptive. The source of instability in both eras was not, as sometimes believed, a faulty distribution of power (Britain too dominant colonially and on the sea and too isolated in Europe after 1763, whereas Russia was too powerful in Eastern Europe; the dangerous growth in Germany's military power and its labile half-hegemony in Europe after 1871). Nor was it simply the fact that certain states in both periods were dissatisfied and revisionist. Britain and Russia seemed invulnerable to any revisionist challenge in 1763, Britain and Germany equally so after 1871. The real Achilles' heel in both systems was the absence of a consensus on a concrete definition of peace and on institutions and norms to embody and sustain it, and the illusory assumption that this lack could be met by manipulating the balance of power.

Normal Operation of the Revised System (1763–1787, 1871–1908)

This section too needs little discussion. As already indicated, the two periods differed significantly in certain ways. There were major European wars in the first but not in the second; the system was certainly better managed in 1871–1890 than in either 1763–1787 or 1890–1908. But the basic principles of operation were the same in both periods. The spirit of realpolitik prevailed; goals were pursued and crises managed primarily by means of shifting alliances and alignments. The overall trends over time were also similar—the rise of more complications, deeper tensions, balanced and unbalanced antagonisms, and threats of general breakdown and war. Three special reasons explain why balance of power politics appeared to make Europe more peaceful and stable in the late nineteenth century than in the eighteenth. These were, first, Bismarck's extraordinary ingenuity, skill, and restraint in managing crises in 1871–1890; second, the fact that in the late nineteenth century European imperialism abroad served initially, until about 1890 or after, as an outlet for European energies, diverting them from Continental quarrels, whereas throughout the eighteenth century overseas imperialism had remained intensely competitive and helped promote war in Europe; and finally, the fact that nineteenth-century industrialization, technology, and demographic growth, together with the rise of nationalism and mass politics, vastly increased the costs and risks of a major or general war for all major governments, making it much harder to justify a decision to go to war in each particular crisis and easier to postpone it, without making leaders or peoples consider war less likely or necessary in the long run.

In other words, the greater peace and stability of the late nineteenth century came from temporary exogenous causes, not from a sounder system. The prevailing conviction in military and diplomatic circles for a decade or more before 1914 was that a great war was coming, that it would be terrible and costly, that it would decide the fate of nations for generations, but that it probably could not be avoided and must be fought and won. This assessment of the situation was, in a tragic way, realistic.

In any case, in neither period did most governments, despite major crises and considerable fear of war, make serious efforts to revive the old consensus on a concrete definition of peace or develop a new one. That was left to fringe groups—peace advocates, women, and socialists.[4] This inaction did not reflect a remnant of the old optimistic belief that the problems of preserving peace would somehow solve themselves or be solved by ordinary balance of power politics. Instead governments and leaders increasingly rested their hope for peace on being militarily prepared for all contingencies (*"Si vis pacem, para bellum"*) and assumed that only fools and swindlers would believe or preach otherwise, or would pass up an opportunity to strengthen their position—another sign of the absence of a practical consensus on peace.

Exhaustion, Collapse, and Destruction of the Old System; Pupal Stage of the New

That exhaustion happened in the 1609–1643, 1787–1811 and 1908–1945 periods is fairly self-evident, a truism or cliché. Some discussion of the central characteristics of this stage, however, will help show how despite their obvious differences these three historic eras are basically alike, and why in each case the destruction of the old system made possible the emergence of a new one.

One central characteristic is that where *sacro egoismo* (sacred self-interest) had already become a leading principle of statecraft in the previous period, *va banque* (going for broke) takes control in this one. Under the stimuli of growing fear, greed, and opportunity, unchecked by consensual norms, and reinforced by the phenomena we know as the security dilemma, positive feedback, and escalation, the dominant strategy among the contending great powers becomes one of aiming for a decisive victory, first in competitive high politics and ultimately in war—this despite the fact that no one really knows or can calculate what the final consequences of war, even victorious war, will be. The game of competition for security and advantage, increasingly tense but still confined within the bounds of a vague general agreement that the game was necessary for everyone's overall security and advantage and should be continued, gives way to a quest for victory regardless of its general consequences and regardless of whether the game can survive.

This escalating, hypertrophic pursuit of victory, driven above all by fear of the intolerable consequences of defeat, causes governments to lose control, first of the game of high politics and then of the wars that ensue. Despite the slogans more or less genuinely believed and propagated to justify the quest for victory (defending the true religion, saving the nation, defeating tyranny, saving a people's culture and way of life, making the world safe for democracy, ending war forever, and the like), the very concept of victory tends to become meaningless, self-encapsulated in the sense that no one can clearly define what victory would accomplish other than to defeat or destroy the foe and avoid defeat or destruction for oneself. Whenever precise definitions and programs are put forward they arouse serious opposition and divisions even among allies.

A growing sense of the futility of war for such ends, heightened by the intolerable suffering produced by its hyperbolic protraction, leads in all three periods to a widespread, though not universal, revulsion against the old politics supposedly responsible for it and a broad, genuine yearning for a new politics of peace. This feeling, however, fails to produce agreement either on a concrete, practical definition of peace or on the specific ways to achieve it. Ideas and proposals for a structure of peace arise in each era, ranging widely from the serious through the impractical to the dangerous or downright lunatic. None, however, produces consensus on the question even on the side of the ultimate winners. What prevails in practical terms is the belief in the primacy and necessity of victory and the hope that it will create and define peace.

What follows is just enough history to indicate why in my view this description fits these three periods, despite their obvious differences, and also offers some new perspectives and insights.

The first point concerns the origins of the great systemic wars of these eras (the Thirty Years War, the revolutionary-Napoleonic wars, and both World Wars). On each there has been endless dispute over what event triggered the final downward spiral, the positive feedback loop leading from tension and crisis into all-out war. These debates are not pointless, the narrow quarrels of academic scribes. The choice of one triggering event rather than another is always connected to larger questions—the nature and causes of the escalation of crises generally, the question of overall responsibilities for the wars, and even the causes of war itself. Regardless of differences of opinion over what started the snowball rolling in each case, however, there is no real disagreement among scholars that in each case a downward spiral developed—a series of defensive-offensive initiatives and responses taken not because leaders were unaware of their risks or confident they would succeed, but because, knowing the risks, they considered these moves the only way to respond to others' moves and the general threat of defeat and destruction. This fact signals to me (others may disagree) that at the beginning of all three periods the prevailing system went out of control, unable to correct itself or be corrected. Va banque was widely seen to be the only serious strategy for deterring an intolerable outcome and/or insuring a desirable one.

This pattern of self-reinforcing downward spiral is not universal in international history. It does not apply to most wars in these three centuries, including some very big and important ones, much less to periods of peace. This is another indication that these particular periods represent cases of systemic collapse rather than temporary outbreaks of violence or partial breakdown and revision.

An even more compelling indication is the way in which in all three instances general war turned into all-out hypertrophic war, war of unprecedented violence and extent in pursuit of unprecedentedly sweeping imperialist aims. Long before the Thirty Years War Habsburg and Valois-Bourbon monarchs had contended over the *dominium orbis* and a *pax Hispanica*, but never with the desperate commitment with which these goals were pursued by Olivares and Philip IV or resisted by Richelieu and Mazarin.[5] No earlier Counter-Reformation prince had pursued the aim of restoring Catholic supremacy in the whole German Empire to the lengths Ferdinand II did, in part because no earlier Protestants had presented so open and sweeping a challenge as the Protestant Union and the Bohemian nobility did.[6] Nothing before 1795 prepared Europe for the ferocious onslaught of revolutionary French imperialism, and still less for the limitless imperialism of Napoleon.[7] Both sides in the First World War, once in, developed sweeping imperialist programs and sought a knockout victory; the democratic Allies on the whole did so even more consistently than the authoritarian Central Powers.[8] Both sides in the Second World War vastly outdid those in the First in the hypertrophic way in which they fought and in the goals that they pursued.

One cannot explain this hypertrophy of war simply as the result of accident, changing technology, or a self-generating expansion of violence in which war feeds on war. Most wars, including many big ones, have managed to stay precariously under political control, limited by the politics of war (negotiations with allies and the enemy over war aims and goals, domestic pressures for peace, the mutual experience of exhaustion leading to changes in policy or governments, and so on). In other words, they fit

Clausewitz's famous definition of war as politics pursued by other means. These systemic wars during most of their course did not. In them, the politics of war as the art of limiting and ending war through negotiation, consent, compromise, and consensus was defeated—in fact, condemned as folly and treason, and politics was reduced mainly to serving the ends of more war for greater victory.

It is nonetheless significant that this kind of systemic breakdown, a constant danger and potentiality in international relations, has been realized only three times in four centuries of international history. Only in these periods do we see a full descent into all-out pursuit of victory and hypertrophic war and imperialism, attended by horrors in each period analogous in character if not in scale; war has troubled and afflicted peace at many times in various degrees, but completely overwhelmed and destroyed peace only in these eras. This fact is not merely worth noting in order to keep one's balance and perspective. It also accounts for something detectable in these three periods and only in them, especially toward their end—signs of a genuine break in the cycle, the emergence of a widespread conviction that the current game of international politics could no longer be endured and that a new kind had to be discovered or invented, even though most contemporaries could not say what the new kind should be and many despaired of its very possibility.

We cannot explore and compare here the signs of a change in collective consciousness emerging in each period (for example, genuine and opportunistic conversions of former adherents and practitioners of the old politics to new ideas, rats leaving the sinking ship while true believers go down with it, ideas once discarded and derided as Utopian being revived, and so on). What matters is that the systemic breakdown at the end of these periods brought an opportunity for a breakthrough to a new system, though without assuring it or making clear what it would be.

The Significance of This Scheme
for the Late Twentieth Century

Even readers willing for the sake of argument to go along with this reading of the long history of international politics from 1609 to 1945 may be asking the obvious question: What good is it? What does it do, beyond dressing up old facts and conventional ideas in new clothing? What keeps it from being just another example of the kinds of periodization, categorization, and narrative lines historians like to concoct and play with? In particular, how does it contribute to our understanding of the Cold War, its end, and its future implications?

These are legitimate questions. My reply concedes certain points while defending the scheme on others (though again without offering much evidence). Admittedly, the scheme could conceivably be sound and useful as history, helping to integrate the historical evidence and answer some of the riddles of the seventeenth-early twentieth centuries, without contributing much toward analyzing the recent past and the current situation. In other words, it could be good history and still be irrelevant for our present concerns. The case for its relevance has to be made. Making this case is not easy, because some superficially plausible arguments in that direction will not do or are insufficient.

One such would be to claim that the scheme is worthwhile because it refutes or at least renders more dubious other broad views on international history, in particular those of realists and neo-realists, commonly used to explain the Cold War and its end. I think it does—but even if that is true, the obvious way to refute these views is by direct criticism, not by constructing such an elaborate scheme as this. A similar claim, possibly true but in any case inadequate, would be that to set twentieth-century international politics, in particular the Cold War and its end, into a broad historical context like this one serves to stimulate new ways of thinking about it and generate new insights. For example, it makes one see both world wars as a second Thirty Years War, which destroyed the nineteenth-century system and opened the way to something new. Once again the reply is fairly obvious: Even if this conception of the two world wars as one long Thirty Years War is true (and the leading American historian of the Second World War, Gerhard Weinberg, in particular challenges it), it is hardly a new or revolutionary idea, and whatever value it supposedly has for understanding the Cold War would lie in the very method rejected earlier, namely, explaining recent international developments by historical analogy and "comparative" history.

In other words, this interpretation of centuries of international history before the Cold War can legitimately interest analysts of the Cold War only if in some important way that conflict and its end can be shown to fit into that long history as an integral component rather than by analogy, so that our understanding of what really happened in the Cold War and its outcome is significantly altered and enlarged thereby. This is a tall order. Nonetheless, I will make the attempt. Others more expert in the Cold War and its end must decide whether it succeeds.

The specific claim is that the Cold War and its end, placed within the long history of international politics, represent another breakthrough to a new system, like those of 1643–1715 and 1811–1820. As in these two earlier eras, the most important thing that finally happened in and through the Cold War was that a transformed kind of international politics emerged and crystallized. The principles, rules, and constituent practices of a new system were worked out under competitive and dangerous conditions until in the end a consensus or at least convergence developed among most of the important players on a concrete, practical definition of peace. This view seems to me a defensible (though controversial) historical interpretation of the Cold War and a useful framework for analyzing the process and considering its implications.

It locates the roots and origins of the Cold War not primarily in a deliberate drive for empire by either side, or in a balance of power struggle for security and advantage, or even in a clash of rival ideologies and worldviews. True, the Cold War quickly became all these things. It started, however, with the parties as allies who intended to continue their cooperation and promote general peace and security but had not reached a basic agreement on a concrete, practical definition of peace (in fact, they had to an extent deliberately avoided doing so). The result of not working out what postwar "cooperation" and "peace" meant during the war in concrete detail was that each major player, when it began to implement its own concept of peace, took moves by others as direct threats and challenges to that concept, and considered them to be incompatible with real peace and intolerable in their long-range consequences.

No doubt these reactions resulted in part from misperceptions, latent suspicions, and hostility left over from prewar and wartime rivalry (among the Western allies, the United States, Britain, and France just as much as between them and the USSR). Yet misperception and the revival of old mistrust was not the main cause of this development, for it has to be recognized that even if the mutual accusations of deliberate hostility and breach of faith were often wrong, one-sided, or propagandistic, the judgments both sides made that the others' moves represented threats to their own interests were substantially correct. In other words, the wartime allies produced the Cold War precisely by trying to construct peace and a new order without first carefully defining what this project meant and what it required in individual and common action. As a result, the initial attempts at postwar cooperation for peace actually produced a Cold War by making the erstwhile allies face the fact that they were really opponents, possibly enemies.[9] In a still more remarkable paradox, that Cold War would finally lead first to limited cooperation among the rivals to keep it from turning hot, and finally and suddenly to a consensus on peace that would permit real cooperation.

This sequence of events makes 1945–1991 resemble 1643–1715 as a breakthrough rather than 1811–1820. In 1945–1991, as in 1643–1715, it took decades of conflict and a decisive military-political outcome to establish the norms, rules, and conditions of the new system and arrive at a consensus definition of peace—which is what one would expect. 1811–1820 was different because the final allied coalition against Napoleon in 1813–1815 did something unique and astonishing in history. It abandoned the policy which previous anti-French coalitions had followed (also followed by the victors in the Thirty Years War and in both world wars) of concentrating mainly on military victory over the common foe and relying on that military victory and the spirit of wartime union to pave the way to peace and postwar cooperation. Instead, the powers in the last coalition in 1813–1814, even before launching a new campaign against Napoleon, negotiated agreements among themselves on a comprehensive, concrete, practical definition of peace. They then fought the war to achieve that particular definition of peace, maintained this consensus on peace through the course of fighting, and made every effort to bring other parties, including their enemies, into it.

They put politics ahead of war, consciously fought for concrete, agreed political aims rather than mere military victory, and after victory translated this wartime consensus into a comprehensive network of treaties and a general alliance. Only because they did this *during* the war, drawing on lessons learned in a generation of earlier wars, could they produce real peace through a single peace settlement at Vienna. The failure or inability to do this, as in the seventeenth century and the first half of the twentieth, means that no matter how much states and peoples want peace and strive for it, it will come, if at all, only out of further struggle.

According to this interpretation, the Cold War itself, like 1648–1713, was an era in which this wartime omission was made good—in which the terms, norms, principles, and rules first for a limited cold peace and then a wider, somewhat more positive but still cold peace were painfully worked out. As in 1713–1715, the process ended unexpectedly and dramatically in victory for one side, but also with most major players converging on a new concrete definition of peace and taking some major steps to implement it. This overall interpretation, though also controversial, is defensible. It does not denature or trivialize the Cold War, downplaying the fact that in the short and middle term, as event and conjuncture, it consisted overwhelmingly of hostile confrontation, fierce competition, and several grave crises with potentially disastrous outcomes. Nor does it require inflating the mutual restraint and sense of limits displayed by both sides during the Cold War, vital for averting war between the two sides, into active cooperation and good will.

It offers no new facts about the Cold War, but rather a different conceptualization of it in a *longue durée* view of international history. Just as a long-duration view lets us conceive the post-Westphalian era not simply as a contest between France's bid for hegemony and European efforts to maintain a balance of power, but as a confused, conflicted process of working out how the new political principles and rules obscurely outlined and foreshadowed at Westphalia would really function in practice; so this view lets us see the Cold War not simply as a struggle over who would rule the world, but over what the rules, practices, and conditions of postwar peace would be and who would set them.

Peaceful coexistence developed not simply out of balance-of-power competition and the fear of mutual assured destruction, nor as a slogan and policy of the superpowers adopted in the course of the Cold War, after Stalin's death or the Cuban missile crisis. The idea was there from the beginning. The conflicts and crises of the Cold War arose precisely from moves and countermoves on both sides to define the terms and conditions for peaceful coexistence in areas and over issues left dangerously undefined by the war and the nonexistence of a real peace settlement—Berlin, Germany, Yugoslavia, Western and Eastern Europe, Japan, China and Korea, Vietnam, the Middle East, much of the Third World.

At every point, moreover, the concern not to go too far, the desire while achieving one's own goals at the same time to keep the outcome minimally tolerable to the other side, controlled the conflict on both sides and kept it from issuing in overt war, though the margin was sometimes dangerously thin. Cold War competition was not a *va banque* competition and descent into the maelstrom like that before and during the Thirty Years War, the revolutionary-Napoleonic wars, or the two world wars. This fact is most strikingly apparent precisely in the most dangerous crises—1948–1949, 1956, 1958, 1962. It does not really matter whether one attributes the restraint which pulled both superpowers back from the brink solely to the nuclear stalemate or explains it (as I would) more as a fundamental recognition reached on broad grounds that, in general, war had ceased to be a viable instrument of politics. In either case, it meant a break with the old politics.

This view also integrates into the history of the Cold War another development of equal or even greater importance, too often seen simply as part of the Cold War or a kind of sideshow and byproduct of it—the permanent pacification and integration of Western Europe. While the terms of cold peaceful coexistence between the two opposed blocs were being defined in competitive, conflictual fashion by the Cold War, the very concept of peace was being redefined, expanded, and transformed within one bloc in a different, essentially cooperative process. The political and economic integration of Western Europe, combined with its economic growth and the expansion of its economic and political ties to North America, the Pacific Rim, and much of the rest of the world, constituted nothing less than a new, concrete definition of peace. A large and growing number of important, highly developed countries redefined peace to mean not merely the elimination of hot war among themselves, but the joint advancement of economic development and prosperity, political and economic integration and interdependence, democratization, human rights, a market-oriented economy, liberal representative government, and a joint approach to common problems.

This new development coincided with the Cold War but was not simply a product of it. In fact, it affected the Cold War as profoundly as it was affected by it. Indirectly it promoted détente and the growth in trade and communication between the blocs; more directly it led to such things as the Helsinki Accords, the work of the Conference on Security and Cooperation in Europe (CSCE), and the encouragement of dissent in the Soviet bloc and the Soviet Union. It is not unreasonable to define the end of the Cold War as the adoption since 1985 of this new concept of peace, developed above all in Western Europe, by the countries of the former Soviet bloc and most of the USSR itself.

To repeat what was said at the beginning: No one should buy this interpretation of the Cold War and its end (as the sudden, unexpected climax of a long-developing subterranean convergence on a new concrete definition of peace) merely on the basis of this brief argument—much less adopt the whole scheme of international history on which it rests. At most it may be suggestive. My further remarks on the implications this scheme and interpretation might have for the future are naturally even more tentative, speculative, and personal. They may be legitimate in a work like this festschrift, however, where they would not be in one of pure academic scholarship.

One obvious way to view what this scheme suggests about the future of world international relations is optimistic. On this reading, the end of the Cold War marks a real, meaningful convergence among many of the most important countries of the world on a concrete definition of peace—a consensus, moreover, potentially far more sustainable and defensible than earlier ones. The definition of peace now includes and is supported by values and principles which, unlike earlier ones, have a real future. That is, they are far more practical, desirable, adaptable, and widely applicable—liberal representative democracy, civil rights and the rule of law, the expansion of trade, interchange, and communication between open societies, market-based economies, governments responsible to their own citizens, and the development of institutions and norms to promote international cooperation in general and to act against at least the worst and most dangerous forms of international outlawry. In other words, this new phenomenon is not just a temporary and partial breakthrough to general world peace like earlier ones, but a real, permanent achievement, like that of manned heavier-than-air flight in 1903.

Another possible reading is pessimistic. Whatever else this history of long duration proves, it shows that breakthroughs of this sort do not last. The mood and spirit that inspired them and the circumstances that made them seem imperative change or disappear. The cycle of decay, crisis, partial overthrow, apparent but deceptive renewal, and further degeneration leading to another great systemic crisis takes over. Nothing suggests, much less proves, that the fate of this breakthrough will be different. The so-called consensus on a concrete definition of peace is anything but universal, and very thin and shaky where it exists. Commitment to its values and norms, even where they have taken root, will not survive any serious political or economic challenge, and many powerful enemies of these norms remain ready to challenge and defy them. Nor is there any guarantee or good reason to believe that this breakthrough, even if it helps solve the problems that caused past wars, can master the new world problems looming in the future.

Both of these views and the respective outlooks they suggest are plausible; neither is necessarily true; and neither slant, optimism nor pessimism, is particularly helpful. The only sensible attitude to take, if this scheme has merit, is a kind of sober realism, neither optimistic nor pessimistic. Something big and real has happened, both different from and analogous to major breakthroughs in the past. We do not know how well the emerging new system will work in an unknown future or how durably it will withstand the unpredictable but inevitable tests and shocks to come. We do know it is the only system for peace we have; that it is better (that is, both more effective and more solidly grounded) than anything that has gone before; and that it therefore makes sense to do everything possible to sustain it and make it work.

That general premise has two slightly more specific implications. The first is that this scheme indicates how important ideas are in international relations (conceptions, visions of the future, understandings of what is possible and impossible, collective mentalities and outlooks, concrete formulations of aims and goals, attitudes about rules, norms, and expectations). Of course material realities influence these, possibly produce them. Nonetheless, ideas not only influence conduct in international affairs, but can also change material realities and what persons, societies, and governments do with them. Just as most of the great material improvements in the life of persons and societies, in this century as before, have come from ideas, mainly advances in science and technology, so the worst international crimes and horrors of the twentieth century (both World Wars, Nazism, Communism, the Holocaust, other genocides, integral nationalism and tribal war, terrorism) have sprung above all from ideas and outlooks. So have the great advances (the liberation of conquered and oppressed peoples, an end to overt imperialism and colonialism, the rise of democracy and civil liberties, more open societies, the emancipation of women, the growth of international cooperation and the institutions to support it, the establishment of zones of peace instead of war).

The implications of this rather banal point are less obvious. First, it places a high priority in international affairs, often treated as a theater of pure power politics, on the arena of ideas, collective mentalities. If, as claimed, a large section of the international community has now reached consensus on a new, concrete definition of peace, one which though fragile and incomplete is still more solid and hopeful than any earlier one, then the most important task becomes to maintain, strengthen, and broaden this consensus. Every action and every policy needs to be considered and decided finally in the light of whether it undergirds or undermines it, at home and abroad.

This consensus on a definition of peace certainly faces major external challenges, but my reading of history indicates that the greatest threats to it are likely to come from within, and that like the Vienna System it will fall to internal decay earlier than external assault. This fall will come about for some of the same reasons as in the nineteenth century, namely, that governments and elites benefiting from the peace settlement will try to preserve it unchanged and use it strictly for their own interests, adopting an ideology of the status quo, and that many of those who initially share the definition of peace or go along with it will rebel against it, believing that it frustrates them while keeping one part of the international community permanently on top. Signs of this happening or already having happened in the former Soviet Union, parts of Asia and Latin America, and elsewhere are easy to see and very disturbing.

Another argument made earlier, that a certain kind of optimism can threaten international consensus and cooperation, also applies here. Neither optimism nor pessimism are good or bad in themselves, of course. The problem here lies in a particular form of optimism or simplistic thinking, the belief that a simple way or magic formula exists for achieving and maintaining peace. Let a certain formula be applied, a given principle be established, a mechanism be unleashed or law obeyed, and peace will be secure. This kind of thinking has always been endemic in international affairs on all sides of the political spectrum from right to left, but although the tendency to rely on nostrums for peace is universal and timeless, the fashion in nostrums changes over time. Many of those common in history seem to be receding in appeal or least remain contested—peace through a balance of power or a preponderance of power in the right hands (the two phrases usually mean the same thing) or through the rule of law, national self-determination, the liberation of oppressed peoples, democracy, constitutional government, economic development, world federation or world government, international organizations and peacekeeping forces, universal disarmament, and so on.

One, however, seems to be gaining ground in the United States and part of the West, and to be reflected in certain of the contributions to this volume: a doctrine one might call economism. This is the belief not simply in the greater power and efficiency of free market-based economies in producing goods and services, but also in the ability of free-market economics to solve the major problems of world order, or at least to render them manageable and ultimately obsolete. Let the ideas of Adam Smith and J. S. Mill (which on examination turn out really to be more like those of Bernard Mandeville and Herbert Spencer) be recognized as universally valid and given free rein; let governments concentrate on their legitimate tasks, which are to provide the institutional and legal frameworks under which the free market can operate, and otherwise get out of the way of market forces, freeing them to work across national and on global lines; let people and governments concentrate on the fundamental needs and requirements of society, promoting human welfare through the material wealth created by the free play of economic competition; and most of the sources of international conflict will decline or disappear. States, economies, even rival nationalities and religious groups will become too closely interdependent in economic activity to be able to fight on a large scale, or to want to.

Put aside all the challenges which could be made to these claims (here admittedly overdrawn and oversimplified) on various general grounds—economic, environmental, social, communitarian, and the like. Concentrate instead on the central issue of international order. Can one rely largely upon the free play of market forces to solve the kinds of problems, economic and other, that have caused international and civil wars in the past? If not, is it prudent to call for governments to abandon attempts to manage problems of trade, national production, unemployment, economic vulnerability, and general economic welfare through the instruments of international politics, all for the sake of the free market? Should one welcome the inability of governments to control the movement of capital internationally and applaud the signs of the putative obsolescence of the state and the takeover of many of its traditional functions by private groups, above all multinational corporations, when one at best does not know and cannot predict what the consequences may be in international politics?[10]

I do not think so. The marketplace is a valuable, in some respects indispensable, servant in the cause of world order. It can help make many problems soluble or manageable that would be insoluble without it.[11] Yet the unfettered marketplace is a bad, dangerous master in world affairs, mainly because there are so many vital tasks it cannot touch and therefore so many promises it cannot fulfill. It cannot defend national territory, or promote vital cultural and spiritual values, or insure the protection of rights and property abroad, or preserve the stability of government and law at home, or do a host of other things citizens everywhere naturally expect their governments to do for them in the international arena. And for many, at least in their perception and experience, the marketplace does not even produce a decent economic existence.

To suppose therefore that the movement toward greater world peace is essentially a shift from politics to economics is seriously mistaken. For one thing, it sets up a false dichotomy, like suggesting that the road to health lies in going from medical treatment to nutrition, whereas any sensible program of medical treatment includes nutrition, while nutrition can never constitute a full program of medical treatment or substitute for it. The more international relations comes to be concerned with economics and tied to it, which is a long-standing, accelerating, and on the whole valuable trend, the more we need international politics in order to keep that trend from going beyond control. The suggestion that economics is the more vital, central, comprehensive sphere of activity in human society, and politics a narrower, less central and more dispensable one, has things just backward. Politics, which comprises the organization and leadership of groups for collective enterprises and the processes whereby their decisions are made, is the most comprehensive, inclusive, and indispensable of human activities, in business and economics as everywhere else.

An even more fundamental conceptual error, however, is to conceive peace and order not as a path or process, but as a certain condition, a state of things brought about when the right policies and actions are followed, whether they be sound market economics or intelligent power politics backed by a good national defense, or strong political ties and friendships, or good treaties and international law well enforced, or something else. The conceptual confusion shows up in the common phrase, "establishing a just and lasting peace." Peace and order are not a condition or set of conditions established by treaties, power politics, economics, or anything else, and then maintained or preserved. Peace and order must be conceived as organic, constantly changing, either growing or dying; something always becoming, being created and recreated.

A just peace can only mean one in which many diverse, conflicting aims, claims, rights, and calls for justice are creatively reconciled, compromised, or held in fruitful balance; a lasting peace can only be one which keeps changing and adapting to new demands for justice. The name for the only process and activity through which this job can be done is "politics." For this reason, the notion of another method or route to peace, economic or any other, is pernicious nonsense, and the widespread contempt for politics and politicians in the United States and elsewhere represents a dangerous trend. The British political writer Bernard Crick, correcting Thomas Jefferson's dictum about eternal vigilance as the price of liberty, has put it well: "Eternal politics is the price of liberty."

This applies still more to the international arena. Eternal politics is the price of peace—and will remain so in the twenty-first century as it has always been in the past.

Notes

1. Some examples of these omissions: no peace made between the two main combatants, France and Spain; no exact delimitation of territory and sovereign rights between the King of France, the Emperor as both Austrian Habsburg monarch and leader of the Holy Roman Empire, and local princes and authorities in Alsace; the exact nature and role of France and Sweden as protectors of the constitution and liberties of the empire; the relation of former imperial territories and circles such as Burgundy and the Low Countries to the empire; and no precise definition of the relation of the emperor and imperial institutions and authorities to the estates. War continued in the Baltic and northeastern Europe, and relations between Christian Europe and the still dangerous and aggressive Ottoman Empire in Southeastern Europe and the Mediterranean remained critical. All these problems caused much conflict and war in the decades after the Treaties of Westphalia.

2. Some examples of progress: the cooperation between Britain and France to enforce and revise the settlement; their willingness to impose peace and compromise on former or current allies and their relative success in doing so; the fact that international congresses and conferences were called to settle crises (even if they proved unsuccessful); and the persistent peace efforts of statesmen like Robert Walpole, Philippe of Orleans, regent of France, the abbé Dubois, and Cardinal Fleury. Perhaps the most striking evidence of change is the long effort made by Emperor Charles VI of Austria to insure the most important goal of his dynasty and reign, the peaceful transmission of all his domains to his daughter Maria Theresia, by means of a Pragmatic Sanction accepted by the various Habsburg estates and guaranteed by international treaties concluded with all the important powers of Europe—in other words, by means of peaceful diplomacy and international law. True, this effort ultimately broke down and proved nearly fatal to Austria in 1740–1741, but in the seventeenth Century it could never even have been tried.

3. This disappearance of any consensus on peace is clearly evident in both cases. After 1763, France, though too exhausted to launch a new general war, remained bent on somehow restoring the balance of power Britain had overturned, particularly on the seas. Austria felt the same way but even more strongly in regard to Prussia, Prussia was equally fearful of Austria, and both feared their growing dependence on Russia, which under Catherine II exploited their rivalry in order to expand its control of Poland and aggrandize itself at the expense of the Ottoman Empire. In 1871, France felt threatened by Germany and was revisionist; Austria felt itself so dominated by the new Bismarckian Reich and dependent upon it that its only chance for security lay in allying with Prussia-Germany and turning its power against Russia; Russia was secretly worried by the new Germany, convinced that Germany would have to show that it was Russia's friend or Russia would have to find ways to check it; and Italy was at once fearful, insecure, and greedy. Only the

British were relatively complacent about the outcome, as they had been after 1763, and in both cases that mood did not last long.

4. Illustrating this inaction in the later eighteenth century was the failure of the French and Austrian attempts to get European cooperation to save Poland or the Ottoman Empire; in the late nineteenth, the failure of all attempts to revive the Three Emperors League and the fate of the Hague peace conferences. On this last point see especially Jost Dülffer, *Regeln gegen den Krieg? Die Friedenskonferenzen von 1899 und 1902 in der internationalen Politik* (Berlin, 1981).

5. J. H. Elliott, *The Count-Duke of Olivares* (New Haven, 1986) and *Richelieu and Olivares* (Cambridge, 1984); R. A. Stradling, *Philip IV and the Government of Spain, 1621–1655* (Cambridge, 1988); Lucien Bely, *Les relations internationales en Europe (XVIIe–XVIIIe siècles)* (Paris, 1992).

6. Robert Bireley, *Religion and Politics in the Age of the Counter-Reformation* (Chapel Hill, NC, 1981); Geoffrey Parker, *The Thirty Years War* (New York, 1984); Bely, *Relations internationales*.

7. T. C. W. Blanning, *The Origins of the French Revolutionary Wars* (London, 1986), and *The French Revolutionary Wars 1787–1802* (London, 1996); Paul W. Schroeder, *The Transformation of European Politics 1763–1848* (Oxford, 1994).

8. For a convincing scholarly defense of this revisionist verdict, see G. H. Soutou, *L'or et le sang: les buts de guerre économiques de la Première Guerre mondiale* (Paris, 1989).

9. This verdict is of course not original, but also not simply a conventional one. It seems to me, moreover, in line with the main outcome of the orthodox-revisionist debate in American foreign policy historiography, strengthened by recent works taking account of new material from the Soviet archives. See, for example, Norman Naimark, *The Russians in Germany: A History of the Soviet Zone of Occupation, 1945–1949* (Cambridge, MA, 1995); Carolyn Eisenberg, *Drawing the Line: The American Decision to Divide Germany, 1944–1949* (New York, 1996); Vladislav Zubok and Constantine Pleshakov, *Inside the Kremlin's Cold War: From Stalin to Khrushchev* (Cambridge, MA, 1996), 276. For an excellent recent survey and interpretation of the evidence, see Melvyn Leffler, "The Struggle for Germany and the Origins of the Cold War," Occasional Paper No. 16, German Historical Institute, Washington (1996).

10. There are striking historical ironies here—that anti-Marxists should now develop a capitalist version of the Marxist-Leninist doctrine of the withering away of the state, or that strong hostility to big government and distrust of its power should coexist with a sanguine confidence about enormous concentrations of power and wealth in great corporations, institutions generally more secretive and less transparent and accessible to the control of law than democratic governments are.

11. It can, for example, help declining states incapable of still acting as independent great powers accept their loss of status and security peacefully by holding out the prospect that their economic future can still be secure even after the loss of great-power status. Even for this possibility, however, a working international market system is only a necessary, not a sufficient condition. It also requires political action and commitment on the part of the military-political victors and losers alike to make this happen.

About the Editor
and Contributors

Alan S. Alexandroff is research director of the Program on Conflict Management and Negotiation at the Centre for International Studies at the University of Toronto and a Director of Navigant Consulting, Inc. in Toronto.

Michael E. Brown is associate professor at the Edmund A. Walsh School of Foreign Service at Georgetown University.

Joseph M. Grieco is professor of Political Science at Duke University.

Carl Kaysen is D. W. Skinner Professor emeritus of Political Economy, Security Studies Program, Massachusetts Institute of Technology.

Deepak Lal is James S. Coleman Professor of International Development Studies at UCLA.

John Mueller is professor of Political Science at the University of Rochester.

Ronald L. Rogowski is professor of Political Science at UCLA.

Richard Rosecrance is professor of Political Science at UCLA.

Paul W. Schroeder is Professor emeritus of History at the University of Illinois.

Arthur A. Stein is professor of Political Science at UCLA.

Cherie J. Steele is visiting assistant professor of Government at Dartmouth College.

Edward Yardeni is Chief Economist and Global Investment Strategist at Deutsche Banc Alex. Brown.

Index